D0464638

THE BONOBO
SISTERHOOD

THE BONOBO SISTERHOOD

REVOLUTION THROUGH FEMALE ALLIANCE

DIANE L. ROSENFELD

HARPER WAVE

An Imprint of HarperCollins*Publishers*

THE BONOBO SISTERHOOD. Copyright © 2022 by Diane L. Rosenfeld. All rights reserved. Printed in the United States of America. No part of this book may be used or reproduced in any manner whatsoever without written permission except in the case of brief quotations embodied in critical articles and reviews. For information, address HarperCollins Publishers, 195 Broadway, New York, NY 10007.

HarperCollins books may be purchased for educational, business, or sales promotional use. For information, please email the Special Markets Department at SPsales@harpercollins.com.

FIRST EDITION

Self-portrait illustration of Chrystul Kizer used with permission.
Photo credit: John R. Boehm Photography

Library of Congress Cataloging-in-Publication Data has been applied for.

ISBN 978-0-06-308507-7

22 23 24 25 26 LSC 10 9 8 7 6 5 4 3 2 1

To my mother, Phyllis Ellis Rosenfeld, Esq.,
whose maternal energy is the river that flows through these pages;
to Kitty, my North Star; and
to Terry, for everything.

CONTENTS

FOREWORD

This book you are holding offers a vibrant vision and a detailed plan for uniting yourself with femalekind in revolutionary coalitions such as those characterized by the least known of the great apes, the bonobos. The promise of bonobos, with whom we share 98.7 percent of our DNA, is to end male sexual violence. Professor Rosenfeld understands that all women experience male-perpetuated sexual violence in our distinct locations of oppressions uniquely and imagines, powerfully and convincingly, that we women can't ignore each other's suffering anymore. Instead, we may learn from our closest living relatives, the bonobos, to form sustainable female-to-female alliances that not only disrupt individual acts of male aggression but render obsolete oppressive patriarchal systems.

The Bonobo Sisterhood offers a jaw-dropping social and legal investigation into the catalysts and custodians of sexual violence, anchored in and informed by Professor Rosenfeld's decades of searing work on the subject. Hers has been both expert and painful work, a public service she has fought to sustain amidst the most twisted and sordid moments of patriarchal oppression. Bolstered by her knowledge that the sexual violence–free bonobos exist and have something to offer us, Professor Rosenfeld has created an arguable and achievable vision for a world in which women are finally liberated from the violence of men.

What could that vision be?

Bonobo society is egalitarian. All females live free from sexual coercion and harassment by all males. Period.

Sit with that.

How, evolutionarily speaking, did a little-heralded species arrive at this radically different outcome, when, for example, 100 percent of female chimpanzees, their closest primate relatives, are severely beaten and sexually coerced? We humans are, too, very close cousins of bonobos (closer than gorillas), and yet, like chimpanzees, we suffer from male aggression and patriarchy.

What have bonobos done to arrive at their singular, male violence–free model? The more important question is, might it be possible for us to look to them for traces of, or even guidance on, how to ameliorate human violence? This exciting book offers a resounding "Yes!"

Without being irresponsible or fanciful with the science, or wishfully extrapolating and overlaying bonobo society onto *Homo sapiens*, we can nonetheless take fact and inspiration from decades of fieldwork by evolutionary biologists, primatologists, and anthropologists who follow and study wild bonobos in the Democratic Republic of Congo, the only place in the world bonobos exist.

Strong female coalitions undergird bonobos' stable, peaceful societies. Dig this: female bonobos coalesce *without kinship ties*. They come together, help each other, share food, groom, cooperate, protect each other, (1) whether or not they are related,

(2) whether or not they even know each other, and (3) whether or not they even like each other (as observable and measured by time spent playing, hanging out, grooming, and sharing valuable resources).

Additionally, when a female reaches reproductive age and is ready to migrate out of her natal group to a new community, she forms an alliance with an older female to help her integrate into her new home. Males gain their status in their communities through the presence of a dominant mother, who helps ensure his reproductive success. In short, females are essential to stable flourishing, fundamentally expressed through coalitions between other females.

Perhaps we women can do what they do. We can build coalitions and issue a bonobo call for each other. Whether or not we are related, know each other, or particularly like each other.

Wow.

I have seized the bonobo call for myself. I originally met bonobos in 2008 during my first trip to the Congo doing sexual and gender-based violence work through a grassroots public health focus. Encountering the trauma caused by the extensive violence against women and children during that first stay in the Congo nearly shattered my soul. Bonobos at the Lola ya Bonobo reserve near Kinshasa loved me back to life. Shortly after, I met my partner, who runs one of only three bonobo research camps in the world. With him, I began spending time in the rain forest to follow the bonobos in their Congolese rain forest basin habitat.

Being with bonobos in the wild has been the honor of a lifetime. I am moved to the depths of my soul when I sit on the fecund earth under the trees in which they have built their night nests and watch as they first begin to stir while the equatorial sun rises. I watch while that first lazy arm dangles out of the nest, or a baby peeks over, or a hungry juvenile slowly brachiates toward its first piece of fruit of the morning. It often makes me weep. When they come down from their nests, we follow them throughout the day, observing their behaviors, feeding, grooming, copulating, sharing, playing, laughing, antics, and highjinks. And notably, wonderfully, we observe a complete lack of sexual coercion, no beating of females, no violence of any kind, no infanticide, no homicide, no harm. We watch as females express choice as to when to copulate and with whom. I have personally witnessed, over and over again, what seems like thoughtful consideration by a female as she is approached and solicited by a male, and how she decides whether or not she wants to take him up on the offer of sex. If she agrees, she chooses the place, somewhere along a high tree branch or perhaps over yonder on a grooming log. When she does not reciprocate interest, he simply wanders off and leaves her be. What we could learn from this! In the rare instances where a male does aggress, the reaction from the nearby females is extraordinary: they stunningly rush together, shriek and bellow, gesture and posture intimidatingly, flinging their arms about and jumping wildly, while all other males scatter hither and yon. They let their brother suffer the terrifying consequences of his misguided social behavior as the females shake him down. The other males do not interfere, but rather observe from a safe distance in fear of the females' coalition.

So herein, open your heart and mind to a fiercely intelligent analysis of patriarchy and sexual violence, and to the exhilarating introduction of our dear closest relatives, the bonobos. They can teach us egalitarianism, the effective social power of female alliances and coalitions, and the benefits and joys of living free from sexual coercion and violence. May it be so with us.

Ashley Judd

Kokolopori Bonobo Research Reserve
Democratic Republic of Congo

INTRODUCTION

Bonobos are living proof that patriarchy is not inevitable.

Our most closely related evolutionary cousins, the bonobos, are peaceful, loving, food sharing, freely sexual, and xenophilic, meaning they love strangers, they do not fear them. Why? Because in their female-led social order, they have nothing to fear.

Here's how it works: If a female bonobo is aggressed upon, she lets out a special cry, and other females—whether they know her, like her, or are related to her—rush immediately to her defense from wherever they are. They form coalitions instantaneously with remarkable speed. Together they fend off the aggressive male, biting his ear or toe, and send him into isolation. When he returns, in a few days or later, they all reconcile, and he does not aggress again. And here is the most significant takeaway: evolutionarily, bonobos have eliminated male sexual coercion.

This model of collective self-defense changes everything.

I first learned about bonobos from Richard Wrangham, a Harvard University anthropologist, when we were on a panel together in 2004. He explained that primates use male sexual coercion to control females as reproductive resources. For example, male chimpanzees batter fertile females; male orangutans force copulation with lone females; male silverback gorillas commit infanticide, abduct the infant's mother, impregnate her, and add her to their harem. We humans hear about this violence and consider how brutal nature is, but we don't question its logic because it fits with our expectation of male behavior. We think of male violence as our legacy, our evolutionary destiny. Bonobos invite us to think again. It might be that bonobos prevented patriarchy from ever taking hold. They might represent a "pre-patriarchal" social order that stopped violence from becoming the organizing principle of society. And it produced instead a harmonious, peaceful, cooperative, and joyful community. This book contends that such a society is not only possible, it is proven by the existence of the bonobos. Bonobos look very similar to chimpanzees, so much so that they were not recognized as a separate species until 1929. They are found only in the Democratic Republic of the Congo and are less studied and less well known than chimpanzees. Nevertheless, the fascinating and developing body of work being done around bonobos reveals possibilities for peaceful coexistence between males and females that we might never have thought possible.

To say I was riveted while learning about our bonobo cousins would be a wild understatement. At that point in my career, I had spent more than a decade as an activist legal scholar and lawyer searching for ways to end male sexual violence. I had tried to do this through asking audacious questions to expose the underlying inequalities of our legal system and social order: "Why Doesn't *He* Leave?," for example, became the title of my master's thesis at Harvard Law School challenging the deeply flawed societal expectation that sending women to battered women's shelters is an acceptable approach to domestic violence. But my new insights into bonobos opened a whole new world of possibilities to eliminate male sexual coercion and with it the underpinnings that cause, support, and perpetuate patriarchal violence.

Patriarchal violence is the term I use to describe the amount and type of male coercion necessary to preserve a male-dominated social order.

Richard and I were mutually compelled by our respective fields, so we created and cotaught a course on theories of sexual coercion to more fully explore the potential of bonobos to inform human law and society. Teaching this class with Richard gave me the opportunity to test the hypotheses about the power and potential of female alliances to change the world. The book you are now reading is the result of that inquiry.

That the idea of female alliance was born of a collaboration with a male colleague is not ironic—though at first glance it might appear to be. Female alliances don't exclude males; quite the opposite. And we will see more of how and why in the coming pages, where I invite everyone to join in new coalitionary forces to thwart, once and for all, the power of violence to shape the world. I call these alliances the Bonobo Sisterhood. This sisterhood excludes no one, and all are welcome as long as they abide by the Bonobo Principle. It is a two-part principle, and if you agree with it, you are part of the Bonobo Sisterhood.

The first part: No one has the right to pimp my sister. With *pimp* I include any form of patriarchal violence from gaslighting to economic, emotional, physical, sexual, and psychological abuse.

The second part: Everyone is my sister.

For now, though, we have to start where we are, in a world saturated with patriarchal violence.

Every day in the United States, three to four women are killed by their estranged husbands or boyfriends. Black women are at a 40 percent higher risk of being killed. LGBTQ people experience intimate partner violence at rates comparable to and even higher than their heterosexual counterparts.

The National Network to End Domestic Violence (NNEDV) conducts a day-long survey once a year to offer a snapshot of domestic violence in the United States. Here's the snapshot from a single day in 2019: Because of domestic abuse and the threat of domestic homicide, almost 43,000 women and children were refugees from their own homes. They were running for their lives, forced to seek emergency shelter, forced to go into hiding. They were escaping from domestic terrorists who had been holding them hostage with threats and violence. That same day, more than 11,000 requests for shelter services went unmet, and 7,732 of those were for domestic terrorism refugees. Perhaps if we recognized them as refugees, we could see domestic violence as a crisis.

This violence is the backdrop of our everyday lives. Part of why we view patriarchal violence as inevitable is that until now we have not had a proven way to eliminate it. We're taught to rely on laws or law enforcement to protect us. But the moment we delegate our safety to someone else, we give up our power to them. Bonobos show us that uniting with other females and allies, coming physically to one another's defense in numbers, will shut down aggression. We have a way out.

The anthropologist Amy Parish, a leading expert in bonobo studies, has said, "Bonobo females live the goals of the human feminist movement: behave with unrelated females as if they are your sisters."

And everyone is your sister.

This approach excludes no one. It includes everyone.

The Bonobo Sisterhood is the missing piece that changes everything. And it's possible that in a butterfly politics sense, Ashley Judd is the bridge that connects it all. When she courageously came forward publicly against Hollywood producer Harvey Weinstein, she reignited the #MeToo movement. Women from all over the world came forth with their own experiences, showing the extent of the problem, and uniting survivors around the world. The Women's Marches, the largest in history, showed our willingness to protest this untenable situation. What was lacking was a solution, and that's what this book proposes: a collective self-defense to protect ourselves and our sisters. This would be unlike anything that has been tried or conceived of to date, at least on a large scale. And it is something we can begin to create tomorrow.

The book is divided into three parts: the Problem, the Pivot, and the Promise. The first part presents the pervasive *problem* of patriarchal violence, identifying how it flows as an undercurrent in our everyday lives. Informed by decades of legal experience and teaching at Harvard Law School, I share my perspectives on why we take for granted or view as inevitable the level of male sexual violence in our society and world. Women think and are taught that law will come to their aid if they are harmed. But as Thelma famously said in *Thelma and Louise*, "The law is some tricky stuff!" When it comes to protecting women from sexual violence, the law slips and slides and ultimately elides the problem, giving whatever justification it can while being careful not to admit misogyny. Women and girls are taught that men will protect them from violence; but this, too, is often misguided.

What will finally enable us to take an unvarnished look at the role of sexual violence in establishing and maintaining gender-based hierarchies is knowing that for the first time, we have a way forward. The bonobos light the way out of this well-worn patriarchal path. We take heed from the way they operate socially.

If one of us is at risk, then we are all at risk. So we work together to eliminate the risk as if it is happening to each of us personally. The *pivot* is learning that you are worth defending; and that you have the power and right to defend yourself. Self-defense changes everything. It is the turning point that corrects the delegation of our protection to men. Instead, we learn to protect ourselves, and this in turn ignites our ability to defend our sisters.

From the pivot of learning we have selves worth defending, we move to the *promise*. The promise of the Bonobo Sisterhood is that we can start enacting the principles now. And that we have all the tools we need. Building the Bonobo Sisterhood is as easy as standing next to a stranger you think might be in trouble because someone is harassing her on the subway car. Building the Bonobo Sisterhood means looking around at your chosen sisters and exploring how together you can forge new bonds inspired by the energy of knowing that we can transform our circumstances by creating our own collective self-defense. We will do this by reframing the question of equality to ask not how women are equal to men, where men are the standard of comparison, but we ask how do we promote equality among and between women? And what happens when we identify and choose to share our resources and protection with other women and girls?

The energy of the Bonobo Sisterhood is palpable, tangible. I had the wonderful opportunity of giving a keynote speech at the Omega Institute for Holistic Studies in upstate New York. The night before my talk, my Bonobo Sisters and I went out to an Italian restaurant. The women knew one another only through me and had only just met the day before. You would never know that from the intense, ecstatic, joyous, hilarious bonobo bonding that took place at that dinner. We were all supercharged by the excitement of having a new theory of life; a new way to confront the status quo and make it so much better.

Everything I learn about bonobos gives me hope, as humans with the capacity for sophisticated language, morality, law, and the ability to articulate rights backed by a collective self-defense.

We can choose to be bonobo. We choose love over fear; abundance over scarcity; peace over war; sexual choice and freedom over coercion.

As we embark on this journey, please know that I am coming from a place of inclusion, love, and respect. The frame of patriarchal violence is premised on male supremacy over females. All our gender relationships take place against this background; and all will change when that changes. The Bonobo Sisterhood gives us the framework for comprehensive gender inclusion. And our new lens on equality among women allows us to transcend racial, ethnic, class, geographic, and other divisions. Through this change in focus, we consciously choose to be bonobo; to share in our abundance in creating a new social order.

I offer you this book with the hope that the bonobos light up your inner power to change the world.

Welcome to the Bonobo Sisterhood. Let's begin.

PART ONE

THE PROBLEM

CHAPTER 1

ANSWER THE CALL

In the Wamba forest in the Democratic Republic of the Congo, a group of female bonobos curled up into the branches of nearby trees to take a postbreakfast nap. However, the male bonobos around them had different plans, swinging and howling in excitement as they observed one particular female who was in estrus. In the blink of an eye, three high-ranking females swung down from the treetops toward the aggressing males, pursuing and biting them until the four ran off.

WHAT JUST HAPPENED?

"What just happened?" I asked, appalled, as I turned to the prosecutor. We were being shuffled aside to make room for the next litigants. It was July 1994, the humidity clinging to us in the barely air-conditioned courtroom at 13th and Michigan in Chicago. This morning call was exclusively for domestic violence cases; the courtroom was packed, standing room only. The prosecutor shrugged as he moved us along. This judge did not care about these cases, he explained; the judge wasn't running for reelection.

I was then the acting chief of the Women's Advocacy Division of the Illinois Attorney General's Office. Donna, a petite woman in her midtwenties, had called the office the day before asking for help with her order of protection hearing. I explained that we were a policy-making office that did not get involved directly in cases, but after hearing the terror in her voice, I agreed to meet her in court, not as her lawyer but as a legal advocate. In criminal court, the prosecutor represents the state and would act as her lawyer. I therefore had no formal role; I was there to provide whatever support I could through my presence.

Donna's fear was palpable and justified. Two weeks earlier, she had obtained an emergency order of protection against her ex-boyfriend Rick. Such an order is available ex parte, which means it can be obtained without the defendant appearing in court. The defendant is then served a summons to appear in court within ten to fourteen days for a full hearing.

After Rick was served with the summons, he was furious. He instigated a car chase, eventually cutting Donna off and blocking her in. When he approached her car carrying a lug wrench, she rolled down her car window, fearful of his shattering the glass. He threatened to "rip her guts out," reached in, and ripped her T-shirt, at which point Donna's father, a much smaller man, jumped out of the passenger seat and tried to restrain him.

Rick, about six feet tall and weighing around three hundred pounds, turned his wrath on Donna's father, beating him so severely that he needed to go to the hospital. That was the story she told me over the phone, pleading for any help I could offer.

I met Donna outside a packed courtroom. Every day the United States' domestic violence courts, which are dedicated to such cases, are filled with women like Donna, women in an abject state of terror. Every day, judges hear case after case concerning men, almost all of them like Rick, threatening violence to women they view as "theirs." It is so common, so ubiquitous, so woven into our everyday existence that nearly all of us accept these assembly-line courtrooms, society's tepid response to domestic violence, as natural and sufficient. As just life.

We have lost the sense of urgency presented by this form of domestic terrorism; our lack of a feeling of immediacy belies the potentially lethal danger created by men seeking to control women. The existence and absolute necessity of special courts dedicated to domestic violence blinds us to the fact that we should not need any such courts. Their existence, with the long queues of terrified women, testifies to a system that routinely fails to provide a comprehensive safety net for endangered women by holding the abusers accountable.

That day, however, standing as an advocate for Donna, I had the visceral realization that changed my life. Donna was not merely a faceless statistic of the many endangered women. She was a five-foot, two-inch–tall mother. She was the terrified ex-girlfriend of a repeat abuser. And Rick, whom she pointed out for me, was no faceless threat; his intimidatingly large frame was encased in a gray suit.

The case was called, and we all stood up and approached the judge's bench. Rick asked for a thirty-day continuance to find a lawyer. The judge agreed, banged his gavel, and called for the next case. The prosecutor did not intercede to tell the judge that Rick had already violated the emergency order of protection and that Donna was in potentially lethal danger. I was incensed.

From the court, Donna and I went to talk to the court's advocate for domestic violence cases. Seated on bare wooden chairs in the advocate's dilapidated cubicle, the three of us discussed a safety plan. Donna's eyes filled with tears as she explained that

Rick had already broken into her apartment, so she did not feel safe there. She did not want to stay at her father's house and further endanger him. So she had been sleeping in her car for the past four days.

We all agreed that she needed to find a battered women's shelter. The court advocate picked up the phone to start calling around the Chicago area. With luck, she said, one would have an available bed.

Luck? At this moment, a proverbial brick fell on my head. The profound injustice of the situation occurred to me with blinding clarity. I represented the chief legal officer for the state of Illinois, and this was the best that I could do for this citizen? The system had just allowed a dangerous criminal to roam the streets freely while I was hoping to put this woman into hiding. How in the world did we get to this place? How was I complicit? What could possibly be done?

I now have answers. But at that moment, what I knew was that the United States has built and staffed specialized courtrooms filled with terrorized and terrified women desperately pleading for protection from their intimate partners. And rather than provide them with any meaningful help, our system is set up to make it their own responsibility to keep themselves safe.

The courts cannot keep up with the demand. Overstretched prosecutors cannot keep up with the demand. The insufficient number of beds in women's shelters cannot keep up with the demand. Where are women to turn when their lives and the lives of their children are at risk?

On a typical day in the United States, domestic violence hotlines receive around 20,000 calls for help. More than half of the 76,525 victims served in one day in September 2020 were women and children fleeing their homes from domestic violence, forced to seek shelter elsewhere. On top of that, 11,047 requests for services were unmet. Fifty-seven percent of those unmet pleas were for shelter. These numbers are staggering.

Even if you are not being terrorized by an abusive partner, you are aware at some level that many of your sisters are. It is a force that shapes women's collective consciousness, keeping us in a state of fear of and subordination to male violence. At some level of awareness, most of us accept an existence that floats between "There but for the grace of God go I" and "Nothing more can be done about it."

We are told, both implicitly and explicitly, that we have to accept this state of affairs. We are lulled into complacency by the sense that the problem is too big and too entrenched to address. This is the way things have been, how they have always been, how they must be. Just look at history, law, and biology, we are told. Shrug and make room for the next litigants.

But we also know that this is unacceptable. We must take a hard look at how living under a constant cloud of patriarchal violence affects women's lives every day. And we must commit to steadfastly refusing to continue accepting it. Along with that refusal, we need to have the confidence of knowing that there is a new, different, proven way forward.

WOMEN NEED AN ARMY

Robin, of average height, weight, and appearance for a recently terrorized thirtysomething-year-old, sat silently in the passenger seat of my mom's car. It is December 2019, and I was a generation older than I was when I worked for the Illinois Attorney General's Office. In the privacy of the car I asked how she was doing. She lowered her head and started sobbing. A minute, two went by. Then she said, "I am a quiet person, and it's hard for me to say." She raised her eyes then. "I can't tell you how much I appreciate what you did for me. You literally changed my life."

We were in the parking lot outside the Lake County Courthouse in Waukegan, Illinois. It was a steel gray, cloudy day. We had spent the morning in court, but now that ordeal was over and she let out a sigh of relief with her whole being. She was experiencing a moment of reprieve. I shared her sense of relief.

It was pure coincidence that I was in town and able to show up for the court hearing. The day before, as I had been boarding my flight from Boston to Chicago to visit my mother, I had received an email from my colleague Michael Bischof. Mike was forwarding a message he had received through the Cindy L. Bischof Memorial Foundation. He had created the foundation, dedicated to helping victims of domestic violence, in honor of his sister, a successful commercial real estate broker who at forty-three had been murdered by her ex-partner. The message was from a close friend of Robin's. It was pleading for help. It said, in all caps, "I AM TERRIFIED HE IS GOING TO KILL HER IF HE GETS OUT."

I heard this as a bonobo call for help, and when I landed in Chicago I immediately reached for my phone. The facts were these. The defendant, John, had been in custody for several days after breaking into Robin's house by disabling her security code. He had also called in a bomb threat to her high school reunion. He had done that while watching her from the parking lot and sending her messages proving that he could see her from where he was. He had sent Robin and others close to her incessant messages from unknown numbers expressing his sexual longing, lewd to angry, for her. It was a pattern of stalking, cyberstalking, and gaslighting, the term for a deliberate effort to make another person think he or she is the one who is disturbed and unstable. Simply, John engaged in a campaign of harassment to keep Robin in a constant state of fear.

I connected with Robin later that night. We'd never met, and she knew nothing about how Mike had received her friend's pleading email or how it had ended up reaching me earlier that day. After introductions, I told her I would be in the court for next morning's hearing. What I didn't try to explain was that I had received the bonobo call just as I happened to be going to Chicago, and I had taken it as a sign that I needed to show up in person.

Robin had not intended to appear in court, as she was too frightened to see John, especially if he was to be released. But when I told her we could meet up first and that she would not have to face him in the courtroom, she agreed.

Then I got to work. I took all the information I had and wrote a letter to the Lake County state's attorney, whose office would be prosecuting the case. In it, I did an informal danger assessment that detailed the threats that John had made against Robin and the laws he had broken. I emphasized that her case had come to my attention through the Cindy L. Bischof Memorial Foundation, a name that carries weight in Illinois. Cindy Bischof's ex-boyfriend, who had several orders of protection against him that he violated many times over, shot her in the head as she left work on a Friday afternoon. Immediately after her death, Michael Bischof and I collaborated on the Cindy Bischof Act to provide GPS monitoring for high-risk domestic violence offenders. This is a simple and effective way to enforce the terms of an order of protection that can save the lives of endangered women. It was one of the legal policy proposals I made in the wake of working on Donna's case, and now over half of the states have laws authorizing such monitoring in domestic violence cases.

Armed with the letter, I arrived at the courtroom early. I asked the bailiff to let the state's attorney know that I would like to meet before the hearing. The bailiff promised he would but warned that it would be a while.

I used the free time to good advantage. Down the hall from the courtroom was a windowless office for the domestic violence advocacy program. It was staffed by three overworked women. Awaiting my turn, I asked one of them if a danger assessment of any kind had been done on Robin's case. She looked at me blankly and said no, she didn't think so. She added that she didn't know what a danger assessment was. Neither did her two coworkers.

I channeled my frustration into a patient explanation. A danger assessment is a questionnaire victims fill out so the court can better assess the level of danger her abuser poses. For example, if he has threatened to kill her, if he has a gun, and/or if she thinks he could kill her, she would be at high risk, and her case would be handled accordingly.

I knew that to level my frustration at those three women crammed into a small office and tasked with helping to address as systemic a problem as domestic violence would be the worst kind of counterproductive action. They were there to help, but they had not been given even the most basic information or training to be able to advise victims effectively. It wasn't their fault that the system is set up to do so little.

The assistant state's attorney finally came out to meet me. He was a short white man in his early thirties, dark hair, round glasses on a round face. His name was Eric. He was carrying a pile of case files in manila folders. I introduced myself and told him that the case against the defendant, John, was very serious. I ticked off the violations John had already been charged with and suggested several more that were being investigated by two different police departments. Robin was in potentially lethal danger, which was not reflected in the very low bond amount that, if John posted it, would enable him to leave the courtroom that day with no restrictions.

Eric evidenced little to no familiarity with the specifics of Robin's case. What he did know was that the case had not been flagged in any way that would have indicated John's potential lethality. Again, I suppressed my frustration, now tinged with fury.

In all likelihood Eric, given his caseload, had only minutes to review Robin's case before the hearing. The same was most likely true for all the cases he had in his files. But in Robin's case a series of almost accidental connections had caused me to hear her call for help just when I was able to provide it. I handed Eric the letter describing the seriousness of the threat John posed to Robin. Flustered, he excused himself, saying he would be back shortly. When he returned, he informed Robin and me that his boss would be handling the case.

The chief of the Felony Division then stepped in to prosecute the case. He was an older man, evidently more experienced. I had a sidebar with him in the courtroom, explaining further the contents of my letter and my assessment. He read parts of the letter to the judge and presented a list of violations charged and potential ones that had yet to be charged. The defendant's bail was increased from $2,500 to $250,000. The judge also ordered that John be held in custody and ordered that a full psychiatric evaluation be done to assess John's dangerousness. He stressed that John's release should not endanger Robin or people close to her.

This is what answering the bonobo call in a country filled with terrified women begging courts for protection from men can look like. And we know this to a certainty: right now it is woefully insufficient.

Sadly, I do not know what happened to Donna. We lost touch after I moved out east, though before I left I connected her with every available resource I could think of. I do, however, know what happened to Robin.

Months after she and I met in that courthouse, Robin wrote to me, "I wanted to reach out and give you an update. I would first like to say that I think of you often. You changed my life. I cannot thank you enough. I will never forget your words as we left the court room, 'Women need an army.' You, without a doubt, were my army. You have forever changed how I think and support someone."

Because we live in a patriarchy, we think in terms of an army. Fine. That's mostly apt. More apt, though, is the fact that we need an army of bonobos or, better yet, a Bonobo Sisterhood.

We must think in terms of sisters coming to a threatened woman's aid. The bonobos offer us a model for how to do that. If you feel you are threatened, you give the equivalent of the bonobo call, and an army of supporters comes to your aid. Just the presence of them will likely be enough to send the message that you are not as vulnerable as your oppressor counted on your being. You're not easy to defeat; you're not an easy target to be hit or kicked or rendered a "battered woman." I want us to be stronger. Together we will be.

I want you never to be struck, but if you are, I want you to know that the violation will call forth the wrath of an army of bonobos. We are coming to stand with you. We will protect you. And in turn, you, too, will answer the call. And the world's Johns and Ricks will be on notice.

To be stronger together, we have to confront the problem. We have to understand that the problem isn't Robin's or Donna's, it isn't that of an individual woman in individually bad circumstances. Nor is it the problem of Illinois or of any other single state or nation. Yes, John and Rick are part of the problem, but they are only a part of it. It is the world of John and Rick that is at the heart of the problem. In recognizing that truth, we recognize something fundamental: that this is our problem, a problem for an army of women to solve.

THE EVERYDAY UNDERCURRENTS OF SEXUAL VIOLENCE

The reality of how sexual violence runs as an undercurrent to our daily lives unfolded for me one semester at the beginning of my Gender Violence, Law and Social Justice course at Harvard Law School. One particularly memorable year, a student shared a narrative about the intergenerational transfer of toleration of intimate partner violence in her family. Once she came forward, she created a space for others to join. It had a contagious effect, similar to that of the #MeToo movement but on the much smaller scale of our classroom. The power of truth telling is transformative. It enables people to release shame that is not theirs to carry. Individual narratives inspire others to share, and before long there are stacks and stacks of stories, all bearing remarkable similarities.

The various narratives by the students included shocking amounts of intimate partner and family violence. The most extreme was a student realizing that her father's suicide that had resulted in the deaths of her mother and a sister was actually a murder-suicide. He had killed himself through carbon monoxide poisoning in his car in the garage, knowing that the fumes would enter the house as well. Another wrote of her ex-partner standing on her neck while holding their infant and laughing, saying, "Look what I can do to your mother!" Another involved abuse in a same-sex relationship; yet another dealt with a father who was in prison for failing to pay child support.

That was in just one class, one year. The sharing of narratives created the kind of consciousness-raising space where revolutions are born.

We were in the hallowed halls of Harvard Law School with its students who, just by entering them, announce that they are at the top of their game, having succeeded in getting this far this early in life. For those who are prone to imagining that sexual abuse, sexual harassment, and domestic violence are the problems of others, know that the women who reach HLS will prove you wrong. They are talented, engaged, fired up, and eager to explore the fields of knowledge and professional opportunity open to them. They are also, as are all women, survivors of patriarchy.

When asked if they personally know someone who has been abused by an intimate partner, every single student in my class raises a hand. We shouldn't be surprised, yet we are surprised when we must confront the extent, the normalcy of the problem. And in a perverse kind of equality, it happens to all of us. No one is immune.

Most of the students who enroll in my course are women. In the first week, I generally have a healthy handful of men, but they fall off by the end of the add/drop period. Many gender-nonconforming folks take the class as well, knowing it will be a safe space. All of the students who stick it out discover that my classroom is a place where they can make sense of their individual experiences in an indisputably patriarchal society.

In this patriarchy, no one is immune to its effects, although it is important to keep in mind the wide range of them as we move through the pages of this book. While I present some of the most horrific and extreme cases, please know that the vast majority of relationships are not violent. Healthy interpersonal relationships abound; we have more capacity than ever to negotiate openly our gender roles. Yet we must take an unvarnished look at the problem to confront its reality and scale in order to honestly address it. Knowing that we have new solutions at hand enables us to do this without despair.

The vast majority of sexual violence goes unremarked upon until it turns into a lawsuit or a murder. And when stories of sexual violence reach the media, they are treated it as something remarkable, sensational, conveyed with an air of shock and resignation. The murder is reported; the underlying, escalating violence seldom is. But domestic violence homicide is so predictable as to be preventable. It is by far the most predictable type of homicide there is. We know who the intended victim is. We know that the motive is to control her and prevent her from leaving. We know that just after leaving an abuser is the most dangerous time for a woman and her children and that her partner's abuse will become more frantic, more violent, more desperate. We know this well enough by now to expect it.

When we read a headline, "Woman Killed, Husband Sought," we turn the page. But stop for a moment and think: Why is the husband or boyfriend always the first suspect when a woman is killed? Why isn't he the last person we would think capable of such an atrocity?

It's because we have become resigned to it. It just happens. Sometimes news articles list a local or national hotline for people to call. But never does an article call for intervention and action at the first signs of abuse. The rare tracking down of foreign terrorists gets top-of-fold, page A1 coverage; the ubiquitous terroristic reign of men against women barely makes the paper.

It does not need to be this way. There should, in fact, be a law. In the nineteenth century, the philosophers John Stuart Mill and Harriet Taylor Mill thought that a crime committed against someone in a position of trust or dependence should be treated as all the more egregious. We have come to assume the opposite. A husband assaults and murders a wife. A boyfriend assaults, rapes, and murders a girlfriend. Turn the page.

In part, we are numb to intimate partner homicide. We never hear about the abuse until it escalates into a homicide, so we think there is nothing we can do about it. If a woman's husband or boyfriend did it, that was between them. The violence is contained in that household, that family, that relationship. Worse, we think that maybe it was the victim's fault for taking up with him, for not getting away from. The media report intimate partner homicides with an air of resignation. The reporting lulls readers into a sense of inevitability, but always someone else's inevitability.

What if the headlines were different? What if, instead, a headline read, "Woman Stops Abuser in His Tracks"? What if there were an army of women who could stop the violence? What if that army of women knew what is a well-established fact: that real intervention will prevent the escalation of intimate partner violence?

A call for help—or for an army—works only if those who can help, who can summon an army, listen. And then act.

"MURDER HAS ABUSE VICTIMS TERRIFIED"

I remember vividly one morning in 1999 when my friend Alexa and I were having coffee over the Sunday newspapers. She handed me the Metro section of the *Boston Globe*. "Di, you have to read this," she said. "Murder Has Abuse Victims Terrified" read the headline. The article that followed told the story of Carol Cross.

Kenneth Emrick had been abusing her for nearly two decades. They had four children. After many attempts to end his violence against her, Carol finally obtained an order of protection. It was Friday. The following Tuesday, she went with a friend and a police escort to pick up her children and her belongings. She waited outside, standing in front of the police car with her friend while the officer went to the front door. Emrick answered from behind the closed door. He told the officer he needed a minute with the kids. He bolted the door. Then he went upstairs, got a rifle, pointed it out the window, and with a single shot killed Carol. The shot went through her neck and into her friend's stomach. She died on the scene; her friend survived. Emrick then turned the gun on himself.

In a country in which three to four women a day are murdered by their intimate partners, the crime was not particularly remarkable, except that it was committed in front of a police officer, thus demonstrating the lack of protection available. Carol had tried to leave Kenneth, so he killed her. What was remarkable about the case, however, was the effect it was having on women in abusive relationships in the town of Lewiston, Maine. It turned out that the Abused Women's Advocacy Project there reported that 75 percent of women seeking orders of protection were too afraid to appear in court. Why? Because their abusers were leaving them clippings of news articles about Carol's murder as a way of terrorizing them, saying, "Go get your goddamn order of protection—you see what it did for her."

To me, this was a crisis in citizenship. For 75 percent of women to have no access to justice because that access is directly threatened by someone who is endangering their lives is unacceptable. It is a call to action.

I had recently moved back to Boston from Washington, DC, where I had served as Senior Counsel in the Office on Violence Against Women at the US Department of Justice. I heard the women of Lewiston making a bonobo call. A loud one. And, remembering Donna and other women I had helped, I offered to marshal whatever resources I had to intervene.

I left a message for Chris Fenno, the executive director of the advocacy project in Lewiston. She called back the next morning, and we talked about options, such as having the police hold a press conference to reassure endangered women of their rights to protection and safety. She arranged a meeting with a small Bonobo Sisterhood made up of her board and staff and a lawyer who helped the organization for me to hear about the situation in their community. I drove the three and a half hours to the secret location of the battered women's shelter where our meeting was to take place. We convened in a small room where we sat for hours as they told me harrowing stories about women's interactions with the police department. Afterwards, as I sat in my car, exhausted and spent from hearing these stories, I realized that this was the case for which I went to law school. A chance to make a real difference—to use the law to address a fundamental question of access to justice.

The organization spent the next few months putting together an impressive report entitled "Voices of Survivors," containing searing data on the domestic violence cases in the area. We called a meeting with the town mayor, the police chief, and the city attorney. I channeled my mentor, Jane DiRenzo Pigott, as I led the meeting to discuss our options for going forward. Rather than take a litigation route, the city agreed to have me convene a national team to retrain their police department and change their policies on how to handle domestic violence cases. It made a difference on many levels. It vastly improved the officers' understanding of the potential lethality of seemingly mundane domestic violence cases, and it reestablished a trusting relationship between the department and the community.

Let's pause to consider what would make that headline more truthful. Notice that the *Globe*'s "Murder Has Abuse Victims Terrified" was a distortion of the facts. An accurate headline would have been "Men Have Women Terrified."

In the United States, more than 80 percent of violent crimes are committed by men. Eighty-five percent of intimate partner violence in the United States is committed by men against women.

Words matter. The wrong words mute the facts. The right words amplify them.

Consider this simple yet brilliant exercise by Jackson Katz, a leading voice in the effort to stop male violence against women, that illustrates how we default to passive voice.

> *"John beat Mary"*—that's a good English sentence. "John" is the subject, "beat" is the verb, "Mary" is the object. Good sentence.
>
> Now we're going to move to the second sentence, which says the same thing in the passive voice—*"Mary was beaten by John"*—and now a whole lot has happened in one sentence. We've gone from *"John beat Mary"* to *"Mary was beaten by John"*; we've shifted our focus, in one sentence, from John to Mary. And you can see John is very close to the end of the sentence, close to dropping off the map of our psychic plane.
>
> By the third sentence, John is dropped, and we have "Mary was beaten," and now it's all about Mary. We're not even thinking about John. It's totally focused on Mary.
>
> Over the past generation the term we've used synonymous with *beaten* is *battered*, so we have *"Mary was battered."* And the final sentence in this sequence, flowing from the others, is *"Mary is a battered woman."* So now Mary's very identity, *"Mary is a battered woman,"* is what was done to her by John in the first instance, but we've demonstrated that John has long ago left the conversation.
>
> Now, those of us who work in the domestic and sexual violence field know that victim blaming is pervasive in this realm, which is to say blaming the person to whom

something was done rather than the person who did it. And we say things like "Why do these women go out with these men? Why are they attracted to these men? Why do they keep going back? What was she wearing at that party? What a stupid thing to do! Why was she drinking with this group of guys in that hotel room?" This is victim blaming. And there are numerous reasons for it, but one of them is that our whole cognitive structure is set up to blame victims.

When we use the passive voice, we lose our power to be effective. We become complicit in the erasure of the source of the violence. This encourages the worldwide focus on the victims of domestic violence. Consider "violence against women" statistics: they all measure victimization. The vast majority of societies focus their attention on the victims, not on the perpetrators. When I worked at the Department of Justice, I sometimes wandered the majestic halls of the main Justice building asking people why my office was called the Violence Against Women Office. From whence, I asked, does this violence arise? Does it fall from the sky? Is it disembodied from its source?

Dorothy Edwards, the founder of Green Dot, made the point that when we use the passive term *violence against women*, we have already given up, assumed the weak position. Our acceptance of this position will not get us to the goal of creating real change. During her presentations on bystander intervention, she shows a slide of the Starbucks logo. She asks what seeing it brings to mind. Most people have some active association with the brand: it reminds them that they need a cappuccino to get through the afternoon or that it is ridiculous to spend five dollars on a cup of coffee. Whatever the response, it is an active one. By contrast, think about the message conveyed when advocates enter a room representing "violence against women" organizations. Using the passive term conveys victim passivity, and the absence of any reference to the source of the violence precludes accountability. The abstract reference to "violence against women" allows us to distance ourselves from it rather than identify with it. The words, the branding, convey no energy, no progressive movement forward, no acknowledgment of who is perpetrating the violence and against whom. Society has branded male violence against women as a problem to track, not to solve.

Language is critically important, especially when articulating a demand for rights. Calls in passive terms do not call forth help, let alone an army. Our current "violence against women" language is standing in the way of real change.

Consider using *endangered woman* in place of *battered woman*. *Endangered* accurately indicates the ongoing nature of the abuser's threat to the woman's life. *Battered woman* conveys the opposite, its past tense suggesting that the abuse is over. Also, it evokes an image of a woman who is beaten down and unable to assert her rights. *Endangered woman*, however, is a call to action. It is a call to protect a woman from future danger. It invites us to examine the source of that danger and to eliminate it.

A step further is to replace *battered women's syndrome* with *male temper syndrome*. We should not pathologize a woman who is trying to cope with the confounding mix of love, hate, and misogyny that animates much male violence against women. Instead, we must address the real psychological problems that are the abuser's. We must pathologize the individual who in 85 percent of cases is male and uses power and control to manipulate and imprison his partner in the home. The syndrome needing a solution rests with the perpetrator, not the victim.

WHY DO WE SUSPECT THE HUSBAND FIRST?

In 2003 in an interview I gave to *Glamour* on domestic violence homicides, I posed the rhetorical question of why, when a woman is killed, the first suspect is the husband or boyfriend. Shouldn't we expect that man to be the last person to harm her rather than the first? The magazine cover listed the story as "Wife Killing Epidemic." I found the issue on the stands in an airport, glad to see the magazine was addressing the issue and hoping that the coverage would effectively raise awareness.

I opened to the story and found two full pages of thumbnail-size photographs of smiling, lovely women of all races. Five hundred women had already been killed that year, and it was only May. In the middle of the next page was an insert of photographs of various high-profile cases in which men were on trial or accused of killing women with whom they were in a relationship. One was Scott Peterson, who had killed his pregnant wife, Laci. Another case was the actor Robert Blake, who was charged with the murder of his wife of six months. He was acquitted but later found liable in a civil suit* for her wrongful death. Then there

---

* In certain instances, family members can bring civil suits for the wrongful death of their beloved one. Civil suits for wrongful death differ from criminal suits in two major ways: (1) the remedy sought in civil suits is typically monetary damages as opposed to a prison sentence and (2) the burden of proof in civil suits is lower than in criminal suits. Because the burden for civil suits is lower, it is possible for someone to be acquitted in a criminal case but be found liable in the civil suit.

was a photo of George Thompson, a lanky white man, in hand-cuffs. He was accused of killing his girlfriend, Julie Grace. My breath caught. I had known a woman named Julie Grace back when I had lived in Chicago. We had worked together at the Illinois Attorney General's Office. No, I thought, this is a national magazine, and that is a common name. I turned the page back to the photographs of the women we had lost, and there was Julie, with her big brown eyes and warm smile.

I felt gut punched. The sadness and shock came in cascades. Could I have done anything to help her? I had not been in contact with her for several years. She was a very resourceful and well-connected woman. What had happened?

Thompson was convicted of her murder. He served only three years in prison.

I held a memorial fundraiser for the Chicago Bar Association to honor Julie's memory and to raise awareness about red flags of potential lethality in intimate partner relationships. Another lawyer who helped with the event lived in the same building Julie had. She had seen George belittling Julie, putting her down. But it wasn't just friends who should have seen, heard, and acted; it was society. And it was certainly, it turns out, the criminal justice system.

Julie had met him in a rehab program the year before. He was in it for "anger" issues. Not long into the relationship, Thompson had thrown a barstool through the window of Julie's high-rise condominium on the twentieth floor. It could have killed someone. Her mother, Ruth Grace, had "received a panicked call from Julie. 'I heard this guy yelling and glass shattering. I didn't know what the heck was going on at first until I realized that Julie was beside herself. . . . I told her, "Julie, you run like hell. You get out of there!"'" Later that fall, Julie looked at real estate in Florida in hopes of moving near her parents and making a fresh start. Soon after returning to Chicago, on November 28, Thompson violently attacked her. Most likely, he knew she was planning to leave him, and separation assault refers to a batterer's attempts to regain control of their victims if they try to escape his reign of terror.

Separation assault, perhaps? He was convicted of domestic battery and ordered to stay away from Julie until June 2004. He was sentenced to eighteen months' probation. But again, Thompson beat Julie on March 7, 2003, and was again convicted of domestic battery. "Although he was given a ninety-day jail sentence, he never served the time because the sentence was postponed until June. In May, he was arrested and charged with Grace's murder."

The conclusion is inescapable: Julie's murder was predictable enough to have been prevented. How I wish she had had a Bonobo Sisterhood to protect her.

MALE TEMPER SYNDROME AND THE PROBLEM OF MALE ENTITLEMENT

How did we get here? For now, let's focus on just two things: male temper syndrome and the male entitlement continuum.

Male tempers are written into the law as if they are a fact of life. Throw a chair out an apartment building's window, and you are charged with destruction of property. The fact is that we live in a society that discounts male temper. There are battered women, not women endangered by male batterers. Our headlines track statistics on the victims of domestic violence, not the perpetrators. There are so many reasons to find this unacceptable, including the fact that focusing only on victims inhibits seeing, confronting, and ending the way male tempers are so often the controlling factor in the patriarchal family unit. The unit is built around this fact, the structure so embedded as to be invisible.

Women and children are not responsible for soothing male temper syndrome. It does not begin with us, and it cannot end with us. Women in abusive relationships will attest that nothing they do pleases their abusers; the rules change as they try to follow them. That's because assuaging the man's temper isn't the point; he expresses his temper to preserve his entitlement. I remember a case where the abusive husband made a list of rules for his wife to follow. "When we dance," one read, "you must look lovingly into my eyes." Another read, "I never want to see you cry." When she broke one of the rules, he had an excuse to punish her. He kept setting the rules and changing them. Compliance with all of them was not possible. And thus he had to punish her.

Male temper syndrome is a key factor in preserving male entitlement.

Imagine you are at home with your extended family. Dinner has just finished. What happens? In a majority of homes around the planet, the men retreat to the living room to do the equivalent of watching sports and shooting the breeze while the women get up to clear the table, clean up, and return the kitchen to a pristine state until the next meal must be prepared. This is what I refer to as SOYAAD, which stands for Sitting On Your Ass After Dinner. Anecdotal data, decades of collected data, all of it captures the fact that the concept is real and universal.

This is the left side, the less threatening one, of the male entitlement continuum. As we look at the right side, we see more dangerous and ultimately life-threatening behavior. But although this left-side behavior, from who controls the finances to who drives the car and chooses what to listen to on the radio, is widespread and seems harmless, I contend that it is not. It can set the stage for and reinforce female compliance. It represents the day-after-day, often minute-after-minute reenacting of the entitlement of men to be served by women.

The relationship of SOYAAD to overall male entitlement is not benign. It represents the backdrop of gender role enforcement, which is the basis of so much abusive behavior. Why? Because even the least violent end of the spectrum is enforced by male temper syndrome. Just the threat of arousing male temper is often enough to secure females' compliance and vast amounts of servitude.

All of this is part and parcel of the undercurrents of sexual violence that pollute the water in which we swim every day. One reason we have not been able to clean up these waters is that we treat patriarchal violence as if it does not have a point-source discharge, meaning as if it has no discernible source; it is, rather, just the way things are and have always been. It is therefore understandable that generations before us were overwhelmed by trying to fight for equal treatment.

This book offers a revolutionary new path. Having a tangible answer and knowing it works will enable us to confront the reality of the situation. Answering the call is where it begins. We must listen to and hear our sisters' stories and not be resigned to accepting the way men treat them. Ending centuries of men controlling women is possible, and within a generation, but the work to end it begins by knowing what must change. And that requires us to confront it head-on.

CHAPTER 2

MEN'S CASTLES, WOMEN'S SHELTERS

The last male bonobo to run off after being attacked by the coalition of bonobo females answering the call was the alpha male of the group. Researchers did not see the male for three weeks after the incident, and when he did return, they noticed he had a toe missing, presumably due to the bites of the females. Yet after his return, he did not take on his old place in the community. Instead, he remained timid and kept to himself, afraid to release the wrath of the females once again.

THUD

The thud of a man's footstep on the stairs. To the wife in the kitchen, it is a signal to be obeyed. As soon as she hears it, she is to get the food onto the table so that its temperature is perfect when he sits down to be served.

She waits in the kitchen, steadying herself with one hand on the cold marble counter, frozen until she hears that thud. Any misstep will be punished. She would like to avoid that if possible.

The woman in the kitchen is Patrisha McLean, and the footstep belonged to her ex-husband Don McLean, the famous musician who wrote "American Pie" and the sweet, sensitive song "Starry, Starry Night" about Vincent van Gogh. That is what the public knows. What Patrisha knew the night she called 911 was that he was going to kill her. "He was trying to shove open the locked bathroom door behind which I had barricaded myself. As it was splintering I pushed the numbers 911. . . . I believed when he broke through he would kill me." A photo of the splintered door chills one to the bone, capturing what Patrisha was going through when she called 911.

The police came, arrested Don, and took him to the police station, where he posted $10,000 bail and was released. He later pled guilty to charges of domestic violence assault, domestic violence criminal threatening, criminal restraint, and criminal mischief. And he paid over $3,000 in fines. But you would not be able to find this in court records, because under Maine's deferred disposition law,* if he did not violate the terms of his bail, such as no contact and no further crimes for a year, the crime he pled guilty to would be expunged from his record.

As in so many domestic violence cases, the punishment does not come close to fitting the crime. The fine is barely a slap on the wrist. The sentence requirements are structured in such a way as to let the offender construct a narrative that completely absolves him of responsibility. It hardly reflects the terroristic control he exerted over his family.

What it does reflect is that the ancient maxim that a man's home is his castle is alive and well. A footstep on the stair, and he was catered to. He exerted his patriarchal authority through

---

* Deferred disposition refers to laws that provide that if no further abuse is committed for a period of time, the case may be dropped from the offender's record.

violence, threats, and emotional abuse, all without any meaningful outside intervention. The inhabitants of the castle all knew their subservient roles. Patrisha worked constantly to keep the peace and to placate him lest he unleash a rage-filled attack. They lived in a house on a hill far enough away from neighbors that no one would hear the screams.

In Don McLean's narrative, he pled guilty not because he was but to preserve the privacy of his family. Yet he admitted in interviews—which arguably he would not have given were he in fact concerned about privacy—to having a temper, to being intolerant of any item in "his" house being out of place, to screaming at people when they were out of place, and to coming from an abusive home. Their daughter, Jackie McLean, has spoken openly about her father's abuse and how she processes it through her music. In an interview with *Rolling Stone*, she recalled how when she was two, her father thought she had hidden a key to a piece of furniture. "He was just screaming in my face. I couldn't leave, I couldn't move, I couldn't say anything. I didn't know where the key was and I was just trapped in that moment having to endure the fear and the trauma until it ended. That was just a normal kind of thing that there would be screaming and yelling." Every stage of her development was "met with some level of trauma." Patrisha recounted a rageful Don telling her he wished he could strangle her. Jackie recalled that "At one point he got really close to me and told me that he wished he could hit me." The fear was constant. Jackie said the experiences had made her "borderline suicidal."

The McLean family was wealthy, white, and living in an idyllic town in Maine with quaint shops and a beautiful harbor filled with sailboats. Yet the type of tyrannical control exerted by this "king" in his "castle" is substantially similar to men's reign in homes across economic and cultural lines.

Patrisha's story is disturbing on its own terms, but consider that most survivors of male temper syndrome are worse off. If someone of Patrisha's race, wealth, and status can be so imprisoned, what does it mean for women who are less privileged and have far fewer resources? Think about women who face institutional barriers that prevent them from getting help out of dire and life-threatening situations. Black women, Brown women, immigrant women, trans women, all report alarmingly similar experiences, including phone lines ripped out of walls or cell phones crushed so that they cannot call for help. Don did that to Patrisha, too, in an attempt to cut off her ability to communicate with the outside world. It is so common a tactic that it's included in forms for orders of protection. The isolation is intentional, not coincidental, a feature, not a bug, of patriarchal violence.

Black women are two and a half times more likely to be murdered by men than are their white counterparts. And more than 40 percent of Black women experience intimate partner violence, compared with 31.5 percent of all women. Black women face multiple and intersecting barriers to accessing help to get out from under their abuser's control. First, institutional racism in police departments means that a 911 call might result in an intervention that is much more harmful than helpful. It is well known that Black women often don't report domestic violence because they do not want to see another Black man go to jail. Also, Black women experience heightened levels of racism at battered women's shelters, which are predominantly run by white women in white neighborhoods. Already full, shelters do very little outreach and are often not an effective option for endangered women who are Black. So whereas men get castles, few women even get a bed in a shelter.

A MAN'S HOME IS HIS CASTLE

What do we mean when we say that a man's home is his castle?

In general, we do not give the phrase much thought. It joins a list of phrases we've grown up with: a man after my own heart, a gentleman and a scholar, be your own man, big man on campus. All of them deserve scrutiny, but few more than "A man is king of his castle."

The very notion of a castle invokes the idea of a fortress, an area protected by walls of stone. Castles are products of war; peaceful societies would not need them.

Here is a quote from the primatologist and anthropologist Richard Wrangham that merits slow reading:

> Human patriarchy has its beginning in the forest ape social world, a system based on males' social dominance and coercion of females. We can speculate that it was elaborated subsequently, perhaps in the woodland ape era, perhaps much later, by the development of sexual attachments with the same essential dynamic as gorilla bonds; women offering fidelity, men offering protection from harassment and violence by other men. From these poorly articulated forms of pairing, language would eventually generate both marriage and the patriarchal rules that favor married men. Men, following an evolutionary logic that benefits those who make the laws, would create legal systems that

so often defined adultery as a crime for women, not for men—a social world that makes men freer than women.

There is a line that runs for millennia from the forest ape to Kenneth Emrick's murder of his longtime partner, Carol, as she waited for a police officer to gain entrance to her home so she could pick up her kids. As Wrangham suggested, we can speculate; we do not have direct evidence of the castle doctrine among primates. But the patriarchal social order of male dominance and males' sexual coercion of females is undeniable. You can trace it through the phrase "A man's home is his castle"—a phrase created and perpetuated by the language of law.

Historically, the phrase reflects a legal designation of the man as king of his castle. Keep in mind that men made the laws to order their relationships among themselves and with their governments. The laws of marriage speak volumes about men's notions of male sovereignty at home and how marriage should be. They firmly established the patriarchal privilege of the man to beat and subordinate his wife. Not coincidentally, the primary place in which women appear in the law is within the institution of marriage.

The castle doctrine not only enshrined in law a man's sovereign right over the women living under his roof, it also established that a man's home was a place where he could be secure from unwarranted government intervention.

The Fourth Amendment of the US Constitution encodes the idea that a man is safe in his home, broadly outlining his freedom from "unreasonable searches and seizures by the government." But in the context of marriage and family law, it adds a crucially important layer of insulation from government interference that facilitates his rule over his wife and children.

Legal history reveals an explicit designation of the man as the "governor" of his "family-state." This designation of the male as sovereign plays a large role in our society's unwillingness to intervene in cases of family violence.

The history of marriage laws illuminates how and why marriage works as a fundamentally patriarchal institution. These legal underpinnings serve as the basis of the inequality in marital relationships. They exist no matter how good the health and happiness of your marriage. The deep roots of male entitlement run under and through all marriages. This is true whether the husband is the breadwinner or not. Beta males rule just as much as alphas, as they comfortably rest in their legally and culturally given entitlements.

"WIVES MUST CONFORM ENTIRELY TO THE TEMPER OF THEIR HUSBANDS"

The first-known law of marriage was formalized by Romulus (credited with founding Rome with his twin, Remus, in 753 BCE) and required married women, "as having no other refuge, to conform themselves entirely to the temper of their husbands and the husbands to rule their wives as necessary and inseparable possessions." "No other refuge," "conform themselves entirely," both enforced by the husband's temper. This law, nearly three thousand years old, speaks to a historical constant: men's tempers.

Men use, and are expected to use, escalating violence to control their wives. Consider this from the fifteenth century, written by Friar Cherubino of Siena:

When you see your wife commit an offense, don't rush at her with insults and violent blows. . . . Scold her sharply, bully and terrify her. And if this still doesn't work . . . take up a stick and beat her soundly, for it is better to punish the body and correct the soul than to damage the soul and spare the body. . . . Then readily beat her, not out of rage but out of charity and concern for her soul, so that the beating will redound to your merit and her good.

From Friar Cherubino to Don McLean, little has changed.

A man is king in his castle. A man is encouraged to use escalating violence to control his wife. These two ancient provisions are still felt. Girls and women are socialized to conform their behavior to the temper of their fathers and husbands, lest they provoke his rage. The rage might be physical violence or its threat, or emotional, verbal, or psychological abuse. The point is that angry men and frightened women reflect their expected gender roles, which are encoded into the law and lived out in so many of our homes.

In the 1950s, American housewives were advised by women's magazines to have the children bathed and ready, the house clean, and themselves presentable to greet the husband-father at the door with a smile and a drink when he got home.

The image, and the presumptions behind it, was ubiquitous enough that decades later, in the 1990s, Verizon ran a public service ad campaign against domestic violence featuring a picture of a bomb. The bomb appears to be making a ticking sound. The caption read, "Honey, I'm home!"

But what the '50s ideal and the '90s public service ad underscore is another inherent fallacy in thinking about male temper syndrome: female compliance will not be enough to stop it.

Abusive men change the rules of obedience so that compliance is impossible. In this world, the satisfaction comes in the gaslighting. Compliance just brings the abuser to his next trick.

This escalation of control calls to mind hamadryas baboons. When controlling their harem and moving from place to place, hamadryas baboon males glare and grimace at females if they try to stray from the group. If the glaring and grimacing do not work to subordinate the behavior of a female, the male bites her on the neck. Though the male's attack on the female is not lethal, it instills enough fear in her to bring her under his control, teaching her the lesson not to stray again.

As scientists such as Wrangham have shown, this pattern of behavior endures. The males will use violence to secure power and control over females. If scolding and threats do not work to intimidate one's partner into subordination, the male is given license, especially within the walls of his castle, to use increased physical violence to establish his dominion. Bullying and terrifying are common tools used by abusers to construct their reign of supremacy.

The idea, enshrined in culture and law, that women must tiptoe around their husbands' temper so as not to provoke them into violence is commonly described as "walking on eggshells." Women learn to self-regulate their behavior to avoid violent incidents. A wife is expected to secure her peace in his home through subordinating herself. Patrisha knew to have Don's dinner on the table at the exact moment he had trained her to serve him. Years of his physical and psychological attacks had taught her that lesson.

JUSTIFICATIONS FOR WIFE BEATING IN LEGAL HISTORY

Women's subjugation to their husbands has a long legal history, deeply ingrained in social practices. The laws of coverture provided that a woman's legal identity was suspended during a marriage. According to Sir William Blackstone, whose famous law treatises published from 1765 to 1769 are regarded as the most authoritative on a wide range of legal matters, the laws of coverture provided that upon marriage a wife's legal identity merged into that of her husband. Her legal identity as an independent human being was suspended during the course of the marriage.

"Femme covert" was regarded as being under the wing of her husband's protection. "Couvert baron" indicated that the wife was under the protection of her lord and baron. This is why, in Anglo-American systems, the wife traditionally took her husband's last name; she became his property. Fortunately, it is now much more common for women to keep their "maiden" names, reflecting a shift away from these outdated notions.

It is important to note that the institution of marriage has undergone tectonic changes over the past few years. Especially with the legalization of same-sex marriage in the United States, there is much good news to report. Yet the structural support beams are still built around male dominance and female subordination. The violence that is used as gender role enforcement within marriages stubbornly persists. We can presume that it is present unless the parties actively negotiate their respective gender roles. Defaulting to gender expectations without consciousness or honest discussions can unwittingly cause friction and marital discord because the roles as given have been based historically on dominance and submission rather than mutual respect and equality.

Think about what it means to lose your legal identity. It wasn't until the Married Women's Property Act of 1882 that married women in England, Ireland, and Wales (but not Scotland) were permitted to own and control property. The law in the United States evolved similarly; it wasn't until the passage of the Married Women's Property Act of 1848 that married women in New York, for instance, could own property. Any economic power a woman might have had before marriage she ceded to the control of her husband. Through the laws of marriage, he gained control over her.

Marriage also placed women's labor fully under the control of their husbands. Even today housework, child care, and elder care have economic value only if someone other than the wife does them. Benefiting from the labor women undertake in men's castles is a presumed prerogative of the resident king.

STATUTES OF CHASTISEMENT

Alongside the doctrine of coverture were the statutes of chastisement. These laws gave husbands the right, if not the duty, to physically "chastise" their wives. The combination of coverture and chastisement meant that what a man did to his wife was distinctly his province; coverture meant that injuries to the wife stayed legally invisible; and chastisement justified every man's control over the inhabitants of his castle.

According to Blackstone, chastising one's wife was regarded

as not only a husband's right but his duty, for "as the husband is to answer for her misbehavior, the law thought it reasonable to entrust him with this power of chastisement, in the same moderation that a man is allowed to correct his apprentices or children." Because the law of coverture suspended the woman's legal status during the marriage, the law effaced the wife and saw only the husband.

Rules in the home were explicitly enforced by the husband. Indeed, Blackstone stated that "the civil law gave the husband the same, or a larger, authority over his wife: allowing him for some misdemeanors, to beat his wife severely with scourges [whips] and cudgels [stout sticks with rounded heads] . . . for others only moderate chastisement." Thus, male supremacy was encoded into the law, which guaranteed that patriarchal control of the family would rest in the husband.

The principle that a man's home is his castle reflects a macropatriarchal architecture of law, culture, economy, and politics that ensures male supremacy. But men's rule within their castles affects women on the microlevel. Because isolation of women within their homes and marriages is such a common tactic of batterers, many women cannot see that it happens on the macrolevel, too. Women often fight to survive individually, not seeing the vast potential of collective actions.

The twin concepts of coverture and statutes of chastisement are the foundation of a man's right to beat his wife. Together, they meant that the state would not intervene to protect a wife from an abusive, violent husband. Think about this legal arrangement made by and between men giving them explicit control over "their" women. Think about the state's complicity in this arrangement, which, after all, was created by the state—not only complicity, but the state is arguably dependent on this arrangement. It secures men's rights in their homes based on a reciprocal agreement of nonintervention by the state. Each man can rule his castle as king without fear of reproach or interference.

Wife beating went from legal entitlement for husbands to legal prohibition. You'd think this would be a win for women, but the historical context helps us understand how the new laws were not strong enough to overcome the patriarchal agreement of nonintervention and thus remain largely ineffectual.

Although the chastisement statutes were formally repudiated, it would be a mistake to understand that "as an indicator of how the legal system responded to marital violence." As historians have noted, "during the Reconstruction Era, jurists and lawmakers vehemently condemned chastisement doctrine, yet routinely condoned violence in marriage."

Law and society move in an intricate dance in which law often lags behind society, in part because of the doctrine of stare decisis, which requires allegiance to laws as written rather than as interpreted by a particular judge. Although statutes of chastisement have not been legally in effect for over a hundred years, we still confront the legacy of these laws. Perhaps it is because we have not replaced them with laws that would create affirmative rights of equality within a marriage.

At no point did society have a collective "Aha!" moment when we—men and women alike—rejected the laws as atrocious and counter to human thriving for women. In fact, these laws are an ever-threatening fault line in the bedrock of the nuclear family: male supremacy instead of gender equality and mutual respect.

To doubt this is to doubt daily facts. Intimate partner violence is illegal throughout the United States, yet the courtrooms are filled with terrified women. Every day, women plead for help. Every day, the vast majority are not provided protection that is anything close to commensurate with the dangers they face. The courts are evidence of the fact that many men—from all walks of life—still think that domination and abuse at home, in their castles, are their patriarchal privilege and right.

To doubt this is to willfully ignore the faulty foundation on which we, women and men, still stand.

In 1868, the North Carolina Supreme Court held that it would not intervene in the "trifling" violence of a defendant who "struck . . . his wife, three licks, with a switch about the size of one of his fingers (but not as large as a man's thumb), without any provocation except some words uttered by her and not recollected by the witness." The case was *State v. Rhodes*. The decision is infamous for what it reveals about a more general unwillingness of courts to interfere with a man's right to rule in his castle. A look at this case offers insight into three key points.

First, a man was designated as the head of his family, and the state gave him the power to govern there without interference. Second, when meted out by a husband or father, life-threatening and life-altering violence is designated as "trifling," a declaration by the state of its devaluation of and disregard for women's lives. And third, *State v. Rhodes* is emblematic of the long history of denying women's basic human rights through "justificatory rhetoric" such as privacy concerns rather than explicitly recognizing how the law operates to protect male privilege to rule over women.

The court was unambiguous: in regard to this tyrant in his castle, this head of the family, the man was considered to be the head of his family-state government:

Our conclusion is that family government is recognized by law as being as complete in itself as the State government is in itself, and yet subordinate to it; and that we will not interfere with or attempt to control it, in favor of either husband or wife, unless in cases where permanent or malicious injury is inflicted or threatened, or the condition of the party is intolerable. Every household has and must have, a government of its own, modeled to suit the temper, disposition and condition of its inmates. Mere ebullitions of passion, impulsive violence, and temporary pain, affection will soon forget and forgive, and each member will find excuse for the other in his own frailties. But when trifles are taken hold of by the public and the parties are exposed and disgraced, and each endeavors to justify himself or herself by criminating the other, that which ought to be forgotten in a day, will be remembered for life.

The claim of not interfering "in favor of either husband or wife" seems equality minded but of course ignores the underlying inequality of a marriage lived in the king's castle.

Far more telling is the designation of domestic terrorism as "trifling." "Trifling" refers to a matter of little importance. But to a woman trapped in an abusive marriage, the husband's tyranny creates a living hell for her and her children. To refer to the lives of women thus situated as "trifling" is a profound insult that runs through centuries of jurisprudential refusal to intervene in a man's sovereignty at home.

Consider the texture of an endangered woman's life. I would argue that one beating could change permanently an intimate partner relationship and that the physical abuse would likely affect the sexual relationship in a profound way. If you know your husband is capable of beating you, you might well not feel able to reject his sexual advances. Moreover, for centuries marital rape was not considered a crime. Rape statutes would exclude marital rape by definition as forcible sexual intercourse with someone not your wife.

Most insidiously, we see the emergence of the privacy doctrine to shield from public gaze what goes on in a home. The court considering *State v. Rhodes* declined to get involved "not because those relations [of husband and wife] are not subject to the law, but because the evil of publicity would be greater than the evil involved in the trifles complained of; and because they ought to be left to family government." The court noted that statutes of chastisement had fallen out of favor in some countries and had met with little favor in the United States. Thus, the lack of uniformity led the court to consider the issue too much "at sea" to announce a clear rule: "For, however great are the evils of ill temper, quarrels, and even personal conflicts inflicting only temporary pain, they are not comparable with the evils which would result from raising the curtain, and exposing to public curiosity and criticism, the nursery and the bed chamber."

Not only did the court protect the man's ability to inflict pain, not only did it declare temporary the pain his wife endures, but it prioritized the man's public reputation over the evil she must suffer. And that is why the nineteenth-century case of *State v. Rhodes* is today visible in the woman putting makeup over a black eye, in Patrisha and Jackie suffering in silence, in family members and colleagues looking away from a bruised lip or a lowered head. They are all reflections of the first laws of marriage requiring a wife, a person with no other refuge, to conform her behavior to the temper of her husband. This conformity is key to our inequality. Because of the importance and social endorsement given to men's tempers, women believe they must tiptoe around men, "walk on eggshells," cajole, defer, and keep their tempers under control lest he prove incapable of controlling his. Women are subordinating to survive.

AN ACT OF TREASON

The most significant of our lessons from legal history is this: the difference between a wife killing her husband and a husband killing his wife. According to Blackstone:

> Husband and wife, in the language of the law, are styled Baron and femme. . . . If the Baron kills his femme, it is the same as if he had killed a stranger or any other person, but if the femme kills her Baron, it is regarded by the laws as much more atrocious crime, as she not only breaks through the restraints of humanity and conjugal affection, but throws off all subjection to the authority of her husband. And therefore the law denominates her crime a **species of treason**, and condemns her to the same punishment as if she had **killed the King**. And for every species of treason . . . the sentence of the woman was to be drawn and burnt alive.

If a woman killed her husband, it was an act of treason, "as if she had killed the King." Are women citizens of their husbands? Are husbands comparable to individual countries in their rulership over their wives? This law shows that it is not an exaggeration but actual legal history that men were designated as kings of their own castles. Men literally wrote themselves into the law as our kings.

So when the Grammy Award–winning musician Sara Bareilles pointedly asks "Who made you king of anything?" in her song "King of Anything," I have an answer for her: men made themselves kings of everything.

CHALLENGING TYRANNICAL RULE AT HOME

The history of white women's struggle for equal rights sheds light on women's collective inequality today. The famous Declaration of Sentiments presented at Seneca Falls in 1848 used the Declaration of Independence to show how white women were positioned beneath men, and how men enjoyed these superior rights at the expense of women's rights to be basic citizens.

In bold language, its writers claimed that men, through their laws, had established "absolute tyranny" over women, including marriage and chastisement and divorce laws. The most significant change to come from the Seneca Falls conference was Married Women's Property Acts.

New York State passed the first one in 1848; Nevada, the last, did so in 1864. Prior to their passage—and generosity toward women varied from state to state—the legal system, created by men, stipulated that husbands took control of all of a wife's property upon marriage. Thus, women's property passed, as women themselves did, from being the property of the father to property of the husband. The transfer of wealth stayed in the hands of men. In the nineteenth century, that law wasn't tossed onto the trash heap but reformed—and by male legislators.

These acts did not address the question of violent, tyrannical rule at home. Laws of chastisement were never repudiated in a direct or affirmative way to give wives, for example, the right to be free from chastisement and rule at home. This helps explain the situation today, where we as a society have failed to provide a safe exit from a tyrannical ruler at home.

NO GROUND FOR ENDANGERED WOMEN TO STAND ON

How can women stand their ground if men are legally entitled to be kings of their castles? Indeed, what ground, exactly, do women have to stand on? What constitutes the castle, and what are women's rights to challenge the designated ruler of her state?

As I write, stand-your-ground laws are on the books in thirty-six American states. Combine them with the inviolate man-in-his-castle doctrine encoded in the Fourth Amendment, and you see the failure of law reform to fix the regime of marriage laws. They are flawed at their foundation. Generations of feminists and legal reformers have tried to fix aspects of the prevailing system in the hopes that in the aggregate, cumulative reforms would reach a tipping point. Given that men throughout the world created the existing laws and men predominate in every hub of economic and political power, an attempt at cumulative reform was the only strategy available. Despite centuries of effort, the hope of reformers has gone unmet.

Here's a line that traces from the forest ape to the present:

men as governors of their family-state. Each man is designated as the head of his family, his little fiefdom: a critical foundation of patriarchy. We can see, because it exists in plain view, that a man's right to rule his wife and to use violence in exercising that right is intentional, not accidental. And although we might think of the laws enshrining that right as old and regressive—which they are—today's legal system is still founded upon them—to say nothing of the social and cultural legacies that persist and bolster them.

New laws to offer protection for women from abusive husbands were added to curb a husband's exercise of his rights to chastise his wife. But at no point did we start over, expressly repudiating a man's standing as governor of his family-state.

We have yet to experience a great legal awakening that strips the right of male domination from husbands and establishes marriage as a state of equality between spouses. The consequences of this enduring inequality and subordination are glaring and grotesque. Evidence of men's continued rights to beat their wives shows through the cracks of our imagined equality. Think about the courtrooms filled with women seeking protection from the tyrants at home.

Consider criminal law's treatment of husbands who kill their wives versus its treatment of wives who kill their husbands. Women face disproportionately harsh sentences for rising up against their kings, receiving on average double the sentence length that men do.

The difference in treatment explains the relative values our legal system places on women's and men's lives. Sadly, this discrimination persists in the law today throughout the world. Men kill women for the slightest infractions. Incels kill women for being women. When women kill their husbands, it is because they are fighting for their lives. Yet even when courts are shown clear evidence of years of abusive treatment by the husband, they are loath to excuse the wife's actions taken in self-defense.

Two well-publicized cases from Florida illustrate the point.

First, consider Marissa Alexander. Marissa, a single African American mother, and her newborn baby had just come home from their local hospital. Her estranged ex-husband was in a violent rage, threatening her after he saw texts on her phone. He had admitted in his deposition that he said "If I can't have you, then no one will": exact words that indicate potential lethality. He admitted beating on the bathroom door hard enough that it could have been broken down, while calling her "a whore and a bitch." When Marissa managed to get free from the bathroom, she was able to get her gun from her car and fired a warning shot upward into a wall of her home. For that she was found guilty and sentenced to twenty years in prison. The initial judge seemed appalled that she had fired the shot at all, even though the gun had not been aimed at the man.

Second, consider George Zimmerman, a white man in the same state of Florida. Zimmerman, who has a history as a convicted domestic violence offender, shot and killed Trayvon Martin, a young, unarmed Black teenager out for a walk. Walking down the street, Martin did not pose any threat to Zimmerman; his offense was simply the color of his skin. After a highly publicized trial, Zimmerman was let off completely.

Racism and sexism go hand in hand. Each is based on white male supremacy and reflects a foundation in law authored by and judged over by, overwhelmingly, white men. White supremacist patriarchy places white men above everyone else.

Consider the two cases. Marissa was in her home when the man, who had a history of domestic violence, intruded. Zimmerman was outside his home and had no prior history with Martin, who was just a Black youth walking near homes predominantly owned by whites. A Black woman stood her ground in her castle and was sentenced for merely firing a warning shot at the ceiling. A white man on a public street shot and killed a Black teen. The law abandoned the former and cocooned the latter. The law allows men to stand their ground even if they aren't acting in self-defense, even if their violence does not take place on their castle grounds. It condemns women for doing precisely what the law says they can.

This poses a question: What is women's ground? Given the explicit divide between the legal consequences of a husband killing his wife versus a wife killing her husband, it is unsurprising that in application, women are not entitled to stand their ground. It is questionable whether we have any ground to stand on at all. A combination of historic legal doctrines and our society's current focus on the wrong question—"Why didn't she leave?"—reveals the underlying lack of ground for women to claim.

HOSTAGES ARE NOT FREE TO LEAVE

A better way to understand the dynamics of domestic violence is to recognize its similarities to a hostage situation. In a case where a battered woman has killed her abuser in self-defense, it is especially useful to employ this frame of reference. This immediately answers the question that so often perplexes judges and juries: Why would a woman kill a man while he is asleep? Many abused wives do so, and courts view this as a negation of self-defense. What could a man, admittedly one who has beaten you for years and threatened to kill you, do to you while he is sleeping? Couldn't you have just left?

No.

Listen to the words of the musician, dancer, and actor FKA Twigs. As I write, she is suing her ex-boyfriend, the actor Shia LaBeouf, for sexual battery, alleging that, among other things, he knowingly infected her with an STD and shot stray dogs to get into character for a film. In an interview about her precarious escape from his violent control, Gayle King had asked her why didn't she leave. FKA responded, "I think we just have to stop asking that question . . . and I'm not going to answer that question anymore. Because the question should really be to the abuser, 'Why are you holding someone hostage with abuse?' People say 'Oh, it couldn't have been that bad else she would have left.' No, it's because it was that bad I couldn't leave."

Compared to the number of men who kill their wives or girlfriends, the number of women who kill their husbands is negligible, with 62 percent of female murder victims having an intimate relationship with their killer compared to 4.9 percent of male murder victims. Yet when women kill men who are sleeping, judges find it absolutely incomprehensible. Why would someone kill a man while he is sleeping? Surely he is no threat to anyone then. But if you remove the frame of marriage and domesticity and instead look at the situation as one in which a captor is holding a hostage, her actions are much more understandable.

Lest you think that the hostage analogy is far-fetched, 69

percent of hostage situations where police are called involve men holding their wives hostage. As just one example, Dorothy Giunta-Cotter, who had taken out several restraining orders against her husband, William Cotter, after he had abused her for nearly twenty years, was shot to death by him in March 2002. According to one news report, despite the orders—one of which had allowed him to go home to get his tools—Billy "broke into the family home carrying a sawed-off shotgun and wearing an ammunition belt. With his daughter watching, he seized his wife. When police stormed in, he fatally shot his wife in the back. Police fired at him in the dark but missed. He then fatally shot himself." It was not even the first time he had held her hostage. On a previous occasion when he had violated a restraining order, he had hidden in the garage, then grabbed his wife, taking her by surprise and telling her, "Stop screaming or I'll shoot you." According to their daughter, Kaitlyn, who was at home and heard her parents struggling, she "ran downstairs to find her mother being held hostage by her father. 'Her mouth was bleeding . . . and she appeared terrified,' Kaitlyn later wrote in an affidavit. 'I . . . stood with my mom and dad to make sure nothing was going to happen.' After two and a half hours, William left."

If we adjust our frame of reference, we see that the captive analogy—which, all too often, is a captive reality—is much more apt than a home in which a marriage between two people has gone wrong. We see the threat for what it is and the woman's choices as few and as dire as they are.

When a woman leaves her abuser, we know that he will stalk her, reassault her, and do everything in his power to bring her back under his control. If she returns under this sort of coercion, she clearly does so against her will. Yet the evidence is that women leave or attempt to leave about five times before they are able to do so effectively. To live with an abusive partner is to confine your life to his temper and controlling violence. It is an ongoing oppression that prevents human thriving. It is a deprivation of basic human rights. Yet it is all too common in marriage.

REFUGEES FROM TYRANNY AT HOME

While men have castles, women fleeing their husbands' castles get shelters.

Imagine what it would feel like to find yourself in a battered women's shelter. Something horrific has happened to you, and now, with no other options, you gather some essential belongings from your home, your kids, and their belongings, and you go into hiding. You are now living with strangers who are also going through their own unspeakable trauma. It is hard to think of anything else when someone—actually, someone who once professed to love you—is now intent on killing you.

When a woman goes to a shelter, she essentially goes underground. She is forced to cut off access to and limit her communication with her friends and family. Because the offender can expect to find her at her place of employment, she runs a real risk of losing her job if she goes to a shelter. If she has children, she has to pull them out of school, disrupting their education. They, too, lose their support systems, the familiarity of friends, classmates, and teachers. If she has an adolescent son, she won't be accepted to a shelter program. And pets must often be left behind.

Why didn't she leave? Because all of these pressures operate to keep women at home with their abusers, trying to placate a violent man, hoping against hope for a peaceful day. This is no way to live a life. It is a diminished state of being in which her right to thrive as a human being is absent.

As a society we view shelters with aloof nonchalance. We can even enjoy a sense of exculpatory pride that they're there to provide help. There is nothing for us to do. A battered woman will go to a battered women's shelter if she needs to escape. I suggest we take a moment to consider the reality of the situation and understand how morally wrong it is and how complicit we are in accepting it as the status quo.

Make no mistake: battered women's shelters exist to preserve the king in his castle. Until we change the world, we must keep and support the shelters. But have no illusion that their existence enforces the damn-the-victim logic of "Why didn't she flee?" (After all, there are shelters, right?) Have no illusion that maintaining safe places for threatened wives and children to flee to allows us to ignore why they're fleeing. Have no illusion that we are not collectively complicit in the agreement that homicidal men get the castle, battered women get the shelter. And have no illusion that the women we are abandoning to the shelter are by definition the ones in the highest lethality risk.

"New news! I left woody, got a restraining order, he violated it by showing up at the house, tried to kill me by choking me, couldn't talk or swallow for 4 days (was in the ER). He committed a felony doing this."

Bonnie Woodring wrote this note to some close family members and friends from the shelter to which she had fled for her life. She was in hiding from her husband, John "Woody" Woodring, but Woody found her. He broke into the insecure shelter, where he shot her to death while her thirteen-year-old son from a previous marriage heard him say to his mother, "You don't want to die, but you're gonna."

This act of domestic terrorism passed with very little public commentary or media attention. When I heard about it, I spent the next two days diving into the case to find out as much as I could. It conformed to so many cases of domestic homicides, which is to say it was a completely preventable and predictable homicide—a very-high-risk case that the judge and the system had regarded as just another petition from another terrified woman in a domestic violence court pleading for help.

The judge had granted a restraining order about a week before Bonnie wrote the note from the shelter. But the first time Bonnie had appeared in court seeking help, the same judge had refused to grant her an order of protection. Three months before the order was issued, Judge Danny Davis in Jackson, North Carolina, had denied her plea for help.

Imagine what life was like for Bonnie, what it took for her to find the courage to go to court to seek protection from a large, violent, overbearing tyrant, only to be turned away. In this case, we have a glimpse of exactly what life was like because three months later she returned to court where she faced the same judge. This time she wrote in her petition:

> I have been in this relationship one and a half years and over the last several months have tried to work on getting out of this abusive relationship including filing restraining order which was denied before. This man has previously been convicted of assault on other wives. Three weeks ago,

when I attempted to leave he choked me twice and ripped off my necklace and tried to remove my rings. He comes to my work and harasses me . . . and keeps tabs on where I am 24/7. It has taken me three weeks to safely plan how and when to leave. He uses his strength, build and Marine ways to intimidate me and my son. . . . I fear for both me and son.

Because suicide threats by an abuser are known lethality factors, a box on the form asked Bonnie for dates and details of any such threats. She wrote:

Last time I attempted to leave, Woody said maybe he was "no good for me" and maybe he should just "kill himself" or "crash his Vette." In June 9, 06 when I tried to leave, he said he would not be alive by morning, that he would take pills and sink the "boat."

She dutifully checked off all of the available boxes. An indication of how ubiquitous his terrorizing of her was, she included the plea, in the box on the form marked "other," "Walmart, 50–100 feet" meaning she was requesting he not be able to approach her on trips to shop for herself and her son.

On the order of protection form that Bonnie filled out, a danger assessment was built into the questions she had to answer. Her level of danger was off the charts: he had threatened to kill her; he had access to weapons; he had strangled her; he had escalated his violence; he had suicidal ideation and a plan; and he had a history of domestic violence against previous wives.

Yet the order, after being granted, was never even served— this despite Bonnie listing the address and hours of his place of employment. By the time of her death it was simply stamped NOT SERVED.

Bonnie was murdered by her husband in the very shelter she had fled to for protection. The state stood by and let it happen.

How pathetic and tragic it is for her to have to beg the judge for fifty feet of space at Walmart so that she might be left alone to shop.

How diminished our set of entitlements is in this situation. When endangered, women check off boxes on a form for an order of protection, pleading for freedom from their abusers' harassment and abuse. Bonnie checked off every available box. She remained unprotected.

Is this, then, the ground on which women stand? When women check off these boxes, what does it imply for their lives outside the boxes? Are we inherently agreeing to the idea that we have no entitlement to safety outside of them? Again, women have acquiesced, in part unwittingly and in part because boxes of freedom are all that is on offer, to subordinating to survive.

Everything is wrong with this picture.

Orders of protection do not protect. Shelters enforce the regime of male temper syndrome. Though I appreciate that shelters have saved women's lives, they are not the answer to domestic violence. Rather, they are "status enforcing regimes," as Professor Reva Siegel at Yale Law School has written. In a brilliant law review article, she theorized that discrimination is often not eliminated through law. Rather, when antidiscrimination laws are passed, they are accompanied by social practices that operate to obstruct the intended effect of the law. She referred to this as "preservation through transformation." The preservation of the patriarchal status quo is accomplished through the strengthening of statutes enforcing regimes that operate to keep women in their place.

Battered women's shelters are the status-enforcing regime of the women's movement.

Our historic legacy of male supremacy is reflected in the societal expectations that men rule their castles at home and women run elsewhere for shelter when those rulers become despotic. We are happy to support a woman in her victimhood as long as she stays in her role. Women are running for their lives from men over whom we have jurisdiction. But instead of exercising it to intervene effectively, we participate in a high-stakes game of hide-and-seek. It is not as if the men are criminals at large. Rather, these are crimes in which the criminal has a particular modus operandi; he is known to the system and easy to identify, yet we fail to hold him accountable. Instead, we place the burden for a woman's safety on the woman herself.

Years of study and experience have shown that when men beat women in relationships, it is not because they want them to leave. Rather, they want them to stay but in a subordinate, servile relationship. They beat them into submission. This truth is reflected in millennia of man-made law, going back to Romulus, and from ancient Rome to the forest ape. Years of study and experience have also shown that when a woman tries to leave an abusive relationship, the man will stalk her and threaten to kill her or himself if she really leaves. Or threaten that she will never see her kids again.

Separation assault—a term coined by the legal scholar Martha Mahoney—describes the way abusers track down their victims and assault them even more violently for attempting to leave. Every state in the United States has stalking laws that anticipate an offender's violation of an order of protection. And just like orders of protection, stalking laws are unevenly enforced at best.

Marriage laws provide the historic context for our consideration of the difficulties in eradicating domestic violence. Laws that gave men the status of kings of their own castles have proven to be intractable. The reason for this is that the laws explicitly permitted—arguably required—the use of violence to ensure a male's supremacy in his castle home. And this particular violence lies at the heart of women's subordinate status. Until we address it head-on, we will not eradicate it.

The usual ways women fight for gender equality, through reform of the existing state of affairs, will not do. We need to take the radically simple approach of saying "No more." Enough. We stand our ground for one another. We claim it. We do not ask permission to own our space. Rather, we assert, collectively, our right to be in the world. We collectively give and answer the call.

Women by and large do not use the language of violence. Of all the women in prison today, 92 percent of them have credible claims of self-defense. This, too, is intolerable. Those are all women who issued a call to a society gone deaf.

Women should have the right to overthrow a tyrannical government, especially where evidence of tyranny is present, and the law has not stepped in to protect her, as it was intended to do. Her acts of self-defense should be understood, not criminalized. And unlike most of the forest apes of our evolutionary past, the bonobos teach us how to bolster that self-defense with cooperative and collective defense as a way to banish the criminal and protect the sister.

CHAPTER 3

THE PHALLACY OF THE MALE PROTECTION RACKET

He is the logical absurdity of the male protection racket.

> Designed as a visual deterrent, Safe-T-Man is a life-size, simulated male that appears to be 180 lbs. and 6' tall, to give others the impression that you have the protection of a male guardian with you while at home alone or driving in your car. . . . When not keeping vigil over your well-being, he can be deflated, stored and transported inconspicuously in the optional tote bag.

"Don't travel," the advertisement's headline warns, "without Safe-T-Man as your bodyguard."

I saw this ad on a flight several years ago. It appeared in the pages of *SkyMall* magazine, which was tucked into the seatback pocket an inch from my knees. I'd finished the book I had brought. I had reread the laminated page explaining the plane's safety features. I opened up *SkyMall*, and there was Safe-T-Man, the promise of protection from an all-too-threatening world.

At first I laughed. Men were marketed blow-up dolls of women they could have sex with; women were pitched blow-up dolls of men who by virtue of the hint of an unshaven jawline and leather jacket provided protection. But then I stopped laughing. The underlying message of Safe-T-Man was no laughing matter. Women need the appearance of a male guardian to protect them. Protect them from what? From other men, of course.

The blow-up doll paradox is too glaring to ignore. Blow-up dolls for men equal sex and pleasure. Blow-up dolls for women equal the promise of a respite from male violence. A female's role is to serve men's pleasure. A male's role is to protect women from other men but not from themselves. Women need men to see us safely home; to walk us to our car; to defend us in our home. Because other men mean to do women harm, men are routinely presented to women as their best line of defense. The absurdist message of Safe-T-Man is that, in a pinch, a facsimile man will do. But the lesson of Safe-T-Man is even more insidious than women needing men to protect them from men; it is the fact that a problem of men's creation—violence against women—is one only men can address.

An extortion racket works like this: pay us when we're reasonable, and we will not burn down your store; fail to do so, and we'll come back when we're unreasonable and burn your store down with you possibly in it. The male extortion racket is no different. Because some men harm women, all women must turn to other men for protection. In all instances, the consequence is the same: a woman must link herself to a man who promises to come to her aid. Some men demand nothing; they walk you to your car and wave you home. Some men demand everything. Because of the racket, all men are in the position to be generous or not. The framework holds throughout gender role enforcement that seeks to impose a strict patriarchal binary of male domination and female submission.

Though the terms of the racket haven't changed much over the millennia, contemporary men are more embarrassed about the fact.

In 2018, the journalist E. Jean Carroll traveled across the United States to cities with women's names (Cynthiana, Indiana; Marianna, Arkansas; Angelica, New York; and others) asking people, "What do we need men for?" The question became her 2019 book's title, in which she recorded the answers.

For example, while in Tallulah, Louisiana, she interviewed Mr. John Earl Martin, a museum curator, and reported the following exchange:

"What Do We Need Men For, Mr. Martin?" I say a little later in the museum tour.

Mr. Martin, who admits . . . that the country might "be better off" if women ran things for a while . . . takes a moment before he answers the What Do We Need Men For question.

"Well . . ." he says. "You need men to protect you."

"Against whom?"

"The enemy," says Mr. Martin, not realizing that, like the Tenth Illinois Calvary, I am setting a trap.

"The enemy?" I say.

Mr. Martin frowns.

"You mean *other* men?" I say. . . .

"Well . . . I suppose . . ." he says warily.

"So we need men," I say, "so they can fight *other men*?"

He smiles. Mr. Martin is too smart to answer.

"But we need men to protect us?" I say. "Right?"

"Yes."

"To protect us from whom?"

Mr. Martin smiles. "You *gotta* have protection!" he says.

"From *other* men?" I say.

"From the bad men, yes," he says.

Then he adds happily:

"And from floods!"

There is humor here, but not much. Rackets work best when no one admits their presence. So, joking aside, we have to ask how women can break out of the male protection racket. Safe-T-Man is an illustration of the situation we're in and a hint to how we can break out of the trap. The first step is realizing that it's a trap, a circular dead end that keeps us stuck in an endless cycle of dependence.

Go back and take a look at the image of Safe-T-Man. Ask yourself, why would the mere appearance of a male guardian be expected to protect you? Because it is assumed that a male accompanying a female will come to her aid. Because it is assumed that a bad man will see the man a woman is with and understand, "Ah, she is under his protection." That assumption demands consideration, critique, and deconstruction—because, like most assumptions informing the male protection racket, it is not true.

In fact, Safe-T-Man represents the phallacy of the male protection racket. There is, again, humor in the word of my invention, *phallacy*, but not much. A phallacy is a fallacy that is propagated specifically to reinforce a patriarchal social order founded upon male-to-male alliances. All humor ends with the truth abundantly caught in every relevant study and statistic that women at risk of being harmed by men would be better off, by far, with Safe-T-Man in their homes instead of flesh-and-blood men.

For women, the home is nine times more dangerous than the streets. The men we know and may live with pose a greater danger to us than strangers do. Likewise, approximately 80 percent of rapes are committed by men who are acquaintances of their victims. We are taught to be afraid of the unfamiliar man on the street, but our efforts to prepare for and fend off attacks by strangers are dangerously misplaced. Women at the gravest risk do not need protection from other men; they need protection from their self-declared protectors. To change this reality, we must confront it.

In *Rape: The Politics of Consciousness*, Susan Griffin put it succinctly: "In the system of chivalry, men protect women against men. This is not unlike the protection relationship which the Mafia established with small businesses in the early part of this century. Indeed, chivalry is an age-old protection racket which depends for its existence on rape."

All men are beneficiaries. All women suffer as a consequence.

The moment women delegate their safety to men, they lose. The loss is all the more galling because it is suffered for a presumed state of safety as hollow as that provided by Safe-T-Man. Just as in all protection rackets, the threat you pay to be protected from is the threat your protector metes out. That many men do not rape the women they know doesn't change the terms of the racket; it only adds to the illusion of safety.

What do women give up in order to gain a man's protection? Everything. Independence, for starters. And then they give up their right to full expression as human beings because they will have to act according to their "protector's" rules in order to be deserving of protection. In all instances, women give up more than they get.

The resulting phallacy is the belief that men are our legitimate protectors when in fact they are our greatest threat. The vast majority of men fall into one of two camps. There are the bad men who abuse women and in most cases abuse the woman who turned to her abuser for protection. And there are the men who do not stop the bad men. Yes, there's #notallmen, but of those, how many actively intervene to protect women from harm? This is among the crueler ironies of Safe-T-Man. No woman expects "him" to stand up and take on an attacker— he's plastic and rubber, after all.

But if good men were in fact protecting women from bad ones, why is the level of male violence against women epidemic? Domestic abuse, spousal abuse, incest, rape: for all the centuries of purported male protection, systemic violence against women is the result.

At least when a store owner pays the Mafia its extorted sum, they don't burn down their store. Women don't even obtain that. The refusal of men to intervene in another man's violence leaves us vulnerable, and this vulnerability is woven into our daily lives. We subordinate ourselves in order to gain male protection not only from men but sometimes from the very man we've subordinated ourselves to in order to gain protection.

Many women would be better off, by far, with only Safe-T-Man in their lives, even if he never came out of his optional tote bag.

Women are accorded safety only in exchange for being some man's property. Some species of baboons have a related social practice where males protect females from other males and then the female is more likely to mate with the protective male. These relationships have been characterized as "friendships"; they call to mind humans' "friends with benefits." Note that the benefits flow to males in terms of increased access to females as reproductive resources.

Let's pause to reflect on this. Men do not shoulder the responsibility to contain their own violence because it increases the flow of benefits to all men, whether they are the perpetrators of that violence or not. When women ask, "If male violence against females is caused by men, shouldn't men protect women without requiring some sort of reward?," they are asking the wrong question. A better question is: Why would a man—good or bad—risk cutting off the flow of benefits? But you don't need to do a thought experiment to see the truth. The law itself provides insight into the harsh truth of the matter.

Rape law was originally a crime of trespass on property—the woman being the property—and the rights were held by her legal guardian/owner, either her father or her husband. This is law written by men, enforced by men, and subsequently amended by men. But its vestigial origins remain.

Most men do not intervene to prevent another man from

harming a woman, instead respecting the other man's owner-ship rights. Consider that women in bars have more success refusing male advances if they claim to have a boyfriend or part-ner than if they just say they are not interested. Therein lies the premise of Safe-T-Man: that a male will defend his rights to "his woman" through the use of violence against an intruder.

I have spent the better part of my professional life trying to figure out how to prevent men's violence against women. But I do often ask myself: Why is this a woman's problem? Why is the entire field of working against "violence against women" populated—with very few exceptions—by women and others who do not identify as cis-gendered white men? Where are the conferences being held for men to own their and their brothers' violence? Of course, there are men who are feminist and strong allies, leading in various ways the efforts to stop gender-based violence. Yet we need to identify and name the barriers to more large-scale leadership by men on men's violence.

Consider street harassment, unwanted public interactions be-tween strangers motivated by one person's gender, sexual orienta-tion, or gender expression. It isn't restricted to streets, for verbal harassment, flashing, groping, and rape happen in stores, on public transportation, in parks. And it is a global problem. Men around the world apparently share an idea of entitlement to public spaces and the right to deny free access of these spaces to women by constantly reminding them of the threat of sexual violence.

Consider, too, that juvenile orangutans will attack and force copulation with a lone female who is foraging by herself. We might think of this as analogous to a woman being alone on a street. What may be important here is that she is vulnerable because she is alone. If she were with a posse or within a group, perhaps the male orangutans might not have established this behavioral pattern of forced copulation, which is comparable to human rape.

The scholar Mikelina Belaineh has written incisively, wisely about the effects of street harassment. They "go well beyond the direct impact on the victims, because repeated harassment eventually leads to women self-policing their actions (where they go, how they dress, what time of day they go out, whether they travel alone or with a male 'chaperone'). This process of internalization . . . leads to women changing their behavior to fit within the rules of how society tells them gender should be performed." And not just women. Anyone who is outside the binary, man-woman gender essentialism central to gender violence is subject to public harassment. As Belaineh's idea of gender policing suggests, harassment is a form of violence that demands the development of real safety and accountability measures.

"Consider the following scenarios," Belaineh wrote.

1) Cis-Woman walking alone gets cat called on the street, experiences vulgar remarks; 2) Woman with a male companion walking on the street, avoids harassment due to a "male" agreement not to disturb one another's "property"; 3) two Cis-Women, in a same sex relationship walking through the city, experience vulgar remarks—treating their displays of affection as real-time pornography for male-consumption; 4) Cis-Woman with a Gender Non-Conforming Female Partner, at first no disturbance due to the perception of her partner as male, but upon shifting perceptions experiences street harassment commenting on their sexuality and making threats in response to the gender expression of the partner; 5) two Cis-men in a same sex relationship, experience street harassment in

the form of hostile comments and threats in regards to their sexuality, and potentially gender expression. Each of these scenarios involves Street harassment, a tool used to perpetrate Patriarchal violence and enforce gender hierarchies. By using a lens of Gender Policing, we can meaningfully acknowledge all of the experiences mentioned.

We cannot miss the obvious. In all of these scenarios, it is men harassing others. And that is because women don't harass. As with violence, men are "overwhelmingly the harassers of both women and men." The data matter, but so, too, does lived experience. When I walk down the street and encounter other women, I never think that one of them will assault me or threaten my well-being in any way. To the contrary, I make eye contact, I might smile or say hello in recognition of another human being. Encountering a man on a street is a wholly different story. A man represents a potential threat. This isn't nervousness on my or your part. This is data-informed wisdom. Per the FBI: in 2012, men committed 73.8 percent of all murders, 99.1 percent of all rapes, 87 percent of all robberies, 77.1 percent of all aggravated assaults, 81.1 percent of all motor vehicle thefts. Now carry those percentages into frequency. Again from the FBI: in 2021, a murder was committed every 35.4 minutes; a forceable rape every 6.2 minutes; an aggravated assault every 41.5 seconds. If you're not nervous, you're not paying attention.

So my first visual encounter with a strange man involves scanning for clues as to whether he represents a threat. I note his age, his size, and how he is dressed, which indicates class. Yes, this is insidious, an accelerant to conscious and unconscious bias. But this, too, is an inevitable consequence of the male protection racket. When I know that in 2014, of two thousand American women surveyed, 65 percent of them had experienced street harassment, 23 percent had been sexually touched, 20 percent had been followed, and 9 percent had been forced into doing something sexual, I cannot help but scan for clues. In short, I and all other women cannot help but lapse into what Belaineh calls gender policing.

Gender policing includes the myriad ways that society conditions people to identify within the gender binary of male/man and female/woman. It is a valuable insight, which begins by acknowledging the perversion of policing that it entails. Because of inadequacies in police preventing patriarchal violence, the rest of us must gender police ourselves and others.

Belaineh cautions us about the consequences of gender policing:

> The paradigmatic scenario of a cis-gender, heterosexual woman suffering from physical, emotional, or psychological violence at the hands of a cis-gender, heterosexual, man dominates our conceptualization of what Gender Violence "looks like." The result is the erasure of marginalized narratives and experiences. Worse, we end up policing our allies. When we participate in, enforce, reinforce, or remain complicit in an essentialist view of gender, we may also be participating in the perpetuation of the phenomenon that underlies all gender violence.

Men's sexual harassment of women commuting to school or work is a problem from Australia to Zambia. One woman wrote to Holly Kearl, an international expert in street harassment, from Perth, Western Australia, saying:

One of the more terrifying things is when a group of men follows closely in a car, having slowed to walking pace, making remarks. . . . There are many other stories of sexual harassment . . . flashing and several "minor" sexual assaults (men grabbing breasts, bottom)—overall I consider myself relatively "lucky" based on the fact that I've never actually been raped by a stranger.

In Zambia, children often have to travel long distances to school and as a result rarely complete twelfth grade. Distance alone isn't the problem; it is the risks they run while traveling.

The risk to girls is so significant that the World Bicycle Relief organization donated bikes to girls so they might get to school more safely. And this is not a problem confined to Zambia. Once when I was riding my bike home from a health club, a white man in a car slowed down to match my speed, rolled down the window, and asked me if I wanted a ride. Afraid, I checked my angry retort. Instead, I offered a blander "No, thanks, I'm happy on my bike." And then, as soon as I could, I turned off the road and disappeared onto the bike path, where he could not follow me. Though it was not a terribly threatening incident, the result was self-policing: I no longer ride my bike to the health club. Again, I am no lone example—far, far from it. Over 90 percent of all women and girls have been harassed at least once on the street. A fact women everywhere live with is that male harassment "prevents women from enjoying all the same freedoms as men when they travel, as most travel guides or study abroad advice sheets show." The message of street harassment is that women and girls don't have a right to walk down the street. If we do, we are considered to be streetwalkers—meaning prostitutes—and thus sexually available to all men.

Harassment is always sexual in nature: it involves a man or group of men proclaiming their opinion of a woman's or girl's sexual desirability. Though street harassment ranges along a continuum from flattery to fear, underlying that continuum is the idea that a man cannot control himself and is therefore not responsible for his own sex drive.

It's not just a question of peace and liberty; the inability to walk down a street unmolested is significant. Street harassment is a constant reminder to women of the threat of sexual violence. On the far side of the flattery-to-fear continuum is rape.

White men take their liberty to walk down the street for granted: it's their world.

My colleague, a scholar and the cofounder of Mentors in Violence Prevention, Jackson Katz, performs the following experiment in an exercise he calls "Sexual Assault in the Daily Routine." In a gender-diverse classroom, he asks the men first what precautions they take when walking alone at night. They remain silent and report that they do nothing.

Then he asks the women what precautions they take when walking alone at night. Hands shoot up as they tell him about carrying mace, gripping their keys like makeshift weapons, holding their phones in anticipation of calling 911 if necessary, and other means of self-protection. There is almost always a straight gender divide between the level of safety consciousness that one must engage in depending on whether a person presents as male or female.

The reason is simple: violence is a language that is strictly reserved to men. This is another lesson Safe-T-Man teaches women. Because violence is the province of men, because men threatening violence can be checked only by a commensurate threat, the appearance of male protection is a woman's best option. After all, from our military to organized crime to policing, violence is mediated by men who decide its acceptable parameters.

Gender policing is the way the language of violence is spoken. It is the vehicle through which gender is enforced as a social construct, a way to compel conformity with a strict binary of male supremacy and female subordination. It polices any gender-nonconforming behavior or appearance. Deviations are punished because they threaten the stability of a patriarchal social order that needs constant reinforcement to survive.

Men commit 85 percent of all crimes and 80 to 85 percent of crimes against women, suggesting a huge gender disparity in the use of violence as a language. Girls and women learn to negotiate their lives around the use of violence so that violence becomes like a second language—an unwelcome but necessary one—to navigate a land where their native language is not spoken.

Jackson Katz points out that white men make invisible their gender and racial hierarchies. He urges us not to accept passively that men commit the vast majority of crimes, pointing out that men are gendered beings who are trained in masculinity. This masculinity is welded to images of violence so that we equate manliness with how well a man masters the language of violence.

If men make the laws defining what is a crime, commit the criminal acts, face the consequences or not for their crimes, what role do women play? Because women do not speak the language of violence, threats mean something different to us. Though we are the victims of male crimes, we are also subject to laws we had no role in making, especially criminal laws. Women are more threatened by men's violence because they have most often not learned that they have the power to fight back.

But the primary game here is between men, and men keep the language of violence to themselves by punishing women who try to speak it disproportionately. When women do speak the language of violence, they overwhelmingly do so in self-defense or in defense of their children. The level of violence originated by women is negligible compared to that originated by men. Whether this gendered differential is evolutionary biology, biological, or cultural is the subject of existential debate. Underlying the debate are the ways in which boys are socialized and expected to be more violent than girls. Boys identify with men and male images in the media, learning that violence is associated with action and that it is their province. Boys don't need T-shirts that say STRONG AND FIERCE! Girls do, because the expectation is that we are weak and placid. To check our own biases, let's try to imagine a boy wearing a STRONG AND FIERCE! T-shirt. We would be confused.

Another aspect of the language of violence learned from childhood on is that boys or men are encouraged to act while girls and women often must ask for permission to act.* Here are two examples.

First, my friend's son, Austin, witnessed another child take a toy away from his older sister, Maria. Maria tried to explain to the other child that it was her toy and she was playing with it. Witnessing that, little Austin went up to the boy who was refusing to give the toy back, grabbed the toy out of his hands, and returned it to his sister.

---

* "Action films," for example, invariably involve violence.

ALL-MALE SPACES

Second, P. Carl told of an interesting incident in his book *Becoming a Man*, a memoir of his journey transitioning from female to male:

> I am a spy. I watch men and how they behave: I am at the pool. A man dismisses a young woman's kind request. She has reserved the lane he is in for the lesson she will teach, the schedule posted on the door to the entry to the pool. "This is my lane." He sneers at her and swims on. The next time he pops his head out of the water I shout at him, "Move the fuck over, buddy," and he does.

P. Carl goes on to describe how he is a work in progress, experiencing different selves in different spaces. Polly, his female, pretransition self, "knows what it is to be treated as a woman and to live inside the confines of the female gender. Carl knows the freedom of being a man and what happens in spaces where only men are allowed to go. . . . When I shout at that man in the pool, it's Polly's memories and Carl's body." The vantage point of Polly-Carl allows us to ask: What does go on in all-male spaces?

All-male spaces and groups are a source of both male power and male violence. They are the spaces where the language of violence is transmitted from men higher up the hierarchy to men and boys below. We know that much of what goes on in these spaces is not good for women. We also know that male-only spaces have been jealously guarded against women.

Does this matter? Does it matter to women what men are hiding? Yes, profoundly. Consider Supreme Court justice Brett Kavanaugh. We know that while he attended Yale, he was a member of the all-male secret society Truth and Courage (TNC), tellingly nicknamed "Tit and Clit." TNC was the only secret society that chose to disband rather than admit women. We know also that he was a member of the Delta Kappa Epsilon fraternity. Years after he left, the fraternity was banned from campus for five years after its members were videotaped chanting outside the freshman girls' dorm, "No means yes, yes means anal."

Yes, what goes on in all-male spaces matters.

For starters, they are homosocial environments. Female-only environments undoubtedly have their own distinctive qualities; however, they are not associated with the kind of toxic homophobia that is evident in all-male groups. Nor are they associated routinely with violent hazing rituals.

A distinguishing feature of male environments is that they all have to do with power gained by speaking the language of violence. The structural features of all-male spaces have alarming similarities whether we are talking about the military, police, fraternities, or men's sports teams. Hierarchies are formed and enforced. Bonds are forged through hazing rituals that are intentionally humiliating, sexually charged, and often violent. But they are endured, perhaps because the ones on the bottom who are not yet full members of the group know that their lowly status is only temporary. After enduring the abuse, they will be admitted to the upper echelon and granted the power to haze others.

A PLEDGE OF MISOGYNY

The ultimate requirement is not to be like a girl; not to be like a woman. In many, perhaps most, cases, a pledge of misogyny—and secrecy—is required as the ticket for admission.

We see such male bonding practices around the globe. In the Sambia tribe of Papua New Guinea, for instance, men force younger men to perform fellatio on them. Young boys are initiated into manhood at the age of ten, when they are taken from their mothers and undergo the first of four steps of initiation. In a special hut, they are taught to perform oral sex on other men in the belief that semen contains an essential life force for becoming a man; the more you ingest, the stronger a man you will become.

The professor of human sexuality and anthropology Gilbert H. Herdt reported that this "flute ceremony" is conducted in absolute secrecy that is enforced through murder. If a nonparticipant witnesses the ceremony, the punishment is death. And if a woman sees any part of the ceremony, the men gang-rape her. Something similar occurs in Brazil, where Yanomami boys play at gang-raping girls and later do it for real.

The logics of gender policing, of the language of violence that supports patriarchy, are ubiquitous. They operate as clearly among gang rapists the world over as they do among the military the world over. Violence, its exercise, and promised restraint are male prerogatives. The doling out and restraining of violence reduce the world to one of two binary genders: (1) heterosexual men and (2) women, a catchall for all those who do not present as heterosexual males. And the institutions that instruct, protect, and sustain patriarchal violence almost always demand a degree of secrecy. Men prefer to keep from view the simple fact that the violence that supports patriarchy is indefensible except as the essential support of patriarchy.

The world's armed services are granted full authority to speak the language of violence. They are also, overwhelmingly, the domain of men. Unsurprisingly, the structure of the military is that of patriarchal violence. The higher up one is in its hierarchy, the more authority one has to direct violence at enemies and subordinates. Many of the military's rituals are cloaked in layers of secrecy. Not coincidentally, the justification for the military, for all military, and for its cost (in 2020, $778 billion in the United States, $252 billion in China, $72.9 billion in India, and so on) is the very same one given for why women need men: the world needs its military because the world needs protection from "bad" men. And, maybe, floods.

For more than a century the Virginia Military Institute (VMI) and the Citadel in South Carolina were the most prestigious private military colleges in the United States. They were all male. In 1996 in the case of *United States v. Virginia*, Justice Ruth Bader Ginsburg wrote an opinion for the Supreme Court holding that it was a denial of equal protection for the state of Virginia to deny admission to women to the state school of VMI. In its defense of the practice, VMI had claimed that women would not do well under its "adversative" training program, which involved spartan barracks, no privacy, and a strictly enforced hierarchal system. It admitted that some women might successfully complete the rigorous program. Still, it maintained that to admit women into its adversative system would "destroy" it. What exactly would have been destroyed if women had participated in the program? Something apparently fundamental to male bonding in the military was at stake. If the all-male environment was breached by the presence of women, the secrets essential to establishing and maintaining hierarchy would be exposed. The adversative system involved the imposition of gender-based hierarchies, even though only men were present. The men who were newest were weakest and designated as women.

We were given a deeper insight into the problem in the case of Shannon Faulkner, decided two years earlier than the VMI case. Shannon was admitted to the Citadel. But when the college realized that she was female, it rescinded her acceptance. She then sued the school.

The suit made transparent that the male-only Citadel was a place where the language of patriarchal violence went unchecked. During Faulkner's court hearing, Ronald Vergnolle, an alumnus from the class of 1991, was asked, "Approximately how many times over your four years did you hear the word 'woman' used as a way of tearing a cadet down?" He replied, "I could not estimate a number. It occurred so frequently. It was an everyday part, every-minute, every-hour part of life there. And if the term 'woman' was used, then that would be a welcome relief, compared to the large majority of the terms you were called, [which] were gutter slang for women."

Recall that the Citadel claims to produce good men who are trained to protect the world from bad men.

The investigative reporter Susan Faludi wrote an article for the *New Yorker* called "The Naked Citadel" that covered the school's objections to admitting Faulkner. In it, Faludi revealed a hierarchal system in which the upperclassmen had unfettered permission to violently haze the "knobs" (the first-year students). The sexual overtones of homophobia and violently denied homoeroticism were striking. They ran from the mild:

> Weighing heaviest on the cadets' minds, it turned out, was the preservation of the all-male communal bathroom. The sharing of the stall-less showers and stall-less toilets is "at the heart of the Citadel experience," according to more than one cadet. The men bathe as a group.

To the perverse:

> Ruthless intimacy, in which physical abuse stands in for physical affection, and every display of affection must be counterbalanced by a display of sadism. Knobs told me that they were forced to run through the showers while the upperclassmen "guards" knocked the soap out of their hands and, when the knobs leaned over to retrieve it, the upperclassmen would unzip their pants and yell, "Don't pick it up, don't pick it up! We'll use you like we used those girls!"

Faludi reported that "one company of cadets recently devised a regimen in which the older cadets tested sophomores nightly with increasingly painful treatments—beatings and stompings and so forth. The process, which they dubbed 'Bananarama,' culminated on a night in which an unpeeled banana was produced—and shoved into a cadet's anus." It is hard to imagine an "adversative" program less likely to produce honorable men who are trained to protect; it is hard to imagine a program more likely to encourage rapists. Suffice it to say that the space between such practices at the Citadel and those of the Sambia tribe in Papua New Guinea is nonexistent.

Around the time Faludi's article appeared, I attended a cocktail party where I wound up talking to a military man about Shannon's case. I asked him what exactly would be threatened if she were to be admitted. "Tradition!" he responded. I pressed, but he couldn't get past that one-word explanation. He started to get red in the face and kind of jump up and down.

It was then I formulated the "jumping up and down" theory: the more a man jumps up and down about something, the closer you are to hitting on something that really matters to patriarchal privilege.

What was it that made the man so adamant about keeping women out of the Citadel, indeed out of the military? What were men so afraid women would see?

It is this: men at the lower end of the gender hierarchy do not want a woman to see them in a submissive position. We know that the incessant use of gender epithets used by the more senior military members against the initiates equates submission with femininity. A woman is defined as something you do not want to be. It makes sense, then, that men would not want women to witness themselves being subordinated by other men.

From the military to police academies to fraternities, hazing practices are alarmingly similar and well documented. The fraternal bonding is forged through the creation of a gendered hierarchy in which the men on top can abuse those who are lower ranked. Men moving up through the ranks are bonded to higher-ups by the twin forces of humiliation and secrecy. The systemic practice of highly sexualized violence in a sexually charged all-male environment is consistent and includes gender policing to make sure that none of the men is gay. In the world of toxic masculine violence, we even witness a seemingly obscene and absurd phallacy, that heterosexuality can be proven by men raping other men.

There is one difference about the military and its practices and sports teams and fraternities and their practices. Women pay for the military. Literally. Part of the taxes we pay go to support the military, where women are not wanted, where women are denigrated, where as a matter of practice the word *woman* is used as an insult.

In Faludi's book *Stiffed: The Betrayal of the American Man*, in which she recounted her investigation of the Citadel, she quoted another former student, Michael Lake: "According to the Citadel creed of the cadet, women have no rights. They are objects. They are things that you can do with whatever you want to." If you live in South Carolina, you should know that the Citadel is a public school that your taxes support.

Men's violence taxes us in so many ways above the purely financial. We pay into a tax system in which police officers have a higher likelihood of abusing their intimate partners than do men in the general population. Studies consistently show that around 40 percent of police officers are batterers. This should cast some serious doubt on whether we can expect them to come to our aid when we are attacked by other men, especially men who claim a possessory interest in us through an intimate relationship.

This is just one example of the safety tax that women pay for men's violence. In fact, the "Pink Tax is a form of gender-based price discrimination. It is the extra amount that women pay for certain products." A study conducted by New York University's Rudin Center for Transportation found that 75 percent of women had experienced some form of harassment or theft while on public transportation, compared to 47 percent of men.

Women were more than twice as likely to be concerned about their safety and were almost four times more likely as men to change their behavior to avoid harassment.

> The results of the survey conclude that using alternative modes of transportation at night for safety reasons adds to monthly travel expenses for women.
> The median extra cost per month for men, due to safety reasons, is $0.
> On the other hand, the median extra cost per month for women is $26–$50.

Men's violence taxes women in so many ways: economically, through a safety tax; psychologically, through instilling fear in us that we are not safe virtually anywhere we may be, that the threat of sexual violence is ever present, yet disembodied; emotionally, as we might be prone to settle for relationships we know are not nourishing, either out of fear or because we don't believe we can find anything better.

Within the male protection racket, within the phallacy that good men are necessary to protect us from bad men, within a world governed explicitly and implicitly by gender policing, Safe-T-Man is the best women can do. One challenge is how pervasive the racket and phallacy are, how difficult it is not just to get out from under it but even to *imagine* getting out from under it. The language of patriarchal violence is no secret. Indeed, it is a fact so widely known and understood as to be the repeat subject of countless popular movies.

The phallic symbolism of guns is not a feminist construct but an acknowledgment of the significance of the relationship between masculinity and violence. The declaration that a real man carries a gun and knows how to use it has been transmitted throughout American history. The famous military chant that American marines bark while marching with their rifles, "This is my rifle, this is my gun. One is for fighting, the other for fun," is the stuff of popular media. In the movie *Full Metal Jacket*, the cadets chant this under the watchful eyes of their drill sergeant while wearing boxer shorts, and when they refer to their penises as being guns for fun, they put their hand over their groin and give themselves a little shake.

Though men might joke about the relationship between guns and penises as weapons, the harm that a man can cause another person using his penis as a weapon is acknowledged by law to be the closest he can come to killing someone without actually causing his or her death. Even the Supreme Court has recognized that rape is the most sublethal crime there is. "Short of homicide, [rape] is the 'ultimate violation of self.'"

Whether the barracks are at VMI or the Marine Corps Recruit Depot on Parris Island, South Carolina, I am certain of this: the true value of a facsimile man made of rubber and plastic is that "he" is forever unable to learn, practice, or exercise the language of violence. And the fact that he would provide protection from other men's violence without exacting any sort of quid pro quo elevates him above far too many human men.

That, obviously, is not the world we live in. In the world we inhabit, men speak the language of violence. They loot, riot, and overturn cars when they protest some government action. Indeed, throughout history, men have used violence to express political outrage and demand change. Women have not. Consider that when Donald Trump bragged about his impunity to sexually assault women, women marched to show their displeasure but no cars were overturned.

In the play *Gloria* about the life of Gloria Steinem, Steinem recounts that the "bra-burning" label given to feminists was meant to discredit them. During a march for women's liberation in the 1970s, women planned to burn garments they thought symbolized their oppression. But because they were not granted a fire permit, they did not actually burn anything! Sisters, need I say more?

Instead of using violence, women act like good girls and ask their (mostly male) legislators politely for help. We turn to our (mostly male) policemen. We turn to our male friends to walk us to our cars, our husbands to walk us across parks. When the legislators come up short, proving to be uninterested, unhelpful, or insufficiently helpful, when no man is there to escort us, we go quietly home, oftentimes afraid for our lives. In some cultures, women are encouraged to leave a pair of men's shoes outside their apartment door to create the impression that a male guardian is present. For those of us in Western societies to gain a bit more freedom of perceived safe movement, we are encouraged to buy Safe-T-Man.

The very existence of Safe-T-Man signifies the way in which male violence is thwarted only by the threat of male violence in return. This fact leaves women at the mercy of men, whose rates of violence against us confirm that such mercy is in short supply. Now that we have identified the phallacies behind this trap, we must work collectively on finding our way out. Let's think outside the trap altogether.

CHAPTER 4

PATRIARCHAL VIOLENCE

Between 1999 and 2008 there was an average of twelve adult males in the Kanyawara community of chimpanzees in Kibale National Park in Uganda. They were ordered in a linear hierarchy under an alpha, who researchers named Imoso. During his reign Imoso tended to monopolize access to the females, siring a disproportionate quarter of the community's offspring. Interestingly, Imoso also had the power to interfere in copulation attempts by lower-ranking males. If other males of the community supported him in conflicts, Imoso rewarded them by interfering less in their copulation attempts. He gave them extra access to the females.

I was sitting in the majestic reading room of the Harvard Law School Library in Langdell Hall in the fall of 1994 reading through the recently passed Violence Against Women Act (VAWA). I was rapt. When I sat down, it was afternoon, but as shadows lengthened, evening came, and more lights were turned on, I did not move from my seat. In addition to creating new laws and providing money to states to protect women, the act created a new federal civil right to be free from gender-motivated violence. I thought it the most potentially transformative civil law regarding women's equality that I had seen in my years of practice. It was as important as the right to vote.

But in 2000, the conservative justices of the US Supreme Court would strike down this civil right in the case of *United States v. Morrison*. And just five years after that, the Court would deal a knockout punch in another case, *Town of Castle Rock, Colorado, v. Jessica Gonzales et al.*, ruling that police have no obligation to enforce an order of protection from domestic violence. Taken together, these cases amount to the reality that at the highest level of US law, women have no right to challenge male sexual violence.

The public is mostly ignorant of this fact. Indeed, the vast majority of law students, lawyers, and law professors are unaware of it. For me, though, these decisions are central to my work, activism, and understanding of the world, and I have pored over and taught these cases for years. These two cases, which I will detail below, go to the heart of the trap of patriarchal violence within which women live.

PATRIARCHAL VIOLENCE

Patriarchal violence is the term I use to describe the prevalence and variation of male sexual coercion that is necessary to preserve patriarchy in a democratic system. The two cases that represent women's inability to access the justice system involved the most extreme forms of patriarchal violence: gang rape and domestic violence homicide. For all my amateur dabbling into sexual coercion in primates, I found few to no examples of these specific types of violence by primates, yet they are enacted by humans every day, even though each is counter to reproductive fitness. In domestic violence homicide, in which a man kills his reproductive partner, he loses her as a reproductive resource. And multiperpetrator sexual encounters result in the inability to determine paternity, thus destabilizing parental investment in children.

In humans, these horrific acts have a larger social significance that gives them meaning: they operate to enforce the patriarchal social order by keeping women down in a society that ostensibly affords them rights. This is why the incredible coincidence that these two cases involved precisely the two most extreme forms of patriarchal violence is so important.

This is the trap from which women must escape. Many men recourse to violence without provocation. Women suffer disproportionately from male temper syndrome. Patriarchal violence is the constant; its extent and timing are the only variables. And under patriarchy, women have few recourses.

The previous chapters help you to see these facts clearly. Many women—and men, for that matter—live day by day in denial about it or accept it as inevitable. The male protection racket, we're taught, is no racket, just the way things are. When male temper syndrome and all of its consequences are acknowledged, male legislators extend to the more privileged among us assurances that, as good men, they will protect your rights from the violence of bad men. This is a belief we accept at our peril.

The strong message is that any woman can be subject to brutality just because they are women. As Catharine MacKinnon wrote years ago, this scheme of violence is akin to terrorism—a brand of terrorism with patriarchy as its motivating ideology:

> Sexual abuse works as a form of terror in creating and
> maintaining this arrangement. It is a terror so perfectly

motivated and systematically concerted that it never need be intentionally organized—an arrangement that, as long as it lasted, would seal the immortality of any totalitarianism. . . . It is at once absolutely systematic and absolutely random: systematic because one group is its target and lives knowing it; random because there is no way of telling who is next on the list. Just to get through another day, women must spend an incredible amount of time, life, and energy cowed, fearful, and colonized, trying to figure out how not to be next on the list. Learning by osmosis what men want in a woman and trying to give it to them, women hope that being the wanted image will alter their odds. Paying attention to every detail of every incident of a woman's violation they can get their hands on, women attempt not to be her.

The message is that men's violent rages cannot or will not be stopped—and that if they happen, there is seldom a remedy for the harm done. In an ironic trap, women are blamed for the very thing they are organizing their lives to avoid: arbitrary punishment for noncompliance with patriarchal norms. So if we try to conform by making ourselves desirable to men, we will be blamed for inciting an attack.

PATRIARCHY IS NOT INEVITABLE

Keep in mind, though, that patriarchy is not inevitable. Recognizing the architecture of patriarchy reveals that in the same way that it is constructed, it can be taken down and dismantled. Barbara Smuts's work on the evolution of patriarchy shows how it is formed through male-male alliances. Such alliances are critical in both primate and human societies. Male sexual coercion of females is the scaffolding of this social architecture. The tacit agreement among men not to intervene in another male's sexual coercion is essential to maintaining a patriarchal social order. We see expressions of this agreement time and time again in law, most significantly in the two Supreme Court cases I mentioned. Law reflects the nonintervention agreement; it does not interrupt male sexual coercion, and it seemingly turns a blind eye to it even when legislatures try to help by passing new laws.

Bonobos are living proof that there is an alternative to patriarchy. Their structure of female-to-female alliances to thwart male sexual coercion is readily adaptable to humans. And a structural response is necessary if we hope to create a society with the true potential for human thriving. The effective and immediate displacement of the patriarchal order is entirely possible.

As the historian Gerda Lerner pointed out, patriarchy is a created social order and historic invention. "The basic unit of its organization was the patriarchal family, which both expressed and constantly generated its rules and values."

The anthropology of law shows that men have historically made and enforced all laws. This means, unsurprisingly, that when it comes to law, men win. A historical and anthropological perspective on male supremacy encoded into the law helps make sense of otherwise shocking decisions. And then it leads to a way forward.

WOMEN HAVE NO CIVIL RIGHT TO BE FREE FROM GENDER-MOTIVATED VIOLENCE

In *United States v. Morrison*, the facts were pled as follows. Alleged facts are taken as true in cases deciding purely a question of law, meaning that the Court will ask whether, if true, the facts would establish a case under the given law. Thus, I recount them here. Christy Brzonkala (pronounced *"bron*-kala") was a newly arrived freshman at Virginia Tech in the fall of 1994. She met two football players, James Crawford and Antonio Morrison, and within a half hour of their meeting, they took turns raping her in her dorm room. In her amended complaint, Christy alleged that a third football player, Cornell Brown, had stood guard by the door during the rapes. He served as an alibi witness for Crawford. She also alleged that their football coach, Frank Beamer, had helped conceal the rape after the fact.

Neither Morrison nor Crawford bothered to use any form of protection. After Morrison had finished penetrating her for the second time, he threatened her by saying "You better not have any fucking diseases." After that horrific night, Morrison was heard loudly stating in the dining hall that he "like[d] to get girls drunk and fuck the shit out of them."

Ms. Brzonkala attempted to seek justice, first by reporting the gang rape to the school. After filing the complaint, she learned that another football player had told Crawford that he should have "killed the bitch." Many students turned against her for having dared to challenge the football team. She became depressed and withdrew from Virginia Tech. She never returned.

During the first school-sanctioned hearing, Morrison was

found to have sexually assaulted Ms. Brzonkala and was suspended for two semesters. He appealed the decision. He was permitted to return to Virginia Tech on a full football scholarship for the following fall term.

In December 1995, Ms. Brzonkala filed suit against Morrison, Crawford, and Virginia Tech in Virginia Federal Court. She brought one of the first claims under VAWA's federal civil right to be free from gender-motivated violence. Virginia challenged the validity of the civil right, and the case made its way up to the Supreme Court. The Court's decision was written by Chief Justice William Rehnquist.

This is significant because Rehnquist, as a sitting justice, had publicly opposed VAWA shortly after it was introduced in Congress. That was a highly unusual act; I can find no other situation when a sitting Supreme Court justice spoke out against pending federal legislation. Indeed, wouldn't that create a conflict of interest if that law was later challenged? Arguably, it would. But no one challenged Rehnquist when he later heard the case and when he wrote the opinion striking down VAWA. The Court's opinion declared unambiguously that violence against women is not a federal issue and thus Congress cannot give women a civil right to be free from gender-based violence.

WOMEN HAVE NO RIGHT TO ENFORCEMENT OF AN ORDER OF PROTECTION

Jessica Gonzales, now Lenahan, lived in Castle Rock, Colorado, with her three daughters, Rebecca (ten), Katheryn (eight), and Leslie (seven). Mrs. Gonzales was in the process of divorcing her abusive husband, the father of the three girls. In May 1999, she obtained a restraining order from the court that prohibited the father from coming within a hundred yards of her or the girls. About two weeks after the restraining order was served, the father abducted the three girls while they were playing outside. Jessica called the Castle Rock Police Department to report the girls missing. When police arrived at the house, she showed them the restraining order and said she believed their father had taken them.

The officers stated that there was nothing they could do. They suggested she call again if the girls did not show up in the next couple of hours.

An hour later, Jessica spoke with her estranged husband, who told her that he was with the girls at an amusement park in Denver. He was admitting to his flagrant disregard of the court's restraining order. Jessica again called the police. The officers again refused to help. They again told her to wait.

Two hours later, she called the police again, and again they told her to wait.

Around 1:00 a.m., now eight hours after the girls had been abducted, she went to the police station herself to file an incident report. The officer who took the report made no effort to enforce the restraining order or locate the girls. Instead, he went to dinner. Around 3:00 a.m., the estranged husband arrived at the police station and opened fire at the officer, thereby committing suicide by cop. Inside the pickup truck, the police located the bodies of the three girls, all shot dead. The gun the father used to kill them and fire on the police officer had been purchased earlier that night.

Jessica sued the City of Castle Rock for failing to enforce her restraining order. The case worked through the court system until it was chosen among hundreds of possible cases to be considered by the Supreme Court.

Justice Antonin Scalia, writing for the majority of the Supreme Court, dismissed her complaint because they did not feel she had a claim through which legal recourse could be sought. They felt that the text in the restraining order, which stated that law enforcement officials "shall use every reasonable means to enforce this restraining order," was not a compulsory statement but instead discretionary. Therefore, the police department was not at fault for exercising its discretion and deciding to not enforce the order. According to the Supreme Court, "shall" is a suggestion, not a command. Therefore, Jessica had no legal recourse, as the police department had done nothing wrong.

To be clear, her case was not heard and decided against her; the Supreme Court simply concluded that she had no case at all. None. What was agreed was that, yes, a court had issued a restraining order against her estranged husband. Yes, she resided in a state that had passed legislation that explicitly mandated its enforcement. Yes, her estranged husband had acknowledged by phone call that he had violated that order. And, yes, her three young daughters had been murdered by their father. What she didn't have, the Court stated, was a case against the police who had failed to enforce the order.

This means that as I write, under US law, you have no right to enforcement of your order of protection, even if you live in a state that has a specific law mandating such enforcement. How can that be? And why isn't this common knowledge? Indeed, why weren't there marches in the streets when that decision came down?

So heartbroken was I about the decision that I carried a printout of the decision in my backpack for about three weeks before I had the emotional strength to read it. I was incensed at Justice Scalia's mocking and dismissive tone toward Jessica and all other endangered women. He actually called "hyperbole" women's claim that an order of protection with no right to its enforcement is merely a piece of paper. But what is the value of an order of protection with no right of enforcement?

Moreover, Justice Scalia was known for his allegiance to states' rights of self-determination. So in many cases when he denied access to federal courts, he would defer to the individual states to make their own decisions. But in this case, he abandoned that position of deference, finding that the state of Colorado could not have meant what it said when it said that police "shall" enforce orders of protection.

After reading the decision in my office, I needed to take a walk. I headed to Harvard Square, the area of shops and restaurants around the school. I found myself in the Body Shop, a store that sells good-smelling soaps and lotions. There was a sign at the register that said, "Donate your used cell phones! Help domestic violence victims call 911!" Incensed, I told the unsuspecting store clerk, "You know, 911 doesn't actually have to do anything when a battered woman calls!" and then proceeded to explain the case and its ruling. By that time, others had gathered around me, and I shared my outrage with them. They were equally enraged and also shocked that they hadn't heard anything about the devasting decision.

THE ONLY MAJORITY WITH NO CIVIL RIGHTS

The *Morrison* case involved a civil right granted to provide redress for all the criminal cases not brought. But lawmakers and judges could not get their minds around how to prosecute the animus that so many men demonstrate against women.

Because men cannot exclude women from all aspects of daily life, the expression of hate through exclusion is less available. Of course, they can intentionally exclude women—think of fraternities, sports teams, the military—but they cannot do it to the extent they can with racial or religious minorities. There are too many of us. Women outnumber men. Consider that: we are the rare majority with no civil rights.

It's that very majority status that puts us outside of the usual categories of those who receive civil rights protection. To offer minority groups some civil rights protection neither threatens nor alters the power structure of a patriarchy. But to afford meaningful equality rights to women—as VAWA did—most definitely could. As applied to women, civil rights are conceived of by men with power as what my friend Pam Coukos called the "too big problem."

To quell the objections of men who were afraid that casting a net over gender-based crimes might ensnare too much sexism—perhaps even their own—women's groups contorted the language of the provision to include only crimes of violence that were motivated by gender. The journey to defining "gender-motivated violence" shows how difficult it is to arrive at a description that people understand and accept.

What made passage of the act so difficult was that male legislators wanted to define gender-motivated violence in ways that would not implicate them in any way. To agree that it was any type of violation, they needed conceptual distancing from the behavior. As men have historically done, the men who drafted VAWA wrote the law with this built-in exclusion for their own conduct. They needed to make sure it would not reach them or infringe in any way on their male sexual entitlement.

Consider this statement by Senator Orrin Hatch, a coauthor and supporter of the act:

> We're not opening the federal doors to all gender motivated crimes. Say you have a man who believes a woman is attractive. He feels encouraged by her and he's so motivated by that encouragement that he rips her clothes off and has sex with her against her will. Now let's say you have another man who grabs a woman off some lonely road and in the process of raping her says words like, "You're wearing a skirt! You're a woman! I hate women! I'm going to show you, you woman!" Now, the first one's terrible. But the other's much worse. If a man rapes a woman while telling her he loves her, that's a far cry from saying he hates her. A lust factor does not spring from animus.

Lust is given to excuse male sexual entitlement and to feed the notion that men cannot control their own sex drive. In fact, the district court judge who heard the original case in *Morrison* wrote that "date rape could also involve a situation where a man's sexual passion provokes the rape by decreasing the man's control."

It is worth paying close attention to what is revealed through language. The idea that lust is somehow tangled up in abuse or the drive to ignore a person's will lies at the heart of men's claim of inability to conceive of what a gender-motivated crime would look like.

The FBI was opposed to adding gender to the category of hate crimes prosecutable by the federal government. This is a different statute from the one involved in VAWA, but the underlying reluctance to recognize federal jurisdiction is the same. In the words of David Evans, the FBI acting assistant director, "The inclusion of gender . . . [in] the Hate Crimes Statistics Act is not recommended. . . . A gender bias motivation would be very difficult to determine, e.g., is the crime of rape motivated by lust or hate?"

Interestingly, the public comments by Senator Hatch and the FBI official nod toward the conflation of lust with some kind of animus with concern not for the potential victims of a civil rights violation but with the unfortunate men who might get caught in a legal trap.

As you read, recall the circular nature of patriarchal law. Women directly endangered by men's violence often appeal to the courts to save their lives. Those courts systemically disregard the seriousness of the threat men pose to women's liberty and lives. A law, VAWA, was passed to remedy this. The Supreme Court eviscerated the authority of the law and of the legislature to pass such a federal law. Women are thus left to be directly endangered by men's violence.

JURISDICTIONAL NO-WOMAN'S-LAND

Jurisdiction means the authority to rule over a particular matter. It turns out that in critical areas of jurisdictional questions, women have no standing. Our rights, our lives, and our experiences exist somewhere in the spaces between categories that were established by men. At each juncture, we have been left out. This includes in civil and criminal law; federal and state courts; private and public acts. *Morrison* involved the hybrid question of civil versus criminal law, based on a civil rights statute one could use to address crimes of gender-motivated violence. It also gave women access to federal court, but the Supreme Court shut that door in our faces, sending us back to state courts. In both cases, the Court refused to intervene in the ultimate privacy zone: the patriarchal family unit.

But before getting into the cases, allow me to explain a bit about the legal distinctions between civil and criminal law, state and federal jurisdiction, and how women's rights do not fit into any category.

You are most likely familiar with criminal laws. Those deal with violence and other acts we as a society deem reprehensible, such that if found guilty a defendant can lose their liberty. In rare cases in the United States and elsewhere, the death penalty is possible. Civil law, on the other hand, involves matters such as contracts, property, divorce, trusts, and estates—conflicts that can be settled with money. The same act can violate both criminal and civil law. Take, for example, O. J. Simpson's murder of his estranged wife, Nicole Brown Simpson, and her friend Ron Goldman. O.J. was famously found not guilty in criminal court but was found liable for the murders in civil court, which ordered him to pay millions of dollars to the Brown and Goldman families.

In a criminal case, the burden of proof is high. The prosecution has to prove all elements of the crime beyond a reasonable doubt. This is warranted because of the potential of the defendant's loss of liberty if he or she is found guilty. In civil cases, the defendant may be required to pay money damages and/or provide injunctive relief (meaning doing or ceasing to do some act). In a civil case, the standard of proof is a preponderance of the evidence. Together, criminal and civil law provide the two principal avenues to obtaining justice. The US Supreme Court has closed both avenues to women seeking justice from gender-based violence.

The federal civil right to be free from gender-motivated violence could be used in either state or federal court. This was significant because federal cases are regarded as the more important ones; recall that the phrase "to make a federal case out of it" means to make a big deal out of something. Also, a person who was subject to gender-based violence could bring a civil rights action regardless of whether there had been a criminal prosecution for the underlying act. This was in recognition of the criminal justice system's widespread and acknowledged failure to address intimate partner violence.

Unfortunately, the fact that women might have access to federal court was so alarming that Chief Justice Rehnquist felt compelled to speak out publicly against the act when it was first introduced. He was concerned that the act would allow a host of "domestic relations" cases to be brought into federal court. What this involves is divorce, which is traditionally a state court matter. Rehnquist suggested that women would use it illegitimately to gain advantage in their divorce cases.

Is this a fair concern? Only if it were true. Rehnquist's language reveals a bias against women that is reflected in a mistrust of the word *gender*. This mistrust has deep roots in American jurisprudence. The legal scholar Deborah Tuerkheimer described this as a "credibility discount" that works as follows: "The rule is simple: credibility is meted out too sparingly to women, whether cis or trans, whatever their race or socioeconomic status, their sexual orientation or immigration status. The discounting of women's credibility is coupled with the 'credibility inflation' we give to men."

THE GOOD-GIRL TRAP OF PATRIARCHAL DEMOCRACY

Imagine, if you will, a board game. There is a large orange infinity symbol with spaces demarcated along which the players move. This game is called the Good-Girl Trap of Patriarchal Democracy. Welcome to the game, and please know that there is a way out. The bonobos show us the trapdoor out of which we can exit altogether once we realize that this is a trap.

Your starting point is the occurrence of a gender-related injury, meaning a crime committed against you because of your gender. A sense of injustice ensues, leading the injured party to seek justice. This leads you to go to your legislator, perhaps along with a representative of an advocacy group, to try to get legislation passed to address the particular situation under which the harm was caused. That legislator will lead you to other legislators, and if that goes well, there will be a committee hearing, or several of them, convened over a period of time correlated with the press coverage of the original injustice.

Let's say the legislation survives the labyrinth of committee hearings and is passed. Though it is now most likely a watered-down version of the original bill, its passage will be celebrated as a victory. Look! Progress! Then the legislation will be challenged in court, not because the folks bringing the suit to strike it down hate women or think they shouldn't have rights but because (pick one): the legislation is either too broad or oops!, the legislature has no jurisdiction to make a law that would cause interference with patriarchal rights.

Now the law will be either overturned or upheld. If it is overturned, the original injured party—you—must start back at square one—unless, of course, you are too exhausted by the original process to regroup and try again. If it is upheld, it will accumulate qualifiers, perhaps be narrowed; regardless, prosecutors in other states may or may not know about its existence. Consider that as I type these words the vast majority of the public does not know that women have no right to challenge male sexual violence at the highest levels of US law. *Morrison* and *Town of Castle Rock* are perfect examples of the Good-Girl Trap of Patriarchal Democracy.

Within a patriarchy, being a good girl means playing by the rules in the expectation that you will be liked and receive the positive attention of, and with it protection from, the boys—the ones with social currency and political power. But as we saw in chapter 3, no amount of being good girls gets women real protection. In the end, it is always the men who decide which women and girls are worthy of such protection. For generations women have asked: What laws will it take to end patriarchal violence? This is not a useful question because embedded in it is the presumption that laws produce social change. In reality, laws advancing women's rights, when pursued within the patriarchy, have largely been an exercise in futility.

The Good-Girl Trap leads to a never-ending game of "choose

your own adventure," in which judges decide how best to shoot down legislation, leaving the injured party to decide if she has the resources to continue fighting. Alas, in a vicious cycle, the Good-Girl Trap can lead to the total destruction of a woman's self. The realization that you are living in a system in which you are at best a second-class citizen is profoundly demoralizing. The rules of the infinite board game, then, are defined by the men in power. If our worth is determined by men, how can we pass laws that extend beyond the protection they feel we require? Especially when they are so invested in occupying the role of our protectors? Or more important, perhaps, how can we leave the board game we never agreed to play?

Recall that there is near-universal agreement that gender-based crimes occur routinely. On the way to passing Congress, twenty-one states conducted their own studies on gender bias in their judicial systems, and every single one of them found that judges subjected women to harmful stereotypes when they sought protection, amounting to the deprivation of equal rights.

Women's groups also initiated and presented studies on the effects of sex discrimination on women's lives affecting every aspect of their ability to participate in our society as full citizens.

Law, and the language of law, is where patriarchy closes its fists around women's rights. From allowing articulation only in men's legal terms, to full-out downplaying of women's injuries in the name of fealty to law, women are left to describe their situation in terms acceptable to men. But this, too, is expected in a patriarchy, where men control the symbols and means of communication. "Male hegemony over the symbol system," Lerner wrote, includes a "male monopoly on definition. . . . The

very metaphors for gender have expressed the male as norm and
the female as deviant; the male as whole and powerful, the female
as unfinished, mutilated and lacking in autonomy. . . . Men have
explained the world in their own terms and defined the important
questions so as to make themselves the center of discourse. This is
particularly visible in the writing and enforcement of laws."

In *Morrison*, language was used to obscure the substance of
the importance of the Violence Against Women Act and reduce
it to a question of interstate commerce. VAWA was passed under Section 5 of the Fourteenth Amendment, which guarantees
equal protection under the laws, and the Commerce Clause of
the Constitution, which gives Congress the authority to regu-
late interstate commerce. Civil rights legislation has traditionally been passed under these dual auspices. But in *Morrison*,
the Court held that Congress could not have jurisdiction of violence against women under the Commerce Clause because it
was insufficiently connected to interstate commerce. The finding was premised on a case it had decided a year before *Morrison* in which it had reversed more than a century of civil rights
jurisprudence by holding that the Commerce Clause needed to be
more narrowly construed.* So convincing was the Court's opinion

---

* The case, *United States v. Lopez*, 514 U.S. 549, 1995, struck down the Gun Free
School Zones Act of 1990. The Supreme Court chooses which cases to accept for
review each year and selected that case. It is plausible, given Rehnquist's objections
to VAWA, that this case was selected and decided in order to create a precedent that
would then require the Court to strike down VAWA when it was selected for review
the next year. In the first paragraph of the decision, Rehnquist wrote, "Believing
that these cases are controlled by our decisions in US v Lopez (1995) and US v
Harris . . . (1883)"; the Court therefore acted as if it had no choice. But notice that
the *Lopez* decision had been only very recently decided, and the next case cited
was from 1883. The Court ignored and entirely disregarded all the significant civil
rights progress that had been made after 1883. Meaning, the Court cited Lopez
as controlling authority that had been decided in 1995, then referred to the Civil
Rights Cases from the 1870s as if no intervening precedent existed that warranted

that most students at Harvard Law School learn the case only for its significance under the Commerce Clause and are shocked to learn instead the substantive importance of the Court's striking down the federal civil right to be free from gender-motivated violence. Other professors who teach constitutional law, with rare exception, stress only the economic analysis of the case.

It is not just that men reserve to themselves the right to determine lust or sexual passion versus hate and animus in rape; it is not just that men reserve to themselves the right to set the terms and the definitions of words—language itself—to determine what is gender-motivated violence. The double bind of the Good-Girl Trap is, of course, that only men are allowed to define what is good. And in that trap, there is little recourse for women to turn for help.

Town of Castle Rock is among the clearest examples of the Good-Girl Trap. Advocates had worked at the state level in Colorado to pass legislation mandating that police enforce orders of protection. That was necessary because police were not, in fact, enforcing those orders, leaving endangered women in even greater danger than if they had not sought protection from the justice system in the first place. Despite the law, the Castle Rock police didn't enforce the order of protection, and eventually the Supreme Court declared that they were under no obligation to have done so. The original advocates were back to square one.

The story of VAWA is the story of the Good-Girl Trap writ large. Women have the most access and success with legislative efforts. However twisted the language may be, the law passed Congress. Women's groups had amassed a mountain of

---

any judicial consideration.

evidence and testimony before Congress over a period of four years, covering in vivid detail the need for this civil right.

The other mechanisms of law enforcement are executive orders by a public official, such as the president or a state governor, and judicial decisions that uphold or strike down a law. Compared to getting legislation passed, women's groups have had less success with prompting executive orders and even less with judicial decisions. So when a law they have worked so hard to get passed is overturned, they are left right back where they began—except that this time, their energy has been depleted and they may not be able to summon up the energy to start all over again. Life under patriarchy goes on.

Like the Good-Girl Trap of Patriarchal Democracy, public communication plays an essential role in keeping women from recognizing that violence is a societal condition under which we all live and that the isolation imposed on us keeps us from uniting to dismantle it. The use of language and the media are two important facets of this.

Women aren't aware of how limited their rights are partly because there's a lack of effective media coverage of cases that concern them. Not only are cases inadequately covered, but when they are, they are rarely contextualized into a bigger picture. Instead, cases of "violence against women" are consistently reported with an air of inevitability. They are also reported as if they are isolated incidents rather than part of a systemic problem.

The way the media portray domestic violence homicide undoubtedly influences how society views violence against women, meaning whether it is seen as a personal matter or a greater societal matter for which there is a public responsibility to create a solution.

For example, when the press reports on honor killings of women, it often does contextualize the crimes in the country and religion under which they are committed. For the most part, this is not the United States. It happens in "other" places and under Islam, not Christianity. But when it is reporting on domestic violence homicide in the United States, cases are almost always treated individually, the crime attributed to the murderer's particular circumstances, rather than being part of any recognizable pattern of escalation of violence that law enforcement has ignored.

By now I hope you understand that patriarchy is sustained by the patriarchal violence within which you live. That is true no matter what your gender. If, however, you are a woman, I hope you now also understand that the Supreme Court grants you no civil right against gender-motivated violence, that your recourse for redress is limited, and that, by design, the Good-Girl Trap will leach motivation and achievement out of you.

There is a solution, a proven one, that is only awaiting our utilization of it.

BONOBOS OFFER AN ESCAPE FROM THE TRAP

In the forest of darkness shines the light of the bonobos. They demonstrate the instability of the patriarchal order and its effective, and immediate, displacement.

In explaining why chimpanzee males might batter females, Richard Wrangham and Dale Peterson cited a study suggesting that females' vulnerability is the key: "Battering in animals occurs in species where females have few allies, or where males have bonds with each other."

Once we recognize the fact of male primate sexual violence and how it preserves males' control over females' reproduction, we can meaningfully juxtapose it against bonobo behavior to understand how the absence of male sexual coercion in bonobos shines like a beacon of possibility.

Hold to these facts: Bonobos—all bonobos—have more wanted sex, sex free of violence, than do any other primates. Bonobos enjoy reproductive autonomy. Bonobos are not xenophobic. Rather than maintaining suspicion and hostility toward others, they are xenophilic, interested in and attracted to others. Bonobos do not rape, and they do not kill their intimate partners. Alone among all primates, bonobos do not commit infanticide. And they have arrived at this way of living without the benefit of laws, governments, police forces, or the military. They did not even need the human primate's larger, more evolved brain.

THE FRAMEWORK OF PATRIARCHAL VIOLENCE

The framework of patriarchal violence is a powerful analytical tool to help us understand what we are up against. It also informs strategies for revolution. The most important aspect of patriarchal violence is how it works at a macrolevel while constructing and shaping relations at a personal and individual level.

In this space between macro and micro, the importance of men's failure to speak out against sexual violence emerges as a truly critical factor in its perpetration. Men are cowed into silence by threats of patriarchal violence by the alpha males at the top of the enforcement chain. Beta males also enforce patriarchal violence through their silence and participation in a misogynist culture. But under patriarchal violence, even the most thoughtful, caring, violence-disavowing man benefits. We note the absence of violence in our own life only because we are aware, at whatever level, of its ubiquity nearby. The patriarchal violence of a large minority of men means that all men enjoy sexual and other entitlements over women and girls. I think that women tolerate a lot of bad behavior by men because they know it can be so much worse. At least he doesn't hit me, they think.

The framework of patriarchal violence also makes it clear that we women need to develop a macro response, a new understanding of the type of solidarity necessary to eliminate the social order sustained by patriarchal violence. In bonobos, their female alliances are not reserved for friends or relatives; they include everyone in their protective network. That is the insight gained from the bonobos, translated into the Bonobo Sisterhood.

When a woman reads an order of protection, she sees her injuries listed on a standard court form. Think about this for a minute. The violence she has suffered is part of a menu of violations thousands (millions?) of other women have suffered, and her experiences are reduced to line items on a court document. Injuries she thought of as unique to her personal circumstances are there reflected in language so common as to allow courts to copy and paste them from form to form. The realization inevitably sets in that she is in fact part of a group, one she never wanted to belong to, never imagined in her childhood that she was statistically likely to belong to.

Now she also knows she is not alone.

The #MeToo movement brought individual injuries into the collective consciousness. Now we need a strategic means to effectively and efficiently build a bridge from the individual to the collective action of sisterhood. The key is to eliminate all sex inequality in all its iterations. Most important, it is to destroy the constant threat of male sexual violence that pervades, shapes, and unfairly limits the lives of women and girls. The question is: What will it take to do that?

Relying on men in a patriarchy to protect women is a fool's game. Instead, we will call on female solidarity and alliances. Bonobos will guide the way.

CHAPTER 5

COMPLIANCE SEX

Deep in the forests of the Democratic Republic of the Congo, researchers observed a group of wild bonobos named E1. The researchers already knew that bonobos are a particularly sexually active species, but they were unsure about how exactly sexual encounters were started and by whom. What they discovered was groundbreaking. Though males did usually initiate sexual encounters, approaching or following females, it was the female bonobos who ultimately determined if they were going to have sex. If a female did not respond with her own courtship behaviors after the approach by a male, the copulation attempt ended and the male moved on. There were no forced copulations and no intervention by other males. The male bonobos understood not only that "No" really means "No" but that *silence* means "No."

But that wasn't the only interesting thing the researchers found. Though most sexual encounters occurred when females were in their maximum sexual swelling period (in other words, during ovulation), they also engaged in sexual activities without swelling, meaning they had sex for reasons other than reproduction. Dare I deduce that they had sex for pleasure?

THE CONCEPT OF COMPLIANCE SEX

The term *compliance sex* describes sex that is not affirmatively wanted but is assented to for any number of reasons, including fear, coercion, and unequal power. It describes much sex that currently takes place under a patriarchy and in hookup culture. In this chapter, we want to take an unflinching look at compliance sex in our search for a better way.

Bonobos offer a promising alternative for what female sexuality looks like outside of a patriarchal social order. Please know that I am not saying that we should all have sex like bonobos. I am merely pointing out different and potentially better possibilities that emerge when we question a framework that we take for granted. For bonobos, sex is frequently initiated and pleasurable, absent male sexual coercion.

Also, please know that as we embark on this inquiry, I am not challenging your right to determine for yourself what you want or how to think and act. This chapter is an invitation to rethink the questions of why we acquiesce in sexual relations and to give you the space and critical distance from which to interrogate your own preferences—and importantly, to know you have the right to act on those preferences.

The term *compliance sex* occurred to me after two publications went viral in the wake of Ashley Judd's allegations against Harvey Weinstein in the fall of 2017. The first was "Cat Person," a short story by Kristen Roupenian that was published in the *New Yorker*. The second was an article on the website Babe about a woman named "Grace" and her account of an evening with the comedian Aziz Ansari that she described as one of the worst nights of her life.

Both involved different versions of a strikingly similar conversation about hookup culture and women performing to comply with male sexual expectations. Discussing these two stories, the philosopher Kate Manne noted that they "[raise] the specter of sex that is unwanted, and even coerced, but not by any particular person. Rather, the pressure derives from patriarchal social scripts and the prevalent sense of male sexual entitlement." This pressure may operate as ambient noise regardless of the gender identities of the people involved.

"Cat Person" described a sexual encounter between Margot, a young college student, and Robert, a thirty-four-year-old man. Although she is disgusted by Robert, Margot feels somewhat helpless to stop the progression of their sexual encounter, afraid of seeming capricious or spoiled. The nonfictional Grace described feeling assaulted by Ansari, leaving the public to debate whether a well-liked, famous actor's sexual aggression constituted assault or the boorish behavior of a bad date. Both stories, striking a public nerve, went viral after their publication.

The coincidence of these two stories—one fictional and one real—led me to develop the term *compliance sex*. But even well before that, I remember overhearing a group of college-aged women talking about giving in to men's sexual advances just to be left alone, to stop the persistent haranguing. When I introduce the term, my students nod in recognition and find it useful in making sense of today's sexual culture. It opens the space for dialogue about sex in the gray area that is experienced by one person as violative yet seen as perfectly fine by the other person. It also counters the shadow box term *consensual sex*. Hookup culture is increasingly said to consist of consensual sex, a deeply problematic standard. Far too often, what passes as consensual sex is nothing more than compliance sex.

Katie Way wrote a long account of Grace's date with Aziz Ansari that was published on Babe.net. Ansari apologized for his behavior and said he would reflect on it; he did not dispute any of the alleged facts. Grace described going out to dinner, then abruptly leaving the restaurant with him although they hadn't finished their wine. They went back to his apartment, where things progressed rapidly. After she had complimented his marble countertops, he suggested that she "hop up and take a seat." And then "within moments, he was kissing her. 'In a second, his hand was on my breast.' Then he was undressing her, then he undressed himself. She remembers feeling uncomfortable at how quickly things escalated." The article described how he chased her around the apartment and that it felt like a "fucking game."

She said she "used verbal and non-verbal cues to indicate how uncomfortable and distressed she was." But she felt that he ignored them and kept persisting, asking questions like "Where do you want me to fuck you?" She didn't answer because she did not want him to fuck her anywhere. She said, "'Next time.' And he goes, 'Oh, you mean second date?' and I go, 'Oh, yeah, sure,' and he goes, 'Well, if I poured you another glass of wine now, would it count as our second date?'" Grace excused herself and went to the bathroom, where she spent about five minutes collecting herself. When she came out, Aziz asked if she was okay and she said, "I don't want to feel forced because then I'll hate you, and I'd rather not hate you." He finally seemed to understand and said, "Oh, of course, it's only fun if we're both having fun."

If we just stop there, we have an account of a man being sexually aggressive with a woman he doesn't know well and has alone in his apartment. This man, in particular, has a public persona built around his being a woke guy who understands and even mocks male sexual aggression, who for a living makes jokes in his comedy routines about its inappropriateness. It is fair to say that we would expect him not to be the person he was being with Grace.

But we cannot stop there because he didn't.

Grace recounted that Ansari continued pursuing her. First he suggested that they just "chill" on the couch. Then "he sat back and pointed to his penis and motioned for [her] to go down on him." She felt pressured and did so, after which he observed, "Doesn't look like you hate me."

Again, let's stop for a moment and consider: Is that really where the bar ought to be for sexual encounters? That the woman not hate the man for his sexual aggression against her? Let's also ask: Does consent feel appropriate here? And if yes, for whom? When Grace felt pressure to go down on Ansari, did that indicate her consent? Like the sexual pleasure, consent seems to have flowed only toward the benefit of Ansari.

The rest of Grace's account details how she left his apartment feeling violated. "In the Uber home from Ansari's apartment, Grace texted a friend: 'I hate men.' . . . 'I had to say no a lot. He wanted sex. He wanted to get me drunk and then fuck me.'"

Note how eerily similar this language is to what Morrison said in the Brzonkala case: "I like to get women drunk and fuck the shit out of them!" he declared in the dining hall. Even the Supreme Court found that statement to constitute gender-based animus. How different is what Grace recounted from what so many men set out to do, especially in male group settings such as football teams and fraternities, on any given night? They all signify the gulf of different understandings of sexual encounters in which one person, usually a guy who declares his intention, pursues sex with a drunk woman who presumably would not consent if she were not intoxicated.

The next day, Ansari texted her: "It was fun meeting you last night." She replied, "Last night might've been fun for you, but it wasn't for me. You ignored clear non-verbal cues; you kept going with advances. . . . I want to make sure you're aware so maybe the next girl doesn't have to cry on the ride home." He responded, "I'm so sad to hear this. Clearly, I misread things in the moment and I'm truly sorry."

Unsurprisingly, following that story, a media storm erupted with people projecting a full range of reactions, from supporting Grace for coming forward and excoriating Ansari for publicly claiming to be a feminist supporter and treating women with such disrespect in private to discounting her story as nothing more than "bad sex" for which she had no right to complain and blanket defenses of Ansari. What, is he supposed to read her mind? Obviously, it was all her fault for complimenting his marble countertops!

When "Cat Person" came out in the *New Yorker* in December 2017, it immediately went viral. The short story about the inner psychological workings of Margot as she navigated her relationship with Robert struck a nerve. Although it was fiction, it aligns with Virginia Woolf's dictum "Fiction must stick to facts, and the truer the facts the better the fiction."

On their first—and only—date, it occurs to Margot while she is in his car that he might take her somewhere and murder her. Just as she thinks that, "he said, 'Don't worry, I'm not going to murder you,'" as if that is a normal thing to think about on a date. And in context it is. The thought of murder isn't as shocking as it should be given today's hookup arrangements of sex between virtual strangers, which puts women in highly vulnerable positions. In hookup culture, constantly aware and vigilant would seem necessary.

In "Cat Person," Roupenian wrote:

[Margot] saw that Robert was watching her closely, observing the impression the room had made. And, as though fear weren't quite ready to release its hold on her, she had the brief wild idea that maybe this was not a room at all but a trap meant to lure her into the false belief that Robert was a normal person, a person like her, when in fact all the other rooms in the house were empty, or full of horrors: corpses or kidnap victims or chains.

Eventually, they go into Robert's bedroom.

Looking at him like that, so awkwardly bent, his belly thick and soft and covered with hair, Margot recoiled. But the thought of what it would take to stop what she had set in motion was overwhelming; it would require an amount of tact and gentleness that she felt was impossible to summon. It wasn't that she was scared he would try to force her to do something against her will but that insisting that they stop now, after everything she'd done to push this forward, would make her seem spoiled and capricious, as if she'd ordered something at a restaurant and then, once the food arrived, had changed her mind and sent it back.

This is the language of compliance sex. She complied with his sexual expectations even though having sex was clearly something she did not want to do. This type of sex is a hallmark of hookup culture.

HOOKUP CULTURE

In a recent book by the journalist Nancy Jo Sales about hookup culture and her foray into it, she questioned:

> Why was I about to have sex with this young man I didn't even like? I think many heterosexual women have had this experience of having sex just because we feel it's expected of us, because it's what we've been taught that we are for: to be fucked. It's technically our choice, sometimes, even when it isn't true agency in the sense of an informed and enlightened choice, and it certainly isn't our preference.

"Like a lot of the time, I feel pressured to," said Melanie, a young woman I interviewed at UC Santa Cruz. "I feel like, okay, this is a Tinder date, this is kind of like what's supposed to happen. And I've talked to so many friends who tell me about times when they've felt so uncomfortable, but they just went along with it.

"Because it's hard to speak up for yourself sometimes, you know?" she went on. "Especially when it's someone you know you don't know that well—like you don't want to be weird, and you don't want them to think you think they're weird—and sometimes it's just a way to get them out of there," said Lauren, a young woman I interviewed in New York. "Sometimes it's a blow job just to end the date and make them go home."

After Nancy Jo had sex with Jack, he zipped up his pants and got his jacket to go.

"So how'd you like your first Tinder date?" he asked.

"We met on OkCupid," I reminded him, and he said,

"Oh yeah, right!"

"Well, I had fun," he said. "I'd say, 'I'll text you,' but if you don't hear from me, nothing personal, you know?"

And that became the title of her book: *Nothing Personal*.

I am aware that sexual culture is a multifaceted, multidimensional amalgam of behaviors, beliefs, attitudes, and social practices. It is not a monolithic or static referent. It is, and has been, central to my work for two decades. I have watched the fight for women's rights and sexual freedom morph into today's hookup culture. And I am concerned. Today's sexual culture, for all its dynamism, for all its amalgamated attitudes, behaviors, and practices, rests atop patriarchy. So do our laws, our governments, our military, our institutions. It's patriarchy all the way down. Though we have been successful at changing some aspects of it, the foundation of sexual rights has not changed.

While women participate in hookup culture, this version of sexual liberation is problematic and soul crushing at many levels. It turns out that having sex "like a man"—meaning with no emotional connection or commitment—fuels women's insecurities, often leaving their self-esteem in tatters. It is far from a vision of what sexual freedom might look like in a feminist utopia.

Women must look under the hood of today's hookup culture. Indeed, a rising tide of voices is calling out its problematic aspects. They are right to do so. Consider: What is the engine driving this culture, who is behind the wheel, who is enjoying the ride, and why? The primary fuels of today's sexual culture include social pressure, sexual coercion, pornography, and sexual scripts.

When I talk about hookup culture, I am adopting the definition that "hooking up involves casual sexual behaviors ranging from kissing to intercourse with a partner in which there is no current relationship commitment and no expected future relationship commitment." (Lewis, 2013) The interesting thing is that it means different things to different people. Typically, men exaggerate the sex that goes on in a hookup and women minimize it, lest they get a reputation for hooking up too much. The double standard still applies, expecting women to walk the narrow line of acceptable sexuality that tells them to be fun and participatory but not to cross over into being too sexually active. It is a line that doesn't exist for men.

The opacity of hookup culture is one of its central features. The lack of definition operates as a veil for much problematic behavior that occurs in the gray area of hookup sex. This leads to the term *compliance sex* to describe sex that is not affirmatively wanted but takes place anyway because one party complies with the other's sexual desires.

TYPES OF COMPLIANCE SEX

The idea of compliance sex captures the range of experiences under patriarchy that are contained in the space between mutual, consensual, healthy, wanted sex and sexual violence. Within this space, there are myriad experiences, but two categories of it seem most salient.

The first type of compliance sex is sex that is not affirmatively consented to or is expressly rejected. It is "complied with" in the sense that the woman does not resist or express her desire not to have sex. Instead, she simply follows along with what the man does. Although her body is engaged in the sex act, psychologically and emotionally she is more a passive spectator than an active participant. She "complies" in the sense that she goes along, not in the sense that she expresses actual consent. Grace's story involves this type of compliance sex. In some places, she gave off "verbal and non-verbal cues" that she did not want to have sex with Ansari. But eventually, she just acquiesced to his demands. This form of compliance sex is more like sexual assault or at least comes dangerously close to it. As we know, many colleges and universities have adopted affirmative consent policies that treat this kind of sex (i.e., without specific verbal or nonverbal affirmations of consent) as sexual assault—with persuasive justifications.

The other type of compliance sex occurs when a woman does not want to have sex but gives affirmative (verbal or non-verbal) consent anyway. This category is defined by the discrepancy between a woman's internal desires and her outward manifestations of consent—essentially, saying or manifesting a desire to have sex when she doesn't want to. She gives consent for another reason, most commonly a fear of saying no, but also guilt, a desire not to seem prudish or deceptive, or simply indifference or resignation. "Cat Person" exemplifies this type of compliance sex—to Robert, Margot is a willing participant in the encounter, but Margot's inner reservations, fears, and emotions show that she doesn't really want to be there, let alone be intimate with him. Margot's internal reservations run the full gamut of reasons for complying. On the one hand, she fears more than once that Robert could be a serial killer. On the other, she fears seeming capricious, as if she had ordered something in a restaurant and then wanted to send it back. There is a moment of resignation right then, too: to stop what she had put into motion would require an amount of energy she did not feel she could summon up.

Yet when you inquire into the pervasive dissatisfactions with compliance sex, when you slow down and study how women act moment to moment, again quoting Roupenian, "you sort of catch yourself acting in a way that surprises and shocks you." If you ask the question "Would you have sex with someone you barely know and find repulsive?," the answer, of course, is "No." It is the smaller moments, when women are conditioned to please men, that add up to compliance sex. This is true and also results in different manifestations for other groups; queer, nonbinary, and trans women also learn to please men. What connects them all is patriarchy.

Such moments are exceedingly common in hookup culture. And they are almost always unbalanced. Imagine a woman alone with a man; chances are good that you perceive him to be physically stronger than she is. Imagine, too, that she is on his turf, in his dorm room, his apartment, his home, his frat house.

It is likely that they haven't talked beforehand about setting boundaries for what might happen. A void opens between this couple. Though women might think that romantic notions will fill the void, many men think that porn fills it. What happens next is often determined by the fact that women are, and understandably so, afraid of pissing men off. Women constantly try to avoid invoking the rage spiral of the male temper syndrome. And women know that a rage spiral is especially likely to happen after a man is rejected.

The problem is that consent seems to be both the floor and the ceiling of hookup culture, a gray zone that may involve something consent-like but very often involves something rape-like. In the stories of hookup culture, the men seem to take in only the positive cues and ignore anything signaling that the woman does not want sexual contact. (Remember the fraternity chant "No means yes, yes means anal.") The women in these stories are often dealing with the very real fear of what saying "No" may involve. The legal system, as it currently is, has no place for these stories, these lived experiences.

Compliance sex, in which verbal and nonverbal cues go ignored and the woman acquiesces, raises the issue of where "the line" should fall between unwanted sex and sexual assault, both legally and extralegally. Should men be criminally or civilly liable for having sex absent affirmative manifestations of consent? Should women who have experienced unwanted sex talk about their experiences? Should they be "allowed" to use the language of sexual assault and rape? (Answers: yes, yes, and yes.)

Compliance sex in which a woman feigns interest to avert other risks raises questions about the role of coercion in dating and relationships. Most of us would agree that men such as Robert (unsympathetic male chauvinist that he is) shouldn't be legally liable for sex that they objectively believed was affirmatively consented to. At the same time, we should be able to criticize openly and frankly the ways in which men exploit the power of patriarchy by soliciting consent in the shadow of gender-based violence. We should ask men to dig deeper than the surface level of women's responses to their sexual advances and perhaps be more attuned to their body language and potential resistance; to think of something other than the satisfaction of their own immediate pleasure. In short, a man should see a woman as a person and not as an object of his momentary desire.

Given that hookup culture routinely ignores such a bare minimum expectation, women must do more for one another. Perhaps more important, we must create space free of blame for women who feel uncomfortable during or after sex acts to reflect on, discuss, and heal from their experiences. We must create a space in which no one talks over them or reduces their experience to "But you said yes." Patriarchy means that there is oftentimes a knee-jerk reaction to protect men or refrain from punishing them, which hinders the ability of women to discuss what they are uncomfortable with.

Most frequently, this line of protection argues that a man didn't know that a woman didn't want sex and therefore shouldn't be severely punished for what he couldn't have known. The philosopher Amia Srinivasan disagrees and argued instead that men always could have known but they choose not to listen. In *The Right to Sex: Feminism in the Twenty-First Century*, she wrote:

> This idea—that the rules have suddenly changed on men, so that they now face punishment for behavior that was routinely permitted—has become a #MeToo commonplace. . . .
>
> It is true that women have always lived in a world created by men and governed by men's rules. But it is also true that men have always lived alongside women who have contested these rules. For much of human history their dissent has been private and unsystematic: flinching, struggling, leaving, quitting. More recently, it has been public and organized. Those who insist that men aren't in a position to know better are in denial of what men have seen and heard. Men have chosen not to listen because it

has suited them not to do so, because the norms of masculinity dictate that their pleasure takes priority because all around them other men have been doing the same.

The goal should be mutually pleasurable sex. This requires creating conditions that are conducive of mutual pleasure. To do this, we need to increase the attention given to female pleasure, which is currently absent in hookup culture.

MIND THE GAP: THE CHASM BETWEEN EXPERIENCES IN HOOKUP CULTURE

Compliance sex, a keystone of hookup culture, is hardly contained there. It is sex that Rebecca Traister described as "an encounter to which I consented for complicated reasons, and in which my body participated but I felt wholly absent." To which Reina Gattuso added that "a lot of sex feels like this . . . sex where we don't matter. Where we may as well not be there. Sex where we don't say no, because we don't want to say no, sex where we say yes even, when we're even into it, but where we fear . . . that if we did say no, or if we don't like the pressure on our necks or the way they touch us, it wouldn't matter. It wouldn't count, because we don't count."

Traister wrote about how consensual sex can still be bad, adding her own observation:

Outside of sexual assault, there is little critique of sex. Young feminists have adopted an exuberant, raunchy, confident, righteously unapologetic, slut-walking ideology that sees sex—as long as it's consensual—as an expression of feminist liberation. The result is a **neatly halved sexual universe**, in which there is either assault or there is sex positivity. Which means a vast expanse of bad sex—joyless, exploitative encounters that reflect a persistently sexist culture and can be hard to acknowledge without sounding prudish—has gone largely uninterrogated, leaving some young women wondering why they feel so fucked by fucking.

In *Sexual Citizens: A Landmark Study of Sex, Power, and Assault on Campus,* Jennifer Hirsch and Shamus Khan got at this point succinctly:

To a nontrivial degree, the basis of society is reciprocity. And yet heterosexual encounters often lack such reciprocity, denying women's equivalent standing to men, and invalidating their sexual citizenship. Consensual encounters of this nature are a training ground for sexual assault, schooling young people to accept as normal sexual interactions in which a guy's pleasure is the only outcome that matters.

FEMALE CHAUVINIST PIGS

How did we get here?

In Ariel Levy's 2005 book *Female Chauvinist Pigs: Women and the Rise of Raunch Culture,* she described how women participate in raunch culture, the culture of pimps and hos and self-sexual objectification, in order to express their sexuality in the "sex-positive" universe.

Levy detailed throughout her book how young women, in order to gain male attention, are buying into raunch culture and participating fully in it. They are learning to have sex like men, to joke about it, to not be "girly-girls," to go to strip clubs with their male friends. In their acceptance of raunch culture, they are learning to please men at the cost of never developing their own authentic sexual selves. Imitating people who are acting out someone else's fantasy gets you further away from your own sexuality.

Raunch culture evolved into hookup culture. And raunch culture, in turn, developed out of sex positivity.

Sex positivity grew out of a rift in the feminist movement over pornography. Since that split, porn has become more mainstream than anyone could have imagined with the advent of the internet. The anti-woman propagandic aspect of porn has only intensified—the misogyny that is now so mainstream that it is barely visible. The 2008 documentary *The Price of Pleasure: Pornography, Sexuality, and Relationships* analyzed the content of more than three hundred mainstream porn films and found that in 89 percent of the films, men verbally and/or physically abused women and in 94 percent, women were targeted as victims. In one memorable clip, a white man pulls a white woman by her ponytail, yelling, "You want something to eat? I'll give you something to eat!," and pulls her into the bathroom, where he shoves her head into the toilet. Why is this in a porn film? What is sexual about it? This is clearly just abusive violence.

Sex positivity was developed to distinguish feminists from anti-porn feminists, despite the fact that, as Levy noted, "all of the feminists thought they were being sex-positive." The anti-porn feminists were concerned about the misogyny and racism in porn and the effects it had on women's subordinate status. In claiming the mantle of "sex positivity," the pro-porn feminists implicitly equated pleasurable sex with pornography, meaning that if you stigmatize porn you're not sex positive, and furthermore you are against sex. This is what has made it so hard for women to criticize pornography—the fear of being labeled "anti-sex." As the professor of sociology and women's studies Gail Dines has pointed out, this is absurd, similar to saying that if you criticize McDonald's, you are anti-food.

Sex positivity won out over the anti-porn feminists in many ways. Third-wave feminism is all about sex positivity, claiming that female empowerment can come from anything from stripping to working in a rape crisis center. By the mid-2000s, the unresolved conflicts within the feminist movement had led to "confusion," which Levy captured in *Female Chauvinist Pigs*. She described how "CAKE parties," named after the now-defunct feminist website CAKE, intended to provide space for women to celebrate their sexuality, became a mark of sex-positive culture. "The new sexual revolution is where sexual equality and feminism finally meet," the organization that started the first CAKE parties claimed. This fully signified "raunch feminism," in which women celebrated their sexual liberation by embracing pole dancing and striptease-a-thons. CAKE offered parties where film actors had intercourse and oral sex inside their "freak box . . . a steel closet with a camera" so that everyone could watch the live stream of the live sex.

At a CAKE underground party that Levy attended, men had to pay double for admission and had to be accompanied by a woman. "The room was packed" with scantily clad women and "young men in jeans and button-down shirts who couldn't believe their luck."

Fast-forward to today's hookup culture, and the same dynamics are evident. Moreover, today's youths are especially susceptible to the influences of pornography. Due to the ubiquity of porn, not only do younger millennials and Gen Zers grow up surrounded by porn, but porn has shaped their entire knowledge of sex. As Amia Srinivasan wrote:

> My students belonged to the first generation truly to be raised on internet pornography. Almost every man in that class would have had his first sexual experience the moment he first wanted it, or didn't want it, in front of a screen. And almost every woman in the class would have had her first sexual experience, if not in front of a screen, then with a boy whose first sexual experience had been. In that sense, her experience too would have been mediated by a screen: by what the screen instructed him to do.

The consequences for our sexual culture of this porn ubiquity are obvious. As Srinivasan posited: "For porn does not inform, or persuade, or debate. Porn trains. It etches deep grooves in the psyche, forming powerful associations between arousal and selected stimuli, bypassing that part of us which pauses, considers, thinks."

Porn is the elephant in hookup culture's bedroom. It provides the sexual scripts that men imagine and women follow. It fills in the spaces that are left unsaid and unnegotiated in a hookup, and its messages of phallocentric sex are constant, loud, and clear. The theme of pornified sex runs through both Grace's encounter with Ansari and Margot's experience with Robert in "Cat Person." Consider this passage:

During sex, he moved her through a series of positions with brusque efficiency, flipping her over, pushing her around, and she felt like a doll again, as she had outside the 7-Eleven, though not a precious one now—a doll made of rubber, flexible and resilient, a prop for the movie that was playing in his head. When she was on top, he slapped her thigh and said, "Yeah, yeah, you like that," with an intonation that made it impossible to tell whether he meant it as a question, an observation, or an order, and when he turned her over he growled in her ear, "I always wanted to fuck a girl with nice tits," and she had to smother her face in the pillow to keep from laughing again. At the end, when he was on top of her in missionary, he kept losing his erection, and every time he did he would say, aggressively, "You make my dick so hard," as though lying about it could make it true. At last, after a frantic rabbity burst, he shuddered, came, and collapsed on her like a tree falling, and, crushed beneath him, she thought, brightly, This is the worst life decision I have ever made! And she marveled at herself for a while, at the mystery of this person who'd just done this bizarre, inexplicable thing.

In the story, Robert's dialogue is taking place between himself and the porn that inspired his actions rather than between himself and Margot as a person with whom he is sexually engaged. This kind of objectified sex is a consistent theme in hookup culture.

We know that media have an effect on our behavior and attitudes. Popular culture is created by the most consumed media, and pornography is one of the most influential forms of media that shapes our sexuality. Because porn is about sex, it escapes much critical analysis that it would receive if the sex part was removed. Porn is increasingly racist, misogynist, and ageist in ways that likely fuel and support negative behavior toward women and girls. When looking at porn, if you remove its sexual aspect, what you are seeing might be quite objectionable.

Pornography is defined by the dictionary as "printed or visual material containing the explicit description or display of sexual organs or activity, intended to stimulate erotic . . . feelings." I do not begrudge anyone erotic feelings. I allow that there are many routes toward stimulating them. Still, I unhesitatingly assert that pornography created atop and overwhelmingly for the benefit of patriarchy is deeply problematic.

First, porn is not benign sex education. It is an industry that is driven by profits. To keep the audience's attention, it must constantly push at the edges of acceptable degradation. And these edges have been pushed beyond our worst nightmares. Mainstream porn is misogynist, racist, and ageist (targeting underaged girls). It not only eroticizes domination but gratuitously throws in demeaning, dehumanizing behavior by men toward women. It gives legitimacy and voice to men's hatred of and contempt for women. And it helps create and normalize this misogyny.

THE PARTY SCENE

Raunch culture seeps into the bedroom not only through porn and the bungled sex ed it provides but also through public, social performances of sexual objectification. In the high school and college contexts, these performances are epitomized by theme parties that reduce women to their bodies and promote men to dominate them. The most classic example of the 2000s is the pimp and ho party: "At these gatherings, men dress in 'pimp' outfits—long coats, jewelry, 'bling,' fur, fake gold teeth, black curly wigs (stereotyping African-American males), and women often dress up in revealing clothing, lingerie, stilettos, fishnet stockings and heavy makeup." Time, and perhaps a late recognition of the racialized costuming, has created endless permutations: suits and sluts, golf pros and tennis hos, lawyer bros and prison hos.

These parties include a dress code—a uniform—that prescribes a particular sexual script: the young women attendees are commodities for the evening, and sexual access to them is presumed. The script primes the students for what will later happen in bedrooms and dorm rooms. That is, after all, their purpose: "When it comes to frat parties, a good theme is everything. If the theme is right, the girls will get drunk, naked, and you'll have more ass than you know what to do with."

The "right" theme conforms with the (surprisingly permissive) sensibilities of a given school's student body. If explicit "pimp and ho" parties are no longer an option, fraternities and social clubs turn to other forms of sexual commodification of women's bodies. Her Campus, self-described as the number one media portfolio for college women and Gen Z, suggests that young women attend CEOs and Office Hos parties or Anything for a Buck parties. But it counsels, "just make sure you control the amount of booze consumed to prevent the bad-decision ball rolling."

Even without a specified gender-segregated dress code, high school and college parties can push the same sexual scripts. As one student who had attended annual Suits and Sluts parties at her private high school in New York City put it, "The party may change its title, but its concept and expectations have stayed the same." She admits rationalizing her attendance by telling herself that this party is just like any other thrown at her school, but this one has a "brutally honest" title.

As Ariel Levy posited in *Female Chauvinist Pigs*, raunch culture pushes women to imitate women in sex work, whose job it is to feign sexual interest in random men with whom they have no connection—except that they are paying her. So women are expressing their sexuality by imitating women whose sexuality is constructed entirely to please a male audience. These parties push this dynamic from an implicit to an explicit one by formulating social performance of the most extreme type of sexual objectification: sex work, the literal commodification of women's bodies. If this is what young women are expected to participate in outside the bedroom, what makes us think that these dynamics don't push on the bedroom walls? When the men take off the suits and the young women take off the few articles of clothing they were allowed to wear as a "slut," the roles remain.

Why is sexualization a bad thing? Because in heteropatriarchy, it stands atop men all the way down; it means that men define and judge women, and their sexuality, in terms of their fuckability. It does not have to be this way; sexuality ought to be a positive, loving force in one's life and identity. It is an energy and life force. Yet it is currently corrupted by white supremacy and misogynoir that are perfectly manifested in hookup culture.

Consider a first-year college student who contemplates going to the pimp and ho–themed party during her first semester, right when she is trying to make new friends in this unfamiliar social territory.

How do you dress for such a party? If you're female, you dress as a ho: fishnet stockings, perhaps, and a hiked-up miniskirt. If you are male, you wear what you normally wear, jeans and a polo shirt. The woman has to embrace the iconography of availability; the man doesn't have to make any particular effort.

Why would she even think that attending a fraternity's pimp and ho party is desirable? Often it is because there are few better options. And absent options, we never learn what happens to the pimp and ho party when it is attended only by pimps. Or what happens when the social events we go to challenge the designation of women—white, Black, and Brown—as oversexualized gold diggers.

Why is it overwhelmingly the case that women don't have a choice on almost every given Saturday? Why are there so few opportunities to party under the understanding that all the women around you see one another and think, say, "She's not a ho, she's my sister!" Because currently it is men all the way down. And within heteropatriarchy, our choices too often range from bad to worse.

TRIGGER WARNING: CHOKING

Nancy Jo Sales shared a personal experience of a hookup that turned frightening:

> Within minutes of him coming into my room, we were in bed and he got so excited, talking dirty, calling me names . . . Stuff like that. And then his hands went around my neck and he started choking me.

I knew from my research and talks with my young women friends that choking had become a thing, a standard move, and so I tried to go with it for a few seconds, to see what it was like and if I had reason to object to it.

But as his grip around my neck got tighter and tighter, I actually wondered—wait, is this motherfucker going to accidentally kill me?

The Choking Boy [her nickname for him] had his big, thick, ham-hock hands around my neck while he was on top of me, pounding away at me pretty hard, crushing me slightly; his thumbs were on my windpipe, pressing harder and harder until I was sure he was going to crack it.

I reacted like an animal—like prey—squirming and scrambling around underneath him, slapping at him with my hands and legs, which he seemed to take as a form of encouragement, choking me harder. So I took my foot and put it squarely against his torso and pushed as hard as I could, catapulting him off me. You know how you get extra strong in those moments when you're fighting for your life? He went flying off the bed, landing flat on his butt on the floor. He looked flabbergasted.

"What the fuck?" he cried. "What'd you do that for?"

"Why the fuck did you have your hands around my neck?" I demanded.

"I wasn't trying to *hurt* you!" he exclaimed, sounding more angry than contrite. "I thought you'd like it!"

"You thought I would like being *choked*?"

"All girls like being choked!"

"And why do you think girls like being choked?" I asked.

But I instantly realized why he thought so: it was porn. [Choking is] [a]mong the most popular searches in porn over the past few years. . . .

Choking is a highly gendered act in porn—almost always it's a man's hands around a woman's throat. Rarely do you see women doing it to men, but men choking women appears so often across categories that many porn sites don't even bother to make "choking" a category of its own.

The sexuality expert Dr. Debby Herbenick and her colleagues noted that "choking is really risky. . . . Even though people call it choking, external pressure on the neck—like from hands or a cord or necktie—is technically strangulation." They continued, "There is truly no safe way to choke someone. As part of my research, I've sought advice from several kink-positive physician colleagues, none of whom feels confident in a 'safe' way of choking as there is too much that can go wrong—from seizures to neck injury to death."

The normalization of strangulation in sexual relationships is alarming. It has become eroticized in porn and normalized in women's magazines. But in fact, even the famous porn actress Stoya is concerned because strangulation—whether you call it breath play or choking—cannot be done safely.

Carvana Cloud, a former chief of the Family Violence Unit at the Harris County District Attorney's Office in Texas, made a bonobo call to me in 2018. The domestic violence homicide rate in Harris County was the highest in the country, and strangulation cases were becoming more frequent. I assembled a team of students and two other colleagues to work with her office. Just a few weeks into our collaboration, a man strangled his fiancée's sister in a hotel room. He claimed in his defense that "she liked it rough." This is becoming a more and more common attitude.

Strangulation is a favorite tactic of batterers. Men use it to show women that they have control over their very lives. It is now regarded as a lethality indicator: women who have been choked by their partners are at a higher risk of being murdered. Most states have raised the penalty for attempted murder in intimate partner cases from a misdemeanor to a felony.

In the early 1990s, one of my favorite colleagues, retired sergeant Anne O'Dell (now McCann), was appointed to lead the San Diego Police Department's new Domestic Violence Unit. Her charge was to bring down the high rate of intimate partner homicides. To learn as much as she could in preparation for assuming that important role, she read through approximately ten thousand police reports on domestic violence, and she was shocked to see how similar the cases were. "It was like all the batterers were reading from the same textbook," she told me. She also noticed that choking had been used in a vast number of cases.

She took her findings to prosecutors Gael Strack and Casey Gwinn, who went on to create Family Justice Centers around the country, all based on their model project in San Diego. They have come to learn the significance of strangulation in domestic violence cases; it is a highly lethal tactic that dangerous offenders use to exert ultimate control over their victims, bringing them within minutes of losing their lives. Gwinn and Strack went on to create Alliance for HOPE International, which includes the Training Institute on Strangulation Prevention.

In 2001, Strack's team in the San Diego DA's Office did its own study of three hundred police reports. The results: domestic violence victims regularly reported being strangled, but with almost no visible signs of outward injury; virtually all perpetrators are men; most abusers don't strangle to kill but to show they can do so.

Strack and other domestic violence experts call strangulation one of the ultimate forms of control over a partner. It's something Monterey County, California, deputy district attorney Elaine McCleaf has seen many times in her own work prosecuting domestic violence cases. "The whole dynamic is power and control," she says. "When a batterer has his hands around a victim's neck and he is convincing her he is going to end her life, he has complete control at that point and then releases her and lets her live. What more ultimate control over another human being can there be?"

Bafflingly, some women's magazines have celebrated choking, which as we now know is just strangulation, "as an exciting form of 'sex play'—even recasting it as a 'daring' sex act which allegedly gives women power. In 2016, *Women's Health* said that choking can 'be an exhilarating experience.' In order to enjoy it, the article said, women just needed to learn to 'relax.'"

In a world of compliance sex, this amounts to risking one's life for another person's pleasure.

Without patriarchy, would we ever encounter such a practice presented as a means of attaining sexual pleasure? The roots of choking are found in misogynistic, unapologetically violent pornography. In the context of male temper syndrome and a culture of coercive compliance sex, any practice that literally robs someone of the ability to summon enough breath to object is objectionable. Perhaps patriarchy, which has near its core contests of dominance, is antithetical to pleasure.

COMPLIANCE SEX VERSUS BONOBO SEX

Bonobos represent an answer to the persistent question of what female sexuality might look like outside of a patriarchal social order. And I don't just mean female sexuality but all sexuality. What would gender and sexuality look like without patriarchal policing and violence? It's hard to imagine, admittedly. But bonobos provide a plausible model of what wanted sex can be. They have frequent sexual encounters that are nonhostile, uncoercive, and, importantly, mutually pleasurable. They are the only primates other than humans who copulate face-to-face.

It is difficult to imagine because all women currently live patriarchy, have lived patriarchy for as long as there has been human civilization. It's all we know. All of the practices we follow, experiment with, endeavor to make work reflect this fact. It's men all the way down. Female sexuality today has developed within patriarchal constraints. Sexuality as we know it is dominated by the male understanding of sex, which emphasizes the primacy of male pleasure and subjects women to sexual subordination. Additionally, the patriarchal state is structured to take away women's sexual independence by positioning their sexual deference as a (at times the only) path to social, economic, and other forms of prosperity.

Once sex is commodified—something to be given for a better life, for money, for social status, or even for mere attention—it becomes detached from the woman itself. What she feels, thinks, or does to protest doesn't matter. The patriarchy has created a barter system in which the knowledge of rules and pleasure belongs only to men.

Bonobos prove that there is another way. Our near-cousin primates followed an evolutionary course that is defined by female alliances. They are cooperative, friendly, affectionate, and highly sexual. Bonobos have sexual encounters that are frequent and mutually pleasurable. The absence of male sexual coercion in bonobos seems to produce a freedom—a sexual liberation, if you will—that is far preferable to what women have tried to carve out of the entrenched human patriarchal social and sexual order. A world of patriarchy doesn't bother with teaching women pleasure-centric sex. A world of sisterhood would. And this is not a far-fetched fantasy.

Bonobos signify something extraordinary: that in nature, there is a model that is feminist, even though we were taught for the entirety of our lives, multiple times over, that men always dominate, whether among humans or animals. So for us women, who are taught that patriarchy is a given, bonobos provide proof that there is an alternative reality. Once we realize that this alternative is possible, it opens up the possibility of existing in a world that we can create ourselves. That promise of a possibility to create a world that serves you rather than crushes you is invaluable.

PLEASURE-CENTRIC SEX ED: KNOW THYSELF

Most sex education, whether undertaken by parents or institutions, glaringly omits pleasure. As a consequence, porn fills the gap. This has the effect of reinforcing patriarchal sex norms that have been the status quo for decades. But what if we imagined pleasure-centric sex, more egalitarian and bonobolike? The journalist Leah Fessler noted:

> Since seeking out pleasure-centric education on women's sexual anatomy, and taking the time to explore the nuances of my body both alone and with my partner, I've realized that sex is inextricably linked to emotions, trust, curiosity, and above all, *self-awareness*. To attempt to separate emotions from sex is not only illogical, given that emotion intensely augments pleasure, but also impossible for almost all women.

If our sexual culture shifted to center on women's sexual pleasure as well as men's, I wonder if hookup culture might not collapse. If we taught pleasure-centric sex ed, imagine the possibilities. Young women who are only beginning to explore physical intimacy would go in armed with the knowledge that emotionless, casual sex is likely to be radically dissonant with their bodies' desires. Men would know that it's their responsibility to care about women's sexual pleasure—which includes caring about their feelings. Pleasure-centric sex ed might even reduce sexual assault and encourage more students to report it, as both women and men armed with a clear understanding of how sex ought to feel would more easily distinguish between assault and "bad sex."

Consider how Nancy Jo Sales's encounter with Choking Boy ended. After she got him off of her and they both recovered from their shock and surprise, he asked if she wanted him to leave. But she did not. Instead, she suggested that they lie down together, and she started touching him gently and sexually, then inviting him to reciprocate. They then had a mutually pleasurable sexual encounter, in sharp contrast to their initial scripted hookup encounter.

Consider what can happen when we, women especially, expand our choices within sexual culture.

BONOBO DANCE PARTIES

Women, imagine that every Saturday you confronted a free and clear choice: go to house number one and join a fraternity party, where you run a one-in-three chance of being raped, or go to house number two and join a bonobo dance party, where you run a good chance that if you elect to have sex, it will be pleasure-centric sex as defined by you and your sisters. Bonobo dance parties would occur only in women-managed spaces, say sororities. If there is drinking, only women would provide the drinks. And if any couple goes upstairs to a room, no fewer than three other woman would know that it is happening and approve. Approve of what? Simple. The Bonobo Sisterhood of three approves that each individual going up those stairs is in command of her decisions, her preferences, her options. And the couple close the door to the room knowing that there is a mindful sisterhood downstairs.

Why would you ever go to anything but bonobo dance parties?

Accepting the pimp and ho party scene and the ubiquity of frat brothers raping women is living the myth of men all the way down. Attending these chimpanzee parties carries a risk of rape, but for too many right now the option is attending them or not attending anything. There is no reason for that to continue. Exercise reason, choose sisterhood, and tomorrow sisterhood will replace patriarchy and bonobo dance parties will be the ones everyone wants to attend. At bonobo dance parties sex positivity might become simply positive, wanted sex.

Women can do this. We just need to be more like bonobos.

PART TWO

THE PIVOT

CHAPTER 6

A SELF WORTH DEFENDING

While observing members of the Bompusa bonobo community, researchers took note of the characteristics of bonobo conflicts. The conflicts varied in sex makeup and size. Though females did form coalitions to defend one another, especially if a young female was being harassed, most female bonobos dealt with their conflicts against males by themselves. And most of them won. Those females knew precisely what they needed to do to overcome the small disadvantages they had against the males, and in the end they were victorious.

Kelly Herron was four miles into a run in Seattle when she had to use a restroom. She stopped in a park bathroom and was attacked by a man who had been hiding in a stall. She screamed, "Not today, motherfucker!" over and over as she defended herself from a brutal assault. Kelly had recently taken a self-defense class provided by her employer. Her skills enabled her to prevent a man from raping her; she fought back and, with the help of a passing stranger who heard the fight, trapped her would-be rapist inside the bathroom until the police arrived. The story of the assault went viral and attracted international attention. Kelly later created a nonprofit called Not Today.

As Gloria Steinem memorably put it, "The most important thing about self-defense is knowing you have a self worth defending."

There are few more immediately beneficial public declarations than "No, not tonight, I have my self-defense class to go to." When a self worth defending and capable of self-defense is declared, heard, and seen, the world shifts to something better—because women's power to self-defend immediately also becomes our power to defend others. And when women who are capable of self-defense start standing up for one another, we start to multiply our power and our message exponentially.

Being able to defend yourself changes everything. When you are armed with a knowledge of self-defense, the walk to your car across an empty parking lot, a night spent out with friends, or the simple act of filling up your car's gas tank is different because it is less dangerous. There may be threats, but you are more capable of meeting them. When you stand in your power to defend yourself, you change the people around you, starting with your sisters.

But let's first start where we are right now: most self-defense courses tend to focus on teaching us how to defend ourselves in the very narrow circumstance of being attacked by a stranger on the street. Such assaults, however, account for approximately 10 percent of sexual assaults. What about the other 90 percent? Take a self-defense course, but be aware of this caveat: you need to learn self-defense from and boundary setting for people whom you know as well as for strangers. Women are encouraged to focus on one problem in a way that takes our attention from the real problem: that men's sexual aggression is widespread, largely unchecked, and most often committed by a man with whom we have some sort of relationship.

The current message—entrenched and understood without its being directly addressed—is that it's permissible for women to use the language of violence in a very limited framework, our attention focused on stranger danger rather than the far greater threat of acquaintance or intimate partner violence. The patriarchal permission to defend ourselves against strangers on the street perpetuates the difficulty we have in enforcing our right to defend ourselves and one another against anyone at any time—even in our homes. We need a different model, one that flows from knowing that we each and all have a self that is worthy of defending—in all circumstances. And that we can help defend one another. We don't have to go it alone.

Most men don't expect women to fight back. Much less do they imagine women fighting back in groups, standing up for themselves and one another. For centuries, men have counted upon their ability to divide us against one another, knowing it prevents us from rising up against the illegitimacy of patriarchy. This expectation encourages the men who are intent on harassment, domestic assault, and murder. It encourages the men who use the belief that only good men can stop bad men to sustain patriarchy all the way down. Both expectations underpin the status quo because, as I've said earlier, all men benefit from it.

To a self worth defending, the status quo is unacceptable. As we have seen throughout this book, the status quo, violence against women, is part of an overall societal structure reinforced by our political institutions, our legal system, our culture, often by our religious beliefs, by histories told that don't include women. It is reinforced through compliance sex. Violence against women is so deeply embedded that we barely know how to see it. A collective response is our only way out: strong and plentiful female alliances to stand up to the extensive male alliances that women confront. The Women's Marches show that we have the ability to unite at unprecedented levels. Imagine what the same marches would be like if it were known to all bystanders that every single marcher is trained in self- and mutual defense.

It starts with each of us individually.

I know I keep repeating it in different ways, but it's worth doing so: the law will not come to our aid because it is conceived of, written by, and overwhelmingly enforced by men. And most men won't come to our aid because nonintervention in another man's sexual relationships is a pillar of patriarchy. There are also costs to men for defying patriarchy. What makes things worse is that women have long been divided against one another, believing that their individual protection depends on winning the competition for a good man who will fend off the bad men. It's a dangerous scarcity mindset that plays right into the heart of the problem. Besides, it's a lie. All our division ends up doing is perpetuating patriarchy.

Ending this cycle of perpetuation of patriarchy starts with us as individuals learning to defend ourselves and thus one another. There is real power in that first step. Even just a quick Google search for "women's self-defense" turns up results that are empowering and practical. Self-defense not only teaches us how powerful our bodies are and how surprisingly fragile male bodies are but also ignites our drive to defend others.

The trope of "mean girls" is that: a trope. It, too, is a lie. Like bonobos, women are xenophilic, even if patriarchy mutes the instinct, encouraging us to extend it first only to our immediate squad of friends. Yet, the opposite trope of women supporting other women is even more visible once you look for it. Many of us have versions of the following stories.

Several years ago, one of my students was being harassed by a former boyfriend. For me personally, that happened during a year of extraordinary bonobo energy—it was the year when my original Bonobo Sisterhood members were all in my class. In support of our harassed sister, five of us signed up for the Rape Aggression Defense (RAD) class that was offered by the Harvard University Police Department. The class was transformative.

Women are taught to fear men. Women are especially—and inaccurately (it cannot be said often enough)—taught to fear men they do not already know. We are taught to fear sharing a street, a deserted hotel corridor, really any place in which one may encounter strange men. We are not taught to fear the men who actually pose the greatest risks to us: the ones we know, with whom we might be romantically involved or who want to be involved with us. The Harvard University police taught us that rather than perceive a strange man on the street as a threat to be feared, we could instead see him as a threat to be neutralized by a series of elbow strikes, kicks, and punches. A few of those delivered with sufficient skill and force would be highly likely to disable him and thereby prevent him from physically assaulting us. An important truth that was not lost on me or my five Bonobo Sisters is that, stranger or not, any man can be neutralized by the same series of elbow strikes, kicks, and punches.

Seeing men this way creates a very different, and empowering, perspective. I could now turn around if I heard footsteps behind me and look a man in the eye, my head held high. The difference wasn't that I knew I was entitled to walk down the street (of course I am) or to be wherever I was, it was that I knew I was capable of defending that entitlement. Instead of seeing and fearing a larger, possibly threatening man, I now saw him in terms of neck strikes, elbow jabs, and kicks, and I assessed him accordingly. I was prepared, if needed, to demonstrate my self-defense capability for him and anyone else to see.

During our last self-defense session, when we had to fight off one or more mock assailants, the young woman who was being harassed assumed her ready stance and shouted "Bring it on!" She then proceeded to execute a series of defensive maneuvers that succeeded in disabling her opponents in short order. After that final class, we all walked outside in Harvard Yard amped, ready, and newly empowered to kick ass and take names. It was a transformative feeling.

Learning your power to defend yourself is a way of gaining self-esteem from the outside in. Taking a self-defense class teaches you that you have, in fact, a self worth defending! Learning the power of your body to defend itself disrupts the lessons we have learned about female fragility and weakness. Consider that most women have learned that men have superior upper-body strength and that they are stronger than us. But self-defense negates that lesson by teaching women the power of our lower bodies, how gravity and body positioning can work to enable us to land kicks and blows that might save our lives.

Fortunately, I have had to use my self-defense skills only once so far. It was a summer Saturday afternoon. I was on my way to Chicago's O'Hare International Airport to pick up my husband when I stopped for gas. I was alone, lost in thought, and so was slow to notice a tall, bald white man with creepy small sunglasses approaching me with a pink piece of paper in his hand. He told me his name, which I couldn't catch and lives forever in my memory as Creepy McCreep. Extending his hand and thrusting the piece of paper toward me, he said, "Here's my phone number, give me a call sometime, what do you think?"

Pause briefly. My right to be lost in thought was disrupted. My right to quickly fill up my car's gas tank and go on my way undisturbed was disrupted. My right to the integrity of my personal space was trespassed. Remember that the threatening undertone in this interaction does not arise for men. Because of patriarchy, a strange woman coming up to a lone man pumping gas is propositioning him. Because of patriarchy, a strange man coming up to a lone woman pumping gas is threatening her.

My reaction was to pivot toward the gasoline nozzle, yank it out of the tank, point it at him like a gun, and say loudly, "I. Think. You. Should. Walk. Away." I enunciated every word through gritted teeth, standing in the ready position.

McCreep got the message loud and clear. Whether he thought I was going to gush gasoline at him or not, I do not know. What I do know is that, alarmed, he backed away, then walked away quickly. Rattled, I replaced the gas nozzle, got into my car, and sped off to the airport. I was definitely shaky. But I was grateful for having been able to make a strong and immediate assertion of my right to defend my personal space.

In a self-defense class, you cannot learn what to do in every single situation that is threatening, nor can you learn every possible response. But—and this is important—you do not need to. You gain a critical set of skills from which your body and mind can choose the appropriate response to avoid an attack. You learn in a somatic way that you are entitled to be free from violence and have the right to protect your personal space from a perceived threat. This is one of the most valuable lessons we can learn.

No self-defense class taught me to threaten McCreep with a gasoline nozzle. Knowing I have a self worth defending, however, taught me that I needed and should be prepared to deflect, end, and survive an attack.

Two of my first-year students were in a criminal law class when the professor was discussing rape. A male student behind one of the women started whispering and then laughing with another male student. My student, Annie, turned around and told them to be quiet. After class, the men approached her, saying aggressively, "How can you tell us to be quiet? You don't even know what we were laughing about!" She responded, "Rape is never funny. It doesn't matter what you were laughing about." Rather than admit that chuckling, even at whatever private joke, while the sexual assault of women was being discussed was inappropriate, the male students didn't back down.

Annie was starting to feel threatened, bullied, when another woman, Kate, came up and stood next to her. And now for a disquieting truth. Kate is tall, athletic, and white. Annie is shorter, petite, and Asian American. With Kate standing beside Annie, the men stopped almost at once and walked away.

Annie and Kate considered that their bonobo moment. It was.

Annie issued a call. Kate responded. It is also an inescapable truth that in a world of men all the way down, most often with white men on top of the pile, ethnicity is significant. It is undeniable that Kate likely demanded more respect from the men because she was white. Certainly, women experience different vulnerabilities based on their race, age, location, etc. We need to be cognizant of this intersectionality as we build the Bonobo Sisterhood. Like the bonobos, we have to protect all who are vulnerable. The belief in a self that is worth defending is effective regardless of race, ethnicity, gender identity, or sexual orientation. Answering the call for our sisters is everything.

The intention, the call heard, the call acted on—that is where we begin.

My publisher and good friend Karen Rinaldi was recently on the subway. It was 2021, and the platform was fairly deserted, with the few people waiting observing covid distancing rules. Karen saw a woman standing by herself. A man went up to her, and it looked as though he was harassing her. Karen exchanged looks with another woman, a stranger, who was also awaiting the train. They both fixed their eyes on the woman in the man's sight and attention to see if she was okay, and Karen started walking toward the man and woman. When the man saw that he was being observed, he walked away, but it was clear that his intent had not been friendly. So Karen and the other woman approached the young woman to ascertain that she was okay. They stood with her protectively until her train came and they got on.

As they stood together, the young woman, clearly shaken, said she knew the two other women had been watching and she was grateful for their protection. She knew she had a self worth defending. Karen and the other woman were ready to answer the call.

Note: Answering the call can happen anywhere, in any circumstances, with anyone. It can be a moment or a commitment. The point is to pay attention to your sisters and help them whenever and however you can.

My friend Nancy lived in an apartment building where she often heard her upstairs neighbors—a man and a woman—fighting. Nancy worked for a domestic violence program in Massachusetts. So she reached out to the woman and helped her create a safety plan. When the man learned that Nancy had done that, he cornered her in a stairway and yelled at her for ruining his marriage. Nancy stood up to him, looked him dead in the eye, and told him that she wasn't afraid of him and that nothing he could do to her would change his marriage. He backed off.

That wife has a self worth defending. So, too, does Nancy. Nancy answered the call as someone capable of self-defense.

A group of my students were at a party one Friday night. Another young woman, who was not part of the friend group, was highly intoxicated. My students were concerned. Their concern grew as men started surrounding the young woman. My students heard the call, and they decided to act. They offered to take her home, but she insisted that she was fine. My students stepped back but continued to observe her. That went on for a while, until my students decided to act again. They intervened, got the drunk girl safely home, and then checked in with her the next morning.

My students answered the call, persistently. What those bonobos did that night might well have saved a woman from a life-altering traumatic attack. The woman, recovering from nothing more than a hangover, expressed her gratitude. She could barely remember the night's events, but she could remember waking up safely at home.

Imagine if women came to one another's aid regardless of whether they knew or liked one another. Imagine how doing so would affect our self-esteem, both physical and sexual. Imagine how it would strengthen our internalized agency to be able to make choices, to move about freely in the world, to know that we women have one another's backs covered. Based on these stories and more, it's obvious that this is already happening. We are already looking out for our sisters, but let's take it further. Let's learn how to see more clearly, to acknowledge and act on the threats that burden us every day. It all starts with teaching women and girls their power to defend themselves and others. When we do that, we disrupt so many patriarchal scripts and assumptions. Most critically, when women act and use our power to protect ourselves, the male protection racket will fall apart. Might this be the reason why in a patriarchy so little attention is given to women's self-defense?

Think about it. The role of male protector is an essential feature of patriarchy. But as we saw in chapter 3, the phallacy of the male protection racket is the idea that we need "good" men to protect us from "bad" men. This arrangement sets us up to fail because it puts the power to defend ourselves into the hands of others, making us vulnerable to their decisions about whether we are worth defending or not. Self-defense is a big part of the way out of this; it is the physical embodiment of the knowledge that each of us has a self that is worthy of defense and, moreover, that we are capable of defending it for ourselves and others.

Consider thirty people in a dance club. One threatens physical and sexual assault to another. The twenty-eight other people immediately come together to protect the threatened from the threat. Gender doesn't matter. Answering the call does.

LEARNING SELF-DEFENSE IS NOT VICTIM BLAMING

Which brings us to victim blaming. Some people fear that encouraging women to take self-defense courses is victim blaming in that it puts the onus for preventing men's bad behavior on women. This argument came to a head when Nia Sanchez, Miss USA 2014, gave a thirty-second answer about campus sexual assault in which she stated that self-defense was a great skill for women to learn. "I think more awareness is very important so women can learn how to protect themselves," she said. "As a fourth-degree black belt, I learned from a young age that you need to be confident and be able to defend yourself." She later explained the importance of teaching self-defense skills to women.

She wasn't saying that a woman's ability to defend herself is the answer to sexual assault on campus. Rather, she was advocating for a skill that she herself has and wants all women to have. She asked, "Why not empower women to feel confident and to feel like she can protect herself no matter the situations, like even something little?" Such as: you are at a bar, someone grabs your arm, and you know the quick sequence of moves to force the man to release his grip immediately.

Sanchez received immediate pushback from women who feared that calls for women to master self-defense would lead to victim blaming. Consider the following response from an article published on Slate:

In a society where women are urged to take on the responsibility for stopping rape through self-defense, it becomes incredibly easy to start to see rape not as a matter
of the rapist's choices, but of the victim's. Which, in turn,
becomes an excuse to let rapists off the hook. . . . It also
discourages reporting because victims understandably
don't want to be told they didn't do enough to stop what
happened to them. Taekwondo is fun and a good way to
stay physically fit. It is not, however, a workable solution to
quell the problem of campus rape.

When I raise the issue of self-defense in my classes, many of
my students' first response is the fear of victim blaming. After a
more in-depth analysis, however, a consensus usually emerges
that as long as self-defense is part of an overall prevention strategy for campus sexual assault that neither requires women to
practice it nor exonerates the offender from responsibility, it is
a good idea. I find that the framework in which self-defense is
presented sparks their evolution in thinking about self-defense.
You can see this in what one of my students wrote in a reflection
paper for class:

> The thing I remember most about the self-defense class
> I took in college was when my instructor asked me "what
> was worth fighting for?" The instructor had just taught us
> how to stick our fingers into potential perpetrators' eyes
> and told us, "that they were the consistency of grapes."
> There was like a collective groan from the class, and a
> couple jokes about how we could never actually do that
> because it was so gross. She then sat us down and had a
> conversation with us about what in our life "is worth" pop-
> ping out an eyeball. She said sometimes you aren't will-

ing to fight hardest for yourself, and she urged us to think about who we would be willing to fight for. I immediately thought of my sister and when she framed it in a way of not protecting yourself, but rather someone else—it became easier to imagine actually poking out someone's eyes.

Even though at first I was not comfortable with the act for myself, thinking about doing it for others made it easier to think about defending myself at those same costs.

The idea that women will act for others even before and with more conviction than they will act for themselves is a recurrent one. Indeed, it starts with our self-esteem; we criticize ourselves so harshly and so unnecessarily. For example, at the 2021 Women & Power Conference at the Omega Institute for Holistic Studies in Rhinebeck, New York, the comedian Amy Poehler suggested that we should treat ourselves with at least as much respect as we do a barista or a neighbor who did not pick up after his or her dog. She tries to "stick up for myself like I would for any friend," noting that we speak with respect to the most awful people! Taking this to heart in the context of self-defense, the bonobo self-defense course will draw upon this principle in empowering women to go to the physical defense of other women. We will act for others in ways we are hesitant to do in defense of ourselves.

Herein lies an answer, however, to the question of victim blaming. When twenty-eight people out of a group of thirty answer the call of someone being assaulted, the concept of victim blaming is moot.

Also moot is the fact that when twenty-eight people out of thirty answer the call, who makes up the twenty-eight doesn't matter. Most important, a perpetrator is going to be less inclined to aggress on another person when he knows that she or they have a posse poised in a defensive stance. This is the antidote to the all-too-common "bystander effect." In a world in which at every moment you know that there are numerous people at the ready to come to your defense, can male temper syndrome survive? No, as men will come to understand that they can no longer act with impunity.

Interestingly, no concerns about victim blaming were raised when the Los Angeles trans community began preparing to defend itself. The Trans Defense Fund in Los Angeles was created to meet the rising threats to the trans community. Privately funded, the organization distributed kits containing a stun gun, pepper gel, an alarm, and a spiked kitty keychain. The kits were cleverly disguised in a trendy tote bag. After its announcement that the kits were available, the group raised thousands of dollars immediately to support the distribution of kits and the teaching of self-defense classes, along with providing those in need with a community and a meal. "The rise of crowdsourced kits for trans people represents a unique, organized blending of values around self-defense and collective care."

What the trans community does have is clarity—cruel, grotesque clarity. To be trans is to stare out on a world presumptively hostile. Nineteen percent of cis-gendered people report being threatened or harassed weekly. Forty-five percent of trans women and men report being threatened or harassed weekly. Researchers at the Williams Institute at the UCLA School of Law found that trans people are over four times as likely as cis people to experience violent crime, including rape, sexual assault, and aggravated or simple assault. They also found that trans people have higher rates of property victimization than cis people.

The Trans Defense Fund estimates that the average life expectancy of a Black trans woman is thirty-five years.

Trans people know that they navigate a hostile world. Because of this, organizations such as the Trans Defense Fund have successfully launched GoFundMe campaigns to give out free self-defense kits. African Americans similarly know that they navigate a hostile world. As Ta-Nehisi Coates brought to the awareness of all Americans, Black parents give Black teenagers "the talk," blunt advice on how to navigate a racist, hostile world more safely. Women need to do the same as they confront a hostile patriarchy. That the world is more hostile to trans women and Black women is undeniable. In a threatening world, we must have self-defense classes and kits. We also need to have "the talk."

I would love to see a kit for women and girls. I also recommend strongly that we give one another blunt advice on how to more safely navigate a sexist, racist, homophic, and hostile world. Self-defense animated by the idea of a shared value—that we have selves worth defending—and collective care, like that of our bonobo relatives, works across orientations and across ethnicities.

When twenty-eight out of thirty people respond to one person's call for help against another person's aggression, there is one Bonobo Sisterhood and one aggressor. Period.

The campaign to provide self-defense lessons in the trans community did not lead to victim blaming. But when discussing heteronormative male violence against women, some women's first reaction is to claim that urging women to learn self-defense is to blame the victim. They argue that we should be teaching men not to rape, not teaching women to defend themselves against rapists. Of course we should teach men not to rape! We must never stop trying to get men to see, as perpetrators or bystanders, how brutish the patriarchal structure is for all genders. But as we have seen in this book and in our collective experience, the process of doing so is slow and not always effective. So we must also refrain from a binary, knee-jerk response because that response puts our lives directly into the hands of those who can harm us. That we are either victims or individuals in control of our fate falls back into a limited and dangerous binary way of thinking. This encourages a history that favors one side only. Not only does this way of thinking hurt us all, but it especially harms the non-white and the nonmale. Absolutely, keep teaching men not to rape. But don't depend on teaching men not to rape to fix the problem. Teaching men not to rape and teaching women self-defense are not mutually exclusive.

Note also that teaching women to use self-defense, both individually and collectively, may actually help to teach men not to rape, because women's exercise of self-defense will make it clear to would-be aggressors that they will face a fight. But it is a fight that we will surely win, if we behave as bonobos do.

My call to embrace collective self-defense as our primary weapon against patriarchal violence is rooted in decades of feminist thought and stories that somehow do not receive the publicity they deserve. Though we consistently hear about victimization, much more rarely do we hear stories about women who have successfully fended off an attack.

History shows us that self-defense for women is not a new concept and can be transformative. Consider twenty-year-old Wilma Berger. She became famous in Chicago for using judo to defend herself against an attacker. Incredulous policemen were shown how the techniques she used worked equally well on them, as Berger demonstrated "throwing a detective as she had her attacker." Berger became a "representative of a new self-assertiveness in women learning self-defense methods." That was in 1909.

Suffragists were willing to defend themselves to advance women's right to vote. That was especially true in the United Kingdom, where they "used their bodies in order to convey their discontent and resist oppression through marches, pickets, and hunger strikes." Arming women with the skills of physical self-defense was the logical extension of urging women to assume, safely, "their place in the public space of the city."

In the intervening decades the importance of learning self-defense waned. The feminist scholar Martha Thompson wrote:

> Indeed, self-defense training was considered in the 1970s to be integral to stopping rape and ending men's societal power over women. However, as government and social service agencies responded in the 1980s to feminist demands for rape victim services, social service professionals replaced feminist activists on the frontlines of anti-rape work, shifting the work from "stopping rape to managing rape," and thus gradually marginalizing self-defense training in the movement.

Let's not do patriarchy's work. It serves the patriarchy to object to women's self-defense, leaving women and girls dependent on male protection, which, as we saw in chapter 3, is a losing proposition. We must realize the urgency of acting. Let us not be complacent and hopeful where we have no reason to be. Instead, we should sound the alarm. But more than that, we should be learning self- and mutual defense because we have selves worth defending.

As the self-defense experts Martha McCaughey and Jill Cermele aptly wrote, "While of course preparation to resist sexual assault and self-defense training provides no guarantee of stopping an attack, it certainly increases dramatically the likelihood of doing so—just as learning to swim increases dramatically but does not guarantee, a person's likelihood of staying alive in deep water." And staying alive—staying less harmed and hopefully unharmed—is the point.

A former student of mine had dreams in which she tried to throw a punch but could never land one squarely. The punches kind of disintegrated on contact, never delivering the intended force—until she took a class in self-defense and learned to shout "No!" loudly while throwing a punch. The first thing women learn in a self-defense course is to stop apologizing for taking up space, to say—even better, to shout—"No!" loudly and with force. When we learn self-defense, we unlearn the lessons of femininity that society has taught us for years: to be polite, to be demure, to be pleasing. To be compliant. Worse, it has taught us that these are strategies to embrace when confronted by a man, including an angry, threatening man. What we must learn is that different strategies, the tactics of self-defense, are required when our lives may be on the line. This begins with acknowledging that all women have lives worth fighting for. That acknowledgment often begins with a shouted "No!" As McCaughey and Cermele wrote:

> Self-defense training is not just empowering for individual women but transformative of the gender ideology that

supports rape culture—whether or not a woman actually has to use it to thwart an attack.

Self-defense training empowers women and upsets the rape culture's scripts of gendered bodies that make rape relatively easy for men to accomplish and rationalize.

Another important lesson of self-defense is that men are vulnerable. At some level, we all know that a kick to a man's groin will disable him, but why hasn't this important lesson been taught more directly? In part it is because when men fight, they tacitly agree not to kick each other in the groin.

"Fighting like a man" most definitely excludes acknowledging how vulnerable men are. But they are. For heaven's sakes, their very manhood is outside their bodies! But fighting like a man means punching the face or the solar plexus or using some form of martial arts. It is almost as though men's physical vulnerability is a secret, well protected by a myth of masculinity that is fiercely guarded in the gendered universe.

Why? Why have men for thousands of years tried to lay out rules of ritual combat that across time and cultures shamed other men for hitting below the belt? Lisa Wade, one of my sociologist heroes, wrote:

> I think it's because it serves to protect men's egos as well as men's balls. . . .
>
> Not hitting below the belt, then, protects the idea that men's bodies are fighting machines. It protects masculinity, the very idea that men are big and strong, pain- and impact-resistant, impenetrable like an edifice. So not hitting below the belt doesn't just protect individuals from pain, it protects our ideas about masculinity.

It's a good thing, then, that we learn to fight like women. Fighting like a girl, from your hips and with kicks, jabs, and punches that are meant to incapacitate an assailant, works surprisingly well against someone who expects to be fought like a man. Nia Sanchez neatly captured this point. When describing a man's disbelief that she could knock him down in a boxing ring, she replied, "Well, I don't know if I could beat you up in a boxing match, but I know how to break your knee and get away."

Sanchez took her Miss USA fame and turned it into a platform from which she teaches self-defense around the world. You can catch valuable demonstration videos on YouTube. Though I endorse taking an in-person, multiweek course in self-defense, even watching a short video could make a difference. It builds on the idea of a self that is worth defending, for a start. It is also the first step in unlocking the power of Bonobo Sisters empowered by the known fact that they have selves worth mutual defense.

"[W]omen may not yet value themselves enough to act individually against their aggressors," wrote Sarah Pongrace, a lawyer, student of mine, and Bonobo Sister, "but they certainly value each other enough to work in groups. One of the most powerful motivators from victims to come forward and pursue action against an abuser is the idea that he might harm another woman in the future." I have seen this proven again and again and again in the decades I have spent defending and advocating for abused and harassed women. "Women are altruistic even in victimhood. We therefore may be just a few steps away from the kind of Bonobo Sisterhood that could protect all women from sexual violence."

PRESPONSE: A PREVENTIVE RESPONSE

I have repeatedly witnessed the fact that women report their sexual assaults to institutions, such as schools or workplaces, or to the police, in the hope that they might prevent the assaulter from hurting someone else. The Bonobo Sisterhood changes that timeline. What a Bonobo Sisterhood does, what it will do on a campus, within a city, internationally, is act before an assault, before there is a victim, before any single sister is assaulted. That is the power of the preventive response to male sexual violence and coercion, or what I call *presponse*. It is the combination of prevention and response. When something is highly predictable, we act beforehand. We take an umbrella along if we expect rain or apply sunscreen if we will be out in the sun. Of course, we also act wisely in the case of even more remote possibilities. We buckle our seat belt, think about whether or not to sit in an exit row of an airplane, go to checkups with doctors and dentists. All of us navigate our lives by exercising some of the power of anticipatory self-defense. Even though male sexual violence limits the lives of women and girls around the world significantly, too many of us do little to nothing in anticipation of the threat of male violence. That is the reason and the need for presponse.

Consider that you have a 1-in-15,300 likelihood of being struck by lightning. Now consider that 1 in 4 women will experience some form of physical violence by an intimate partner. Houses are required to have lightning rods, and all of us have been instructed—by parents, teachers, friends, even strangers—not to stand under a tree in a lightning storm and even to, ideally, go indoors. Now ask yourself why so much is done to ward off an event with a 1-in-15,300 probability and less than this for an event with a 1-in-4 probability.

The threat of future assault is a central weapon of patriarchy that is used to limit women's ability to move in public spaces, while simultaneously reinforcing the male protection racket. Yet there is little to no collective presponse to prevent or avoid harm. The presponse I imagine is a proportionate response to male aggression that will be effective at stopping any assaultive behavior.

The rates of sexual assault should translate into action, not just further study. This involves meaningful self-defense. It means facing facts and being prepared to meet a potential assault, rather than just hoping that if you curb your own behavior and play by the rules, you might be lucky enough not to be sexually assaulted. It's a crime in itself that we don't teach self-defense and other presponsive moves that we know are effective at stopping men's violence and aggression.

We can do better. Parents should encourage their daughters to take self-defense classes. After they have done so, they need to put a bumper sticker on the car declaring the fact that they have done so right alongside the sticker proudly touting the school their child attends. Imagine the message: "My daughter attends this high school, this college, and don't even think of messing with her or her friends." They must make public the fact that they took steps to make sure that their kids weren't sent unprepared into harm's way. Self-defense should be taught on campuses in a public, visible, celebratory way. In addition to a presponsive action to thwart an attack, we need to put pressure on the system to ensure that it steps up to defend women who defend themselves and then who often face charges for doing so.

Despite its all-too-frequent erasure from public discussion, self-defense is another dot to be connected, a crucial piece of the overall puzzle of equalizing women's human status. The physical embodiment of our right to exist without harassment or coercion is at the core of learning self-defense. The power of presponse, of a Bonobo Sisterhood skilled in self- and mutual defense, is a productive repository for our collective rage.

A former student, Amanda Odasz, put this point powerfully. She said that when you're in a room with a man, he has the whole patriarchy behind him. But forming public, visible, self-defending female-female alliances to confront individual males will break down that structure. Imagine, instead of a lone female against the whole patriarchy, a female solidarity such as that described in *Herland*, the 1915 feminist utopian novel by Charlotte Perkins Gilman. Five women easily restrain one man, then anesthetize him and put him into a safe place where he poses no further threat of harm to them. What is fiction we can realize in fact through numbers of women standing in peaceful solidarity, exerting their collective power in a nonviolent way.

BONOBO SISTERHOOD SELF WORTH DEFENDING COURSE

Which brings me to the idea of a Bonobo Sisterhood Self Worth Defending course. Currently available self-defense courses can, by individual or group, be converted into a Bonobo Sisterhood Self Worth Defending course. Only two essential elements need to be added: First, you declare your own and others' self-esteem on the principle that we all have selves worth defending. Many men purposely erode the self-esteem of their partners to make them more dependent and less secure. The first step in converting your self-defense course into a Bonobo Sisterhood Self Worth Defending course is the clear announcement that you have a self worth defending and no one has the right to erode your or your sisters' worthiness as a human being.

The second element that will turn a regular self-defense course into a Bonobo Sisterhood Self Worth Defending course is shifting its focus from threatening strangers to preventing the men we know and even trust from assaulting us. The self-defense courses that are currently available focus on stranger rape scenarios in the hope that the lessons will apply to acquaintance rape situations as well. But the dynamics of target rape and acquaintance rape are significantly different and thus require a different level of preparedness. The more a self-defense course admits this truth, the more it becomes a Bonobo Sisterhood Self Worth Defending course.

As with so many aspects of self-defense, the first change is psychological. A Bonobo Sisterhood Self Worth Defending course takes this further. Self-defense often means that instead of presuming the good faith of people with whom we have some acquaintance, we are well advised to be somewhat suspicious of them, somewhat guarded around them. This is statistically more true of your male acquaintances than of any others. You might think that because someone is a fellow student at your university, he would be disinclined to harm you. The obscenely high prevalence of campus rapes belies this assumption and indicates that the opposite is true.

One of my former students was molested by a close friend of hers after years of friendship and what she thought of as a mutually respectful relationship. When the assault began, her response was to ask him, in shock, "What are you doing?" rather than to fight him off with outrage, as she might have done a stranger. Because they were acquaintances, she was disarmed and disabled. Just by calling out the fact that this is the more likely scenario a woman will confront, the Bonobo Sisterhood Self Worth Defending course starts to counter the disarming effect of acquaintance assault.

Here's another example that haunts me in a similar way. A young white woman at a prestigious southern university was out partying with friends. The friends wanted to move on to another party and were concerned that she was too drunk to take along. So they dropped her at a male friend's room and asked him to take care of her. Instead, he called another male friend of his to come over and they raped her, using her passed-out body as a vehicle for reprehensible male bonding.

The number of acquaintance rapes on campuses—and this represents only a subset of all rapes—speaks to the reality that predatory men use acquaintanceship with women as an access ramp to rape. They do this knowing that our current victim-blaming society will excuse their behavior because of their acquaintance with the victim and the presumption that friends do not rape friends. Patriarchy stacks the assumptions against women. But the Bonobo Sisterhood Self Worth Defending course will reverse this.

On a microlevel, individual women will have to learn not to assume the safety of their acquaintances; to start from a place of prolonged skepticism until he earns your trust. At a more macrolevel, men will be on notice that the world is changing, that old ways of sexual aggression will be met with physical force. They will get the message that aggression hidden behind the cover of an acquaintanceship, friendship, or relationship will no longer get them what they want. Rather, it will get them ostracized and isolated.

How can we attain this? Simple. We can be like bonobos.

The fact that women need to be knowledgeable in the language of violence does not at all mean that women need to be more like men. Like female bonobos, we need to learn self-defense as a preventive response—a presponse—to answer aggression with commensurate force. Learning this will negate the idea that we have to be good girls who are polite and compliant and afraid of offending men. Compliance will no longer be the default; mutual self-care of selves worth defending will be the default. Bonobos are interested in and concerned about others. They answer the call, en masse, to mutually defend themselves. Our self-defending Bonobo Sisterhood will be like that.

Consider the Bonobo Sisterhood Self Worth Defending course. It teaches communal self-defense, a coordinated action of solidarity based not on friendship, kinship, or relationship but rather on the premise that if violence can happen to one of us, it can happen to any of us. This new approach to self-defense is animated by the realization that we have selves worth defending. The bonobo model recognizes that women face different barriers to the use of self-defense based on their race, gender identity, geographic location, and access to resources, to name just a few factors. Yet underlying these differences is the principle that we can and must stand up for one another in an unprecedented, unbreakable solidarity. When women learn to come to one another's aid—without hesitation, without judgment—to help another woman fend off an aggressor, the ripple effects will be felt everywhere.

When we have a friend, family member, acquaintance, or loved one whom we know or suspect to be in an abusive relationship, now we can reach out with this invitation: Come take a Bonobo Sisterhood course with me! This skips over the steps of reaching out and convincing someone that she is in an abusive relationship. Instead, it joyously extends an invitation to be bonobo, to join a sisterhood as big as the globe in celebration of a reclaimed right to human thriving. So much positivity can flow from such a class; imagine what a relief it will be for women to have a new place to go where they will be fully welcomed, supported, and celebrated.

We know it works—bonobos prove that. You know it can work from Take Back the Night campus events to #MeToo and the Women's Marches. Each is an example of a self worth defending being tried here, there, but not everywhere all the time. Not yet. And it can work everywhere. In India's Uttar Pradesh, Sampat Pal Devi, the founder of a group called the Gulabi Gang, taught women to dress in pink saris—the color of sisterhood—and to act in concert, sometimes armed with bamboo sticks, to combat domestic violence. All these are examples of bonobo moments.

Embracing the model of Bonobo Sisterhood everywhere, however, has never been tried. Yet there's no reason not to. We need to stop wishing for something better when centuries of wishing have delivered so very, tragically little.

PART THREE

THE PROMISE

CHAPTER 7

BUILDING THE BONOBO SISTERHOOD

In a sanctuary for rescued bonobos in the Democratic Republic of the Congo, researchers designed an experiment to determine the extent of bonobos' willingness to share food. The researchers set up three connected rooms, the middle one of which held a food pile. A bonobo would be placed in one of the end rooms, which had a mesh door that allowed it to access the food easily. On the other side of the food pile, there would be a door leading to the other end room, containing another bonobo. The door to that room could be opened only from the outside. Overwhelmingly, the bonobo in the room with the mesh door opened the door of the other room in order for the other individual to share the pile of food. The bonobos exhibited no signs of aggression or frustration after opening the door.

Abundance versus scarcity. Love versus fear. Peace versus war. Bonobos versus chimps. Let's choose to be bonobo.

Here are some building blocks for the Bonobo Sisterhood.

ACT ON THE BONOBO PRINCIPLE: NO ONE PIMPS MY SISTER. EVERYONE IS MY SISTER.

As I write, Chrystul Kizer is awaiting trial on charges that she shot Randall Volar, a white man twice her age who trafficked and sexually abused her from the age of sixteen. Her case is one that keeps me up at night. It represents the compounded vulnerabilities of racism, poverty, and misogynoir—misogyny directed at Black women and girls—that produced her tragic situation. It also represents the urgency of acting on the Bonobo Principle. No one had the right to pimp Chrystul; Chrystul is our sister.

I first heard of Chrystul's case from Jessica Contrera's in-depth investigative report in the *Washington Post*. Here's what I learned. Chrystul was a sixteen-year-old sophomore in high school who needed money for snacks and school supplies. Her family had recently moved to Milwaukee and stayed in a shelter because they were fleeing her mother's abusive ex-boyfriend in Indiana. Chrystul had been selected for the performing arts academy in Gary, Indiana, before she left; she was a talented violin player.

A friend of hers suggested she post an ad on Backpage.com, a site that has since been shut down for its role in commercial sex trafficking. Randall Volar was the first to respond to the ad. He bailed her out of jail for $400 a few months after meeting her and then demanded sexual acts that she did not want to do. He took her to hotels and motels in other cities and sold her to other men.

Chrystul's boyfriend Delane was abusive and had publicly

struck her head several times. That same boyfriend continued to be abusive; Chrystul would bounce between his abuse and Volar's, having nowhere safe to be. Delane got her a gun and told her to keep it with her. He knew that she complained about Volar's unwanted sexual advances.

After he was shot and his house was set on fire, police investigated. And they learned that Volar was the suspected child sex trafficker on whom they already had extensive video evidence of his crimes. It began from a 911 call to the Kenosha Police by a fifteen-year-old African American girl who had called from Volar's house. Contrera reported that the girl

told dispatchers that a man had given her drugs, and now he was going to kill her. Then, she hung up.

Officers found her wandering the streets, wearing only a bra under an unzipped jacket. Her pupils were dilated. She said she had taken LSD.

She gave police details that mirrored Chrystul's situation. They too met on Backpage.com when this girl was only fourteen and he began paying her for sex. Ten days after police received her report, they searched Volar's house. They confiscated laptops, hard drives and memory cards, along with women's pajamas, bikini bottoms and underwear.

They arrested him but curiously he paid no bail and was released the same day. At that point, police had "'hundreds' of child pornography videos, featuring girls who appear to be as young as 12, and more than 20 'home videos' of Volar with underage black girls." And here is the most telling aspect of the case: Volar was never charged; he hired a defense attorney for

$20,000 and until his death was able to continue the child sex trafficking ring for which the police had extensive evidence. It took three months for the police to turn the case over to the Kenosha District Attorney's Office, and they had taken no action by the time Volar was killed.

Pause here to consider that after law enforcement officials had found a young girl drugged and scared for her life, had identified her pimp and trafficker, and had learned that he was running a child sex trafficking ring involving several other underaged girls, they did nothing to shut him down. The district attorney, whose office similarly did nothing to protect the girls by even charging a known sex trafficker, took it on himself personally to prosecute Chrystul for the man's death. Michael Graveley, the district attorney, is putting all the resources of his office into this prosecution, litigating it all the way to the Wisconsin Supreme Court.

Why was Chrystul left to continued abuse by Volar? Because the fifteen-year-old's call—which should have resulted in his arrest—was ignored by the people with the power to stop it. Graveley said his office was trying to figure out the age of the girls so they would know what to charge Volar with. But the fifteen-year-old and the others were all clearly adolescents, underaged and not capable of consent. The other telling moment? The officer taking the report on the fifteen-year-old described her as "prostituting herself out," as if that is something a child can do.

Chrystul's bonobo call came too late—after she did what she felt was all that was left for her to do to stop Volar. We hear it now and are trying to answer it. Her story has sparked outrage and public attention from lawyers, activists, and journalists. But if the Bonobo Principle had been widely understood, we would have come to her aid a long time ago. We would have heeded the call when Chrystul's peer raised it. Instead, it went unnoticed and Volar was free to continue his reign of abuse.

No one had the right to pimp Chrystul or any of the other girls Volar was abusing. They are our sisters, and all of our sisters deserve protection from commercial sexual exploitation, especially children.

Chrystul drew her self-portrait while awaiting the outcome of her trial.

The sign she holds reads "We have the right to protect otherself. We shouldn't be punished for doing so. We shouldn't be define [*sic*] by our crime, but who we are as a human being."

It was the first time I had encountered the word *otherself*. As of 2022, Chrystul's case is still pending. I am unable to contact her directly, so I am left to guess her meaning. However, from all that I know and all that I hope, and inspired by Chrystul, I choose to understand *otherself* in two ways.

One: We are different selves at different times. This idea has powerful resonance for victims of abuse, for your otherself might be an earlier version of your current self, one affected and informed by what you know now but did not know then. There are power, compassion, and healing for this otherself. Two: It means a feminist conception of self that refers to a self in positive relationship to others. Your otherself recognizes a sense of yourself that can be located among others with shared experiences.

Chrystul's sign, I feel, pushes us toward that second understanding. In her self-portrait she is alone, but her sign is addressed to a collective "we." We have rights. We should not be punished when we protect and assert those rights. We should not be defined by victimhood or its consequences but rather should be seen as human beings. We should not be alone.

The "we" Chrystul speaks of and to is caught powerfully in the words "Me Too Movement" written across her chest.

The #MeToo movement, founded by Tarana Burke, is all about a recognition of "otherselves." The #MeToo movement is for the self that looks back on the otherself who was abused and speaks out on her behalf. #MeToo is also communal, a movement for the many millions who have been sexually abused or harassed in some way. Tarana Burke, who had been abused and raped as a child, and the #MeToo movement she began touched Chrystul in a profound way.

Perhaps her identification with the #MeToo movement is where she draws the knowledge, strength, and power we see woven into her hair. The knowledge that as a survivor, she is not alone, the strength in numbers that #MeToo represents, and the power of a collective voice.

No one had a right to pimp Chrystul. The law is unambiguous: child sex trafficking is illegal. The facts are equally unambiguous: there was a lack of enforcement, a lack of care or urgency. By example, the Kenosha Police Department's failing to hold Volar responsible or even to charge him with sex crimes after it discovered hundreds of hours of videos of his sexually abusing underaged girls smacks of its granting him impunity. Or, worse, it reflects the world we inhabit, the world of men all the way down, where the safety of girls' lives doesn't matter as much as the criminal Volar's freedom. The racism underlying the failure to protect Black girls and instead viewing them as "prostituting" themselves out should not escape our notice. That Volar was released, that he was able to continue to abuse Chrystul and other girls, and that Chrystul is now on trial for his murder is the way patriarchy works. We must demand better.

Applying the Bonobo Principle to Chrystul means acting on the fact that no one had a "right" to pimp her and the other girls ensnared in Volar's abuse. Acting on the Bonobo Principle means embracing each of these girls as your sister. Envision someone—your best friend, your younger sister, your daughter—for whom you would "bring it," someone for whom you would muster up all the protection you and your other sisters could bring to bear, someone for whom you would answer the call. Now know that Chrystul is that someone. For this, too, is a meaning of otherself: your otherself is the self, the sister, who is under threat and for whom you answer the call.

When I first heard Chrystul's call by reading the article in the *Washington Post*, I reached out to Jessica Contrera and conveyed an offer to help in whatever capacity I could. I included the article in my teaching materials, and one of my students, Brianna Banks, shared my outrage at the injustice of the case. She wanted to do something to help.

In the summer of 2020, Brianna worked for Legal Momentum in New York. This group is led by Lynn Hecht Schafran, a veteran women's rights lawyer. Brianna and I talked with her about Chrystul's case to see how we might collectively help. Then Lynn enlisted the law firm Boies Schiller Flexner to act as pro bono legal counsel. Together, we stepped in as amicus (friend of the court) on the case and filed a brief. We also enlisted the help of other lawyers in Wisconsin, with a consequence being that everyone involved in Chrystul's case is aware that a widening community of bonobos is watching, bringing attention to her case, offering to intervene.

No one pimps my sister. Everyone is my sister. A choice is made to issue the call. A choice is made to answer it. Where there was a scarcity of power, strength, and knowledge, there is now an increasing abundance of all three. That is the Bonobo Sisterhood.

Brianna took Chrystul's case to heart. She published a law review article called "The (De)valuation of Black Women's Bodies." In it she contextualized Chrystul's case in the historical hypersexualization of Black women's bodies within the criminal justice system. Brianna's article, and the work that went into it, became the impetus for her consciously becoming a bonobo. Two other law students who were editors on her article were also coincidentally research assistants of mine. Together they helped produce scholarship animated by the Bonobo Principle.

Within a patriarchy a single bonobo call can get lost in a cacophony of bonobo calls. When a call is heard, however, the choice is to answer the call in the best way you can amid the cacophony. The choice is to be bonobo.

PROTECTING OUR BONOBO SISTERS

For this book, Brianna shared a personal, different story. It is worth quoting at length. Truly meeting the call that no one pimps my sister includes that no one abuses, sexually insults and demeans, and otherwise uses the privileges of patriarchy to belittle my sister. And everyone is my sister.

> In May of 2021, my best friend, Lori, invited me on a family trip, something akin to a family reunion. As Lori's best friend since we were both fourteen, I had become an extended member of her family. (I probably spent more time at her house in high school than my own.) Anyway, this trip included me and Lori, Lori's twenty-year-old sister, Maya, their god-sister, Kennedy, who was nineteen years old, and a host of aunts and uncles.
>
> About halfway through the trip, we rented out a restaurant for a celebratory dinner. We put on our best dresses and heels and spent hours on hair and makeup. Maya and Kennedy were walking down the hotel's long hallway

that connected the rooms to the restaurants. They were on their way to join their parents at the festivities. With their fine hair and clothes, they were beautiful. Both were wearing heels, so naturally they walked a bit slower than normal. I thought them regal.

As Maya and Kennedy walked down the hall, a group of men started catcalling them, asking them to stop and talk. We had encountered them earlier, near the hotel pool. They were groomsmen here for a wedding. They were in their early thirties and had once already catcalled Maya and Kennedy. Anyway, Maya and Kennedy kept walking, ignoring them. The catcalling turned mean and words like "bitch" and "tease" were used. These men felt entitled to the attention of these young women and entitled to verbally abuse them when they didn't get it. Maya and Kennedy began to walk faster to escape the gaze of these men and reach the comfort of their parents.

There is a certain point where the hallway slopes downward. When Maya and Kennedy reached it, Kennedy lost her balance in her heels and teetered over a bit—breaking the shoe and almost twisting her ankle. Seeing this, the men began to laugh and say things like "That's what you get." Mortified and in pain, Kennedy hobbled into the restaurant. She approached her dad crying that she had broken her mother's favorite pair of shoes. She no longer wanted to socialize, was no longer looking forward to having a good time—she just sat on a couch with her arms crossed.

Shortly thereafter, I arrived with Lori. I saw that Kennedy was upset and her father told me about the shoe. I approached her to give her a hug and asked what was wrong. That is when she told me about the men. Immediately, and I cannot stress this enough, I switched into protector mode. I hugged Kennedy, this girl I had met only four days prior, and told her that it's not her fault and the shoe doesn't matter—all that matters is that she's ok. I then looked her square in her eyes and said, "when you see those men again point them out to me. I will handle this."

After dinner, we were all sitting at the bar—the whole twenty of us, including the parents, aunts, and uncles. Kennedy pointed out the group of men. When I began to approach them, Kennedy's father and Lori's father stopped me. "What do you think you're doing?" they asked. I told them the whole story, to which they responded that Kennedy's father, Dwight, should handle it. I very sternly but respectfully insisted that this is something I must do.

It's worth noting that I am six years older than Kennedy and by this point I was no longer dressed in heels and a short dress. I had changed into a Harvard Law T-shirt, biker shorts, and flip-flops. I intersected one of the guys outside the bar. I started off with pleasantries—hi, how was the wedding, how's your trip, etc. I then articulated the reason for this encounter. With a smile on my face but fire in my eyes I said, "Someone in your wedding party harassed my sister tonight, and she said that it was you. I just want you to know that it is never ok to harass a woman or to mock and demean her. For one, she is only nineteen. But most importantly, that behavior will not be tolerated because now you have me to deal with."

His response was typical. First, he cut me off before I could finish to give me excuses. He said that it was not him. He said it must have been the other groomsman, the one with dreadlocks. He then told me that the guys he was with don't travel much, and that they get a little too loose when the bar is open, and then he said the night was young.

My response was simple: none of that is an excuse and

it is never acceptable, no matter the circumstances, to harass a woman. But, and this I said bluntly, directly, "You are your brother's keeper. You are responsible for the company you keep and if your friends are acting damn fools then that is on you." I would not let him cut in. "Because it is your job to tell them to do better and to hold them accountable." I looked him in the eyes as I spoke. And this is where things got interesting.

On the word *accountable*, he started to yell in my face, asking how old I was, declaring he's my elder, in his early thirties. He felt the need to assert that he knew more than me, that I'm a child, oblivious to the fact that hours earlier he and his friends were hitting on a nineteen-year-old. His speech devolved into a "You're just a silly little girl" type of assertion. And, yes! He even wagged his finger at me.

As his voice rose to a level that crossed into disrespectful, I noticed Lori's Aunt Dina standing behind me. She had also just met me 4 days prior, but she also felt protective over me. She had been standing in the corner during this whole conversation, and as this man's voice rose she came closer to me, standing behind me, ready to jump in.

At which point Dina touched my back and said, "I know what you're trying to do, but, hunny, he is never going to hear you." She then turned to him and said something I don't remember. As she pulled me back to our group, the tears in my eyes begin to appear. It is at that moment that I had a realization: I was Kennedy's exact age when I was raped.

I wanted desperately to protect Kennedy in a way no one had been able to protect me.

And then Aunt Dina said the precisely right thing.

She ushered me to the restroom and looked me square in my eyes. "You should be proud. This wasn't for him—it was for Kennedy. Kennedy saw a beautiful, brilliant woman step up for her today. Now she knows that she is worthy of someone fighting for her—someone defending her."

Brianna now looks back at that moment with a full heart. The image of her defending Kennedy while Dina stands in the wings ready to swoop in and defend Brianna remains inspiring. Three generations of women all aligned. It didn't matter that they were not blood relatives, that some had met just days before for the first time. All that mattered was as women they were bonded. They had acted instinctually and deliberatively. They didn't just let the abuse go. They didn't defer to men. They heard the call and they acted with care toward their sister, with conviction toward the offending male. They were bonobos, a sisterhood that helps girls and women understand that we are all worth defending and if we can do this thing, we will all *be* defended.

Brianna and Aunt Dina embodied the fact that Bonobo Sisters have a choice: to issue the call, to answer the call. That's it. Do it, and everything will change.

PROTECTING OUR YOUNGER OTHERSELVES

In the documentary film "Rape Is . . . ," Salamishah Tillet says, "There's a person before you are raped and a person after you are raped. And the person after you are raped always wants to go back to being the person before the rape." That earlier otherself is a different person; the desire to return to being her is understandable, to say the least. What the victimized are often left with, however, is answering that otherself's call by their subsequent actions. The best answer starts with self-love and compassion for one's younger self.

Tarana Burke described her conversations with her younger self in *Unbound*, which recounts her journey from internalized shame for having been sexually assaulted to seeing that the assault was not her fault. Burke is wisely compassionate toward her younger self, identifying, for example, the way adults send young girls conflicting messages. Girls are told not to mess around with boys, especially the "wrong" boys, and if and when harassment and abuse happen, the chances are good that girls will internalize the blame. If they report the harassment and abuse, they are reporting that they broke the rules others gave them. The assumption of complicity is a given, something girls learn everywhere from their home life to popular music and culture to navigating a world built by and for men and boys, almost from birth. Best to keep quiet.

Tarana's #MeToo movement traces back to her experience of sexual assault as a child. This is the most critical point: child sex abuse makes its victim more vulnerable to future victimization. It is a constant predictive factor in continuing sexual exploitation. Experts across the board agree that 70-75 percent of prostituted women were sexually abused as children.

What finally broke down the wall of secrecy that Tarana had built around her own sexual abuse was learning that her own child, Kaia, had been similarly violated at the age of five. *Five.* Kaia confessed to Tarana in a note that "it was a boy at camp. He made me do bad stuff with his brother and I didn't want to. I'm sorry mommy."

The last words were the most painful for Tarana because her child thought she had "broken a rule," just as Tarana had thought she had in her youth. Finally, Tarana was able to say to Kaia, "My baby, listen. When I was a little girl, a similar thing happened to me. That's why when I tell you that you are not to blame, I know what I am talking about."

The #MeToo movement is the place where the two other-selves meet. It is the place where the self after the assault can meet the self before the assault surrounded by a supporting, defending, listening community of our otherselves. Survivors are resilient. Even though seven-year-old Tarana thought it was her shameful secret to bear, she went on to excel in school and to participate in a youth leadership program, rising through the ranks to become one of its leaders. Her otherself did not stop with achieving personal excellence, though. It also launched #MeToo, the movement that created a new sisterhood in its many millions, structure, and form.

The power of survivors and the power of survivors' alliances cannot be doubted and should not be underestimated.

PROTECTING OUR OWN SELVES

#MeToo connects our otherselves. It helps heal our otherselves that exist before and after abuse. It connects them to a vast community of empathetic, emphatic, defensive otherselves. It creates the space for the victimized to come forward, to learn, and to be told that what happened to them as a child, a girl, a woman was not their fault. Learning this is the first step in learning that you are entitled *not* to have this "happen" to you. Most critically, the fault is not yours; it is entirely the person who caused the harm.

There is abundance in a community. It has an inherently healing effect. Knowing that you are not alone, that you stand alongside many, many millions of others, allows you to understand that you are not to blame. It enables you to see that sexual assault is epidemic and systemic rather than aberrant and personal. This realization in turn connects you to a thoroughly justified rage at the patriarchal structures that provide the immunity for perpetrators to continue with impunity their efforts to eviscerate the souls of women and girls.

#MeToo has been the organizing principle for the twenty-first century's mass uprising against sexual violation. The systemic epidemic of abuse has been made visible, damning patriarchy and proving the hollowness of the idea that "good men" will stop "bad men." What will stop them is what comes next. The Bonobo Sisterhood takes the movement to the next level. It is the means of prevention commensurate with the epidemic of abuse.

Do that, and everything changes. In #MeToo you enter a safe space for healing. In the Bonobo Sisterhood you are granted a safe space for protection and innovation. And joy is possible when we are safe.

BE ANTI-RACIST

No one pimps my sister. Everyone is my sister.

To address the patriarchy, we also need to address race. Xenophobia, fear of the other, is based on false ideas of scarcity. This is what drives racism as well—fear that there is not enough to go around; fear that someone is coming to take what is "rightfully" yours; that the alpha male will take the lion's share.

In a patriarchy, women are taught about the scarcity of male protection and that they must be compliant good girls in order to receive it. Only then will they be eligible for its rewards. Whatever the rewards, however, they are still given in a patriarchy that is structured to dominate women rather than to recognize them as equal human beings. Refuse the logic of scarcity, trade the violence of the lion's share for the equal protection of the bonobo's share, and all of patriarchy's competitive divisiveness comes undone.

The Bonobo Sisterhood will work only if white women get on board. Centuries of scarcity within patriarchy—scarcity of power, strength, knowledge, influence—has had its effects. White women, following white men, are part of a race. And many of them—about half of all women who cast a ballot—voted their race over their gender in the 2016 presidential election, aligning themselves with a man who was the embodiment of patriarchal xenophobia. What will it take to change this? A lot of consciousness raising, to be sure.

What privileges white women do enjoy under patriarchy, they enjoy only at the whim of patriarchy. To exercise those privileges for the benefit of patriarchy, to acquiesce in the verbal and real violence that sustains white patriarchy, is to sustain patriarchy itself. The Bonobo Sisterhood cuts this off root and branch.

Men abuse women in intimate partner relationships on all socioeconomic levels. So ask yourself: Are you better off hoping that you'll be one of the lucky women to escape abuse, or will you be better off being part of a system in which women have actual rights and present a united front?

In the book *Not to People Like Us: Hidden Abuse in Upscale Marriages*, the psychologist Susan Weitzman described intimate partner violence in upscale relationships. The men are as cruel and abusive as other men; the main differences are that the abuse and entrapment are more economically highlighted. The essential features of the abuse are the same: the gaslighting, the emotional abuse, the isolation.

Furthermore, systematic male sexual coercion of one group of women implicitly authorizes male sexual coercion and abuse of other women. As Angela Davis noted in *Women, Race & Class*, racism and sexual violence feed upon each other:

> While Black women and their sisters of color have been the main targets of these racist-inspired attacks, white women have suffered as well. For once white men were persuaded that they could commit sexual assaults against Black women with impunity, their conduct toward women of their own race could not have remained unmarred. Racism has always served as a provocation to rape, and white women in the United States have necessarily suffered the ricochet fire of these attacks. This is one of the many ways in which racism nourishes sexism, causing white women to be indirectly victimized by the special oppression aimed at their sisters of color.

As white women claimed rights on the backs of Black women—as they prioritized whiteness over gender—they suffered collateral harm from racially motivated sexual violence. Turning our backs on other more vulnerable women does not keep one safer. Instead, all of us must honestly confront the damage caused by gendered racism. We can find our way out of this trap by creating a sisterhood that stands for the proposition that we are not divisible anymore.

White Bonobo Sisters have unique work to do. White women have to identify, confront, and question our role in perpetuating white supremacy in a patriarchy. In addition, all women need to ask if we are better off scrapping among ourselves to gain rights in a patriarchy—white women especially. #MeToo has shown us in our millions to be harassed, abused, raped. The landscape of women's shelters and men's castles, of backlogged domestic violence cases, of insufficient and ineffectual policing reflects the scraps earned by our scrapping. Women in a patriarchy are conditioned to fight among ourselves to distract us from the real issue: our collective lack of power, citizenship, and equality under a patriarchy. Racial, class, gender, ethnic, religious, cultural, and geographic divisions are always stressed in our current social order so that maybe we won't notice that we can actually be fierce and loyal allies of one another.

A Bonobo Sisterhood that ends patriarchal violence does not end relationships with men or even gendered traditions that you may like. What it does do is enable women to negotiate powerfully from a stronger position rather than simply conforming to expectations. What it means is the sharp curtailment of violence, the increase of joy, and the real likelihood that you will have a happier relationship: the end of sexual coercion. Wanted sex will replace compliance sex. Abundance will replace violence.

The foundation of the Bonobo Sisterhood will be stronger if white women consciously confront the myriad ways our racial privilege works on a daily basis to our advantage and disadvantages our sisters of color. This work will be individual as well as systemic, and importantly, we need not wait for white women to do their deep racial reckoning before successfully building the sisterhood. Because we live in systems of racism and white supremacy, the work will be necessary as long as those systems remain in place. But the Bonobo Principle offers us a shortcut. By acting on it, we can begin to actualize its power to change reality for us all.

So, too, white women must consciously reckon with how we claim privilege on the backs of our Black and Brown sisters. It was no accident that the white man Volar chose to traffic young Black girls. They are the most vulnerable; they are the least likely to be protected. There cannot be any comfort in the idea that because someone else's daughter is being trafficked, my daughter should be safer. In a similar way to men disclaiming their sexual entitlement to our bodies, white women need to disclaim the privileges we enjoy at the expense of women of color.

Consider how complaints work within a patriarchy. When we claim that in our workplaces we should not be subject to sexual harassment, we are saying, in effect, "You can't treat me like that, I am not a whore." But when is it ever okay to treat someone as if she is a whore? When is it ever okay that any portion of humanity should exist for the sexual use of and abuse by another portion of humanity? The horrid and not-hidden suggestion behind "You can't treat me like that, I am not a whore" is that somewhere out there, there is a whore you *can* treat like that. And a grotesque fact of patriarchy is that women of color, especially Black women, are disproportionately prostituted and commercially sexually exploited.

Women who have economic resources at their disposal can make a world of difference for their exploited sisters. Take Swanee Hunt, the heir to a Texas oil fortune and the US ambassador to Austria from 1993 to 1997, who has dedicated her life and substantial funds to lifting up women in politics, aiding them in conflict zones, and helping them exit the commercial sex industry.

Hunt leads Hunt Alternatives, her family foundation started in 1981, and has leveraged the organization's resources to launch campaigns that center on survivor activism. One such program, Demand Abolition, seeks to end the "illegal commercial sex industry in the U.S.—and, by extension, the world—by combating the demand for purchased sex." Guided by a board of survivor-leaders, the campaign focuses on changing the way policy makers and law enforcement officials respond to the commercial sex trade: instead of going after those whose bodies are bought and exploited, they should go after the ones who buy and exploit.

No little girl says she wants to be exploited when she grows up. Girls who grow up within a patriarchy, which is to say all girls born to date, avoid becoming commercially exploited only because others are not so lucky.

By sharing protection resources, we refuse to accept any safety predicated on the misfortunes of other women. We declare that even one exploited sister is too many.

PROTECTING THE LAST GIRL

"Where are all the women?" asked Ruchira "Ruchi" Gupta. She was in the hills of Nepal when she noticed the absence of women and girls in many towns. "Where are they?" she repeatedly asked the men. They would look down, laugh uncomfortably, or just not answer. Until one finally said, "Don't you know? They all are in Mumbai."

Ruchi found that alarming, for Mumbai was very far away

from those rural towns. As she began to explore the mystery, she learned the hard truth that the slave trade in women and girls was very much alive. Procurers would go to families offering money for their daughters, even hinting at marriage, saying that their daughter was starving and in Bombay she would have food and a bed. Fathers sold their daughters for as little as $50.

Once purchased, the girls were passed through a series of middlemen who beat, starved, and subjugated them, all to get them ready for their ultimate destination: brothel imprisonment.

Traveling to Mumbai, Ruchi set out to interview the enslaved women. No one would talk to her at first. For many days she patiently waited in a café, until eventually, some women came forward to ask her why she was there. "I want to tell your story," she told them. They asked why. "Because storytelling can bring about change. It can only make it better because you are in such a bad situation. For all women, we have to help each other because we need change in all our lives. We need change." And so twenty-two women talked to her, telling Ruchi their stories, which she captured in a documentary, *The Selling of Innocents*. And then she set about to change their lives.

Together with those women she founded Apne Aap Women Worldwide in 2002 to share her "vision of a world where no woman would be bought or sold." Since then, they have set up 150 self-empowerment groups in brothels, red-light districts, slums, and villages as part of a community-centered solution to end sex trafficking. More than ending sexual exploitation, the program helps the most marginalized women become leaders in their communities working for change and social justice.

Ruchi is the originator of the term *the last girl*. The last girl is the most vulnerable of all girls because she is not only poor and female but also a teenager. In India, she is low-caste, in the United States she is African American or Native American, in Europe she could be a refugee, in Africa she may be an ethnic minority. . . . She exists everywhere. She has little control over her life, decision making, and her body. She lives in conditions that are akin to slavery. She is the nineteen-year-old woman in the brothel who "chooses" to stay in the prostitution system. There is no effective or comprehensive justice system to prevent her exploitation or help her exit this system, to watch out for her when she is pulled out of school, runs away from the brothel, or tries to leave the brothel to go back home. Her "agency" in her own enslavement is routinely accepted at face value by the state and singularly construed as "choice," as it fails to help her attain her basic needs or increase her choices.

Beyond protecting the last girl, Ruchi and Apne Aap have embarked on a huge project to feed women and children in India. 1 Million Meals has delivered more than 12 million meals to more than a quarter million vulnerable women and children.

MOTHERS AND DAUGHTERS

The power of mother-daughter relationships in humans is another building block in the creation of the Bonobo Sisterhood, and it can produce an even stronger coalition. In bonobos, the females emigrate from their communities at an early age, around six to eight years old, while they are still quite immature. Yet they are received warmly by other groups who quickly adopt them into the fold. In humans, we remain with our mothers, and our relationships can bear an incredible resource of strength and support.

Examples abound of maternal energy as the source of female bonding in humans. In my work on campus sexual assault, countless mothers have sought my help on behalf of their daughters. Fiercely protective, they are often the daughters' strongest ally. Let's draw on the power of mother-daughter relationships as a foundation of support for the Bonobo Sisterhood. Maternal energy is evident in the ways in which older bonobo females protect younger ones. And we can activate this force intentionally to create our sisterhood.

One of my favorite examples of bonobolike coalition building is Valerie Jarrett, her daughter, Laura, and her mother, Barbara Bowman. Valerie was the senior advisor to President Barack Obama. Her daughter, Laura, was my student beginning in her first semester at Harvard Law School and she became part of the original group of Bonobo Sisters, as my teaching fellow in her last year, with the other bonobos in close range. We all brainstormed and formed coalitionary strategies in law and society that have animated many ideas throughout this book. I taught Laura for over a year before learning that she was Valerie's daughter. I was privileged to witness the exceptionally close and important bond between them, and also to see what a thoroughly dedicated daughter Valerie is to her own trailblazing mother, Barbara Bowman.

Valerie served as the chair of the White House Council on Women and Girls created through executive order by President Obama. The Council included all the heads of federal agencies and major offices at the White House. Not just the women. And she headed the United State of Women, another unprecedented effort to raise the voices of women and girls, creating a beautiful umbrella of sisterhood in which all were welcome.

MOTHERS AND SONS

Male bonobos derive their social status through their mothers. They maintain close bonds with their mothers. Doesn't that sound lovely? Their mothers sometimes help them select mates, but they will not take sides against their sons if they become aggressive. Astounding. We could learn something from this example, starting with the reverence given to mothers by bonobo sons.

A dear friend and Bonobo Brother exemplifies this quality. Nick Sensley is a male human bonobo who has worked to stop human trafficking. A former police officer with twenty-five years of experience, he once swooped in to respond to a bonobo call from another close friend of mine whose psychotic father was threatening her. He pulled together protective resources and offered a place in his own home for her to stay until her safety plan was in place. And he had a touchingly close relationship with his mama. He is working on a book provisionally titled *How's Your Mama and Dem?* about her and her signature phrase of caring for others.

MEN IN THE BONOBO SISTERHOOD

We will of course welcome men in the Bonobo Sisterhood. The Sisterhood is not a reverse sort of patriarchy. We explicitly invite and include men, recognizing that we will all be much better off. As Gerda Lerner pointed out, patriarchy is flawed at its base due to its exclusion of women. I take this to heart. It means, though, that the men we include will have to recognize and disavow the illegitimate benefits they enjoy under patriarchy at our expense.

Bonobos give us many reasons for hope, not just for women but for men and, frankly, everyone. Men will also do better in a Bonobo Sisterhood. And while sexual access to females might be a top concern for men contemplating the end of patriarchy, male bonobos initiate sex often. If the female does not respond enthusiastically, he retreats. And his initiation is positively received around 70 percent of the time. That's a pretty high average. Bonobos show us that males do not have to use coercion to have sexual encounters with females.

More seriously, though, countless men and boys now and through the centuries have also suffered from the violence of other men to the women and girls they love. Think of all the sons of mothers who were abused and murdered by men—often by the children's own fathers. Think of all the heterosexual partners/husbands of women who are sexual assault survivors from previous relationships. Think of all the men whose daughters have been sexually harassed in school or the workplace, or been raped, or even been murdered by men. These men have suffered the terrible consequences of this system, not merely reaped its rewards.

As Jackson Katz says, "The same system that produces men who abuse women, girls, and non-binary individuals also produces men who abuse other men, boys, and non-binary individuals."

Moreover, the Bonobo Sisterhood will be a space free from the male-on-male gender policing that so often restricts and harms the lives of men and boys, preventing them from developing their own gender identity.

PROTECTING SISTERS FROM PATRIARCHAL VIOLENCE

City of Joy is a woman-only refuge in the Democratic Republic of the Congo (DRC), which coincidentally is the backyard of the bonobos. The activist, playwright, and feminist V, formerly Eve Ensler, is a beautiful Bonobo Sister who is constantly and radically answering the call. You might know her/them as the creator of *The Vagina Monologues*, the hilarious and simultaneously serious play that changed the world.

In 2011, V cofounded City of Joy to help women who had been brutalized by male militias. The DRC is home to mineral-rich earth that is the object of global corporate competition. Militias are created and supported to mine these minerals and to facilitate access to them. To do this the soldiers use grotesquely inhumane violence, including the gang rape of women and girls as a routine act of war.

Instead of running from this violence, V ran courageously toward it to see how she could help. She partnered with Dr. Denis Mukwege, a gynecologist, and Christine Schuler Deschryver, known as "Mama C," a women's rights activist whose village was torn apart by the militias. To provide women with care, Dr. Mukwege founded Panzi Hospital after militias raided and burned his other hospital to the ground. The victims he treated were grotesquely damaged, their vaginas brutalized and permanently disfigured. "They are killing the vagina," he told the United Nations in 2012. First tens, then hundreds, then thousands of women sought his care.

Dr. Mukwege found Mama C walking on the side of the road, desolate and alone. She had reached the point of hopelessness. He picked her up in his car; they later collaborated with V to create the City of Joy.

It is a place exclusively for women, a safe place where they learn to heal from the sexual violence inflicted upon them, where they transform their pain into a strong bond of sisterhood. They go through leadership training that encourages them to tell their stories with honesty and to inspire empathy and compassion in others when they return to their homes after graduating from the program. Nearly two thousand women have gone through the program. The power of their collective joy is radiant and world changing. Watching them dance, Dr. Mukwege was transformed into believing in the hope, the resilience of the human spirit. For his efforts to end the use of sexual violence as a weapon of war and armed conflict, he won the Nobel Peace Prize in 2018.

Their sisterhood is the Bonobo Sisterhood. Dancing and joy can be restorative. And to heal from sexual violence, to focus on preventing it in the first place, is the path forward. That is explicitly the work of the Bonobo Sisterhood we are currently building.

In our multitude, we are abundant and offer abundance. The divisive scarcity of patriarchy, which leaves so many girls alone and in want of strength, power, knowledge, and help, is replaced by us with our collective strength, power, and knowledge. White patriarchy has ensured that these are unevenly distributed among women, and it encourages gendered racism. It offers the perverse equality that all women are under some extent of threat all the time. The Bonobo Sisterhood answers this with an equality of women-women alliances. And it starts here: No one pimps my sister. Everyone is my sister. And when the call is heard, we answer in our multitude.

PROTECTING THE BONOBOS WHO PROTECTED THEM: RETURNING THE FAVOR

In a striking parallel, both Ruchira and Dr. Mukwege were the subjects of death threats. A man pulled a knife on Ruchira while she was filming *The Selling of Innocence*. When he did, the twenty-two women from Apne Aap defended her, saying, "You'll have to kill all of us first!" The man retreated. After Dr. Mukwege testified to the United Nations in 2012 about the conflict in the DRC, five armed men broke into his house in Bukavu and held his family hostage. His security guard and friend was killed. Once freed, Dr. Mukwege and his family fled to Belgium. A group of women petitioned the government to bring him home, then offered to buy airplane tickets for him and his family to return, then created a market outside Panzi Hospital to raise money for the tickets. To do this they traveled long distances, carrying fruits and vegetables to sell in the market. He returned two months later, touched by their appeal. The women had said, "Come home, we will protect you." He heard them and answered their call.

When he arrived home, there was a formal ceremony to welcome him that, overseen by the government, at first felt insincere. Government officials, after all, had done nothing to protect him or his family or to investigate the assassination of his security guard. Then the "mothers and grandmothers of Idjwi" gate-crashed the party. They arrived with shrieks and ululations. Heads turned; the signboards and banners in the crowd twitched; part of the crowd shifted, then parted. A group numbering in the dozens, some carrying children on their backs, pushed past the chairs and up to the stage. They wanted the microphone, which was passed down. "If you won't protect the doctor, then we will!" said one woman, gesturing toward the governor and the police chief. "Tonight there will be twenty-five of us guarding the hospital, and if someone wants to kill the doctor, they will have to kill twenty-five defenseless mothers first!"

All of us, no matter our skin color or gender, will help build the Bonobo Sisterhood by answering the call.

THE EVER-EXPANDING BONOBO CIRCLE

Bonobo circles can be thought of as starting from the individual, expanding to your sisters and outward to society. Think about how you have acted to protect your loved ones and how that circle might expand to protect others facing some vulnerability or crisis. The chances are good that you already know a great Bonobo Sister, one you call upon when you're in trouble. Chances are you have been a great Bonobo Sister to a friend in need.

My life is populated with exceptional women who have done remarkable things to help other women and girls, as well as several men who help answer the call. Here are a few examples.

In 2007, I proposed teaching a seminar on Title IX and campus sexual assault at Harvard Law School. Supreme Court justice Elena Kagan, who was dean at the time, approved the request even though Title IX of the Education Amendments Act of 1972 was not yet widely known to have anything to do with campus sexual assault. At the time, most people recognized it only for its application to allowing women to play sports. In fact, Title IX prohibits sex discrimination in educational institutions that receive federal funding, which includes nearly all of them. This is one of the strongest civil rights that women and gender-nonconforming people have, and in my opinion, the aspects of the law concerning sexual harassment in an educational context needed to be much more widely known. Justice Kagan's approval of my course led to the establishment of a campus Bonobo Sisterhood comparable to a #MeToo movement.

My students and I developed legal policy suggestions for the enforcement of Title IX rights on campus. We were able to convey our ideas to the Office of Civil Rights of the Department of Education, the agency responsible for Title IX enforcement. President Obama was the first president to take seriously the importance of preventing sexual assault on campus.

In late 2010, I heard about fraternity pledges at Yale loudly chanting "No means yes, yes means anal" outside the freshman girls' dorm on campus. A YouTube video reveals other men goading the men to be "louder!" I was incredulous at the hostile environment they were creating, mocking the idea that women have any sexual autonomy or right to say "No" and be respected. I wound up representing several current and former Yale students in a federal civil rights case based on that incident and numerous others. One of those students, Alexandra

Brodsky, went on to cocreate with Dana Bolger, then a student at Amherst College, Know Your IX, a student-led survivor initiative that is beautifully bonobo. They heard each other's call and started the organization based on the principle that if they had known their rights under Title IX when they had entered college, their experiences might have been different. Schools have obligations under Title IX to remediate a hostile environment and to ensure equal access to educational opportunities. But neither of them knew about their school's obligations, and each experienced negative impacts on their education that were in violation of Title IX. Through courageous and clear-eyed leadership, they went on to provide resources for thousands of students in need of bonobo assistance. They heard the call and answered it. Each went on to Yale Law School and is now engaged in feminist legal advocacy. Alexandra authored a book called *Sexual Justice: Supporting Victims, Ensuring Due Process, and Resisting the Conservative Backlash.*

Amanda Nguyen is the founder of Rise, a phenomenal organization that has promoted the rights of survivors to access rape kits throughout the country. Her fearless and bipartisan leadership is exceptional, and she has emerged as a leader on the world stage. Some of the law students associated with the Gender Violence Program and I helped Amanda with issues concerning her own rape kit when she was a senior at Harvard College. She went on to build on her experience and dedicate herself to promoting the use of and access to rape kits for survivors and victims. She created a truly bonobo response.

Catharine "Kitty" MacKinnon is a Bonobo Sister extraordinaire who has answered the call with her life's work. She is a renowned legal scholar who is the foremother of feminist legal theory. I owe her more than I can say. Somehow, she is behind or knows about everything that is happening in the women's movement around the world. And she, along with some of her Bonobo Sisters, is responsible for creating the right to be free from sexual harassment.

When I told her in 2013 that I would be traveling to India to advise the government on gender violence, she insisted that I meet Ruchi Gupta. So, two days before I was to leave, Ruchi and I met, and by the end of our conversation I had arranged for her to speak at a conference I had helped plan. I was traveling with colleagues who had been advising a High Powered Committee (HPC) of the Indian government on amendments to criminal law after the horrific gang rape and murder of Jyoti Singh, often referred to as "Nirbhaya," a name used to protect the identities of rape victims. She was a twenty-one-year-old medical student on a date with her boyfriend when she was brutally raped, sodomized, and tortured by six men on a private bus. Once finished, they left her for dead on the side of the road. She died thirteen days later in the hospital.

The case ignited national protests in India. The Indian government appointed an HPC chaired by former chief justice J. S. Verma; other members were Gopal Subramaniam, a former solicitor general of India; and Justice Leila Seth, the first woman judge on the Delhi High Court and the first woman to become chief justice of a state high court, Himachal Pradesh High Court. To advise the committee, I worked with some colleagues to form an interdisciplinary group that included Professor Jacqueline Bhabha of the Harvard School of Public Health and Meena Hewett, the executive director of Harvard's South Asia Institute. Together we created the Harvard Gender Violence

Project. With our contacts in India, we planned a conference with the members of the Verma Committee to explore how our collaboration might help.

A remarkable thing happened while I was in India. I arrived on a Thursday; the conference was to open on Friday evening. While in my hotel, I received a call from the mother of a good friend of mine who lives in Delhi. She wanted to know if she, too, could attend the conference. I arranged for her to do so. At the opening session, we heard from the uncle of a five-year-old girl who had been gang-raped and was fighting for her life in a Delhi hospital. Everything about the story was horrific. *Five?*

A local legislator introduced the girl's uncle at the conference. The uncle told the story through a translator. His family were very poor and could not afford costly medical interventions. Afterward, at the reception, my friend's mother, Rasha, and I talked to the uncle. It turned out that Rasha and her husband, both doctors, had worked at the hospital where the little girl was being treated. Without hesitation, Rasha arranged for the five-year-old's medical care to be provided in full. No questions were asked; she held in abundance what that five-year-old victim needed in extremis; she heard the call and came to the girl's aid.

The next day, Ruchi gave a stirring presentation at the conference and was able to connect with Gopal and others who could, and did, support her organization. Ruchi's organization, Apne Aap, has helped thousands of women and their children escape prostitution and the abject poverty that leaves them extremely vulnerable to it. All of that resulted from the moment Ruchi heard the call and answered it.

An abused five-year-old girl cared for. An organization, Apne

Aap, dismantling the more horrific practices of patriarchy and empowering the vulnerable through material support. Kitty's helping me by way of an introduction to Ruchi and everything else she has done for me through the many long years of our friendship. This is the Bonobo Sisterhood at work. This, too, is *how* the Bonobo Sisterhood works. It builds on itself—a call and an answer—and it will change the world. It was in Ruchi's living room that the actor Ashley Judd first met Jodi Kantor and Megan Twohey, the *New York Times* journalists who won a Pulitzer Prize for their reporting on Harvey Weinstein, the now-imprisoned serial rapist and longtime abusive Hollywood producer.

Ashley Judd was enrolled in the midcareer program at the Harvard Kennedy School when she cross-registered for my Gender Violence, Law and Social Justice course at the law school. She proved to be a capable and provocative student, intellectually curious, considerate, and anchored by the practice she calls "exquisite listening."

Coincidentally, she knew about bonobos. She had first met some bonobos years earlier at the Kokolopori Bonobo Reserve in the Democratic Republic of the Congo. As a global ambassador for Population Services International, she traveled throughout Africa educating people about AIDS prevention. During that work, she visited the reserve. She showed me photos of her with the bonobos, telling me that in the midst of her difficult work "they loved me back to life."

Ashley is a Bonobo Sister extraordinaire who has studied the bonobos in the rain forest firsthand, trekking miles through the early-morning darkness to observe them in their natural habitat. For years, she has used her power as a celebrity to give voice to women and girls, to bring healing, to educate, to see people in the unique way that she does, to hold children in orphanages around the world, to bring her light to the world's darkest places. She is visibly, powerfully, a woman who hears and answers the call.

The year she was in my class, Ashley won the Dean's Scholar Prize for her final paper. In it, she developed a model of introducing bonobolike behavior into communities to create a peaceful society. "The crux of the experience would be for each participant to identify core patriarchal wounding in their life, begin to recover from it and accept responsibility for advocating feminist social justice change in their communities in whatever way is most meaningful to their personal narrative; once we begin to recover," she wrote, "we can be most useful in precisely the ways we have been most hurt."

Seven years later, Ashley, hearing the call, was courageously the first to come out against Weinstein. And because she came forward publicly, the world learned that Weinstein had a well-established pattern of making vicious counterattacks against anyone who dared challenge his "right" to abuse. Many of his victims were wealthy and white, powerful yet still afraid. Ashley put her professional life on the line. And the #MeToo movement was forever changed, energized, and vastly expanded, becoming the #MeToo movement that is changing the world.

That is how we build the Bonobo Sisterhood: we witness the work of those around us, the power of our numbers visible through #MeToo, and we call, listen, answer. *No one pimps my sister. Everyone is my sister.*

And it is joyous. One day in December 2019, Ruchi, Ashley, and I sat in Gloria Steinem's writing chair, one on top of the other, and took a selfie. Our stated goal, amid laughter, was to "get good writing vibes." It was the morning after we'd all gone to see *Gloria* on Broadway, all except for Gloria, who had stayed home nursing a cold. Kitty, packing her things in the next room, laughed at our silliness. Each of these women is a treasured member of the Bonobo Sisterhood. So are you.

CHAPTER 8

LAW IN BONOBOLAND

Back in the Wamba forest, researchers focused on observing female bonobo coalitions. All of the coalitions they observed had male bonobos as their target, and the majority of them were a response to aggressive behavior by a male. Interestingly enough, female bonobos did not form coalitions just with their close friends but also with other females with whom they did not regularly associate.

Bonobos need no law, court, or enforcement mechanism other than female-female alliances. Someday, humans could be so lucky. To speed our reaching that goal, I offer a Declaration of Unified Independence from Patriarchal Violence and a Preamble to the Bonobo Sisterhood Constitution.

Declaration of Unified Independence from Patriarchal Violence

We hold these facts to be alarming and urgent:

———————

that men kill three to four women a day in the United States;

———————

that men rape women in such alarming numbers that one in four female college students reports having been sexually assaulted during her time in school;

———————

that every day in America around forty thousand women and children are forced to flee their homes to avoid being killed, assaulted, stalked, or otherwise attacked by their intimate partners, effectively making them refugees;

———————

that women experience measurably diminished lives due to inexorable conditions of living under patriarchal rule in our democracy;

———————

that the omnipresent threat of male sexual violence causes a state of constant fear and vigilance in women and girls, infringing upon our rights to life, liberty, and the pursuit of happiness, thriving, and fulfillment;

———————

that a patriarchal democracy is not true democracy in that there is no sex equality in a patriarchy;

———————

that a patriarchy preserves its social, political, legal, and economic order through patriarchal violence;

———————

that men are profoundly harmed by gender policing and patriarchal violence and that the silence imposed on them exacerbates that harm;

———————

that institutions created under patriarchy are designed to prevent the full participation and thriving of half the population;

———————

that the time has come for women and their allies to rise up collectively to reject our enforced designation as subordinate beings;

———————

that the Bonobo Sisterhood recognizes its power to prevent patriarchal violence.

PREAMBLE TO THE BONOBO SISTERHOOD CONSTITUTION

We hold one another to be fully entitled to a life of human thriving, and declare:

---

that all women are created equal;

---

that we share a state of unfreedom living under patriarchal rule that makes us unequally vulnerable to patriarchal violence and positions us unfairly and falsely in competition with one another for the illusory promise of male protection from male violence;

That such social status and imposed isolation prevents us from recognizing the true power and potential of our alliances with one another.

Thus, we commit to one another:

---

that we must institute a new framework of women's equality among one another and our allies;

---

that each of us has a self worth defending;

---

that we will stand up for one another and for those in need;

---

that we will identify our resources and readily share them with others from a perspective of abundance rather than scarcity;

---

that we recognize that protection of one another is a resource;

---

that no one should go hungry.

To anyone who reads the declaration and preamble and worries, or imagines, that their provisions are impractical or impossible, I say flatly: stop thinking like a chimpanzee; think like a bonobo. Recall that bonobos have already achieved such a society. And how they did it illuminates the way of how we can do it.

EQUALITY AMONG WOMEN

Here's our new central premise: that all women are created equal. What happens when we think about equality among women rather than about women's equality with men? All of our thinking about equality compares us to men. Changing that will lead to new possibilities, new power, new everything. Imagine what can emerge from changing our framework and focus.

Consider this as an invitation, not a directive: when you want something to get done, give it to a woman. What I want to see happen is women and their allies getting together to determine what the new sisterhood looks like to them. I offer the above declarations to start the flow of energy toward thinking anew about the meaning of equality.

Look, men convened somewhere, went off and talked feverishly for weeks on end, and came up with a document saying that all men were created equal, even though they knew they had no intention of putting that principle into practice. Why would we think that the solution to women's equality would be found through women's copying men? This is an opportunity to identify at all junctures where we think something should be done a particular way because it was done that way in the past under a patriarchy. We can break our path dependence. What we want and need will become apparent once we start actualizing the power of the Bonobo Sisterhood.

WHAT THE CONSTITUTION MEANS TO ME BY HEIDI SCHRECK

In her award-winning play *What the Constitution Means to Me*, Heidi Schreck reenacts the debates she competed in during high school on the topic of the US Constitution and her personal connection to it. At the end of the performance, the audience votes on whether we should scrap the current Constitution due to all its flaws and its failure to address people other than propertied white men whose interests animate it or should work instead on amending it. It is usually a close vote, with the preference for keeping the Constitution winning by a slight margin.

This question is relevant to the creation of the Bonobo Sisterhood. It is worth noting that the bonobos have achieved their peaceful society without a constitution or laws. This fact gives us hope. As humans with language, laws, and the ability to articulate complex conceptions of rights and morality, surely we can choose to build on the bonobo model. Just as the development of language was used to consolidate and propagate patriarchal gains in the past, it can be used to create a different social order between and among women and their allies.

After discussing the way "centuries of laws told her she was worthless" (referring to her mother), Schreck says:

Maybe we shouldn't think of the Constitution as a crucible, in which we're all fighting it out together, in which we go in front of a court of nine people to negotiate for our basic human rights, which is what we have been doing for two hundred and thirty years. Because if this is a battle, or even a negotiation, then the people who have always been in power, always dominated, always oppressed—men, white people—will continue to dominate and oppress.

Schreck tries to find herself in the Constitution and is constantly shut out, frustrated by the ways in which it ignores her. She plays recordings of some of the Supreme Court arguments in hearings on abortion and domestic violence homicide.

Discussing the 1965 decision *Griswold v. Connecticut*, in which the Supreme Court held that a married woman had a right to use contraception in consultation with her doctor under the Ninth Amendment's right to privacy, she posits that Justice William O. Douglas needed to reach that conclusion because at the age of sixty-seven, he was having an affair with "a twenty-two-year-old college student! And two other justices may have been having sex with young women as well." She plays a tape of a bit of the argument, and we hear a lot of uncomfortable pauses between the white men who are debating whether or not women should have the right to access contraception.

She plays a tape from the argument in the *Town of Castle Rock* case, the one in which Justice Scalia held that Jessica Gonzales had no right under the Constitution to enforcement of her order of protection from domestic violence, even though the State of Colorado had a law mandating exactly such enforcement. In that clip, Justice Antonin Scalia questions whether the word *shall* in the statute actually meant *shall*.

It was hard for me to listen to the exchange, to the parody he was making of the statutory language. That should have been an easy issue for him. First, he was a strong proponent of state's rights, jealously guarding federal jurisdiction from involvement in any issues that he could send back to the states. Second, he was a textualist and an originalist, a stickler for exact adherence to language, opposed to attributing meaning to it that may not have been there. And yet. In this case, he abandoned both of his usual juridical approaches to deny Jessica's right to police enforcement of her order of protection against her estranged husband, who kidnapped and murdered her three daughters over the course of an evening during which she had pled with police to arrest him. At one point she called with the exact location of his truck, asking that he be arrested so her daughters could be returned to her. The police did nothing. As a result, Simon Gonzales, the man against whom the order of protection had been taken out, shot the girls with a gun he had bought that night.

Confronted by the grotesque facts of the case, representative of the grotesque facts that had spurred the Colorado State Legislature to pass a statute stating that state police shall enforce orders of protection, Scalia still found room to doubt that *shall* was anything other than a suggestion. As a result, police throughout the United States were granted discretion as to whether or not to enforce an order of protection.

As Schreck notes:

> This ruling is most devastating for Black women, women of color, trans women, binary, and nonbinary trans folx, women with disabilities, immigrants—people who are less likely to be helped by police than I am. It's especially devastating to indigenous women, who suffer the most violence in our country.

She notes that the number of women killed each year not just by men but by men who are supposed to love them is "such a staggering figure that I just kind of have to . . . forget it, to get through the day. Except, I think you can't forget about it. Even if you don't know the statistics, I think you can feel the truth of that underneath everything . . . humming."

This is a profound point. That it occurred to a playwright and not to a Supreme Court justice is alarming. In a patriarchy, every human lives with the cognitive dissonance of knowing the prevalence of patriarchal violence, yet ignoring it as best we can. But Scalia, a man, experienced its benefits without any of its costs. Schreck, a woman, knows only its costs. That is unacceptable precisely because we know we have the means not to accept it. With a Bonobo Sisterhood plan in place to create a collective self-defense, we will never again have to accept dissonance as anything other than the gaslighting it is.

One last point about the play: Schreck shares with us an experience of compliance sex that defines and represents and that is a perfect example of what I mean by the term:

At the first rehearsal this senior boy asked me if I wanted a ride home and I said sure, and as soon as we got to my dorm he said: "I've been wanting to kiss you for so long," which was weird because we'd known each other for three hours but he was cute so I kissed him, and then suddenly he took off my pants.

I was really smart when I was 17. I was! I was way smarter than I am now. Plus, I had read everything—I thought. I had read Audre Lorde and Gloria Steinem and bell hooks. I was taking advanced feminist studies. And

219

yet I just decided to go ahead and have sex with this guy because it seemed like the polite thing to do, I think.

Or maybe . . . now, I don't know.

When I think about being in the car, I remember how dark it was outside. I remember there was nobody on the street, my dorm was way, way out on the edge of campus. I remember having this kind of sick feeling in the pit of my stomach and then this fleeting thought—so quick I almost can't put it into language. But if I had to say it out loud, it would sound something like "stay alive."

Which is . . . It's strange because this guy would not have hurt me. I know he wouldn't. We're friends to this day. Well, we're Facebook friends. I'm ninety-nine percent sure he would not have hurt me, so why did I feel like my life was in danger?

There it is again: the reflexive retreat to the basic human desire to live involuntarily pressed up against the equally reflexive fear that being alone with a man can easily lead to loss of life. We shouldn't have to live that way. Our sisters shouldn't have to live that way. Our daughters shouldn't have to live that way. Not one woman should have to live that way. Not ever. And certainly for not one minute more. I think we are at the limit of what rights we can achieve under the US Constitution. This could change if the Equal Rights Amendment is passed. Even still, however, we would be amending, rather than creating, the law.

BUILDING ON WOMEN'S HISTORY

Consider what we have already tried and done.

The first Women's Rights Convention in the United States

was held in Seneca Falls, New York, in 1848. It was flawed from its inception, for it entailed the efforts of white women on behalf of white women. That they were attempting to correct a Constitution authored by white men, a majority of whom owned slaves, is an explanation, not an excuse.

The convention's Declaration of Sentiments was a feminist build on the Declaration of Independence, strongly noting the absence of women from that founding document and demanding that a new one reflecting (white) women's inclusion be considered.

Some of the white suffragettes were abolitionists, but their arguments were inherently racist, complaining that they had less rights than a "Negro," referring to Black men. Black women were not even mentioned, except that Sojourner Truth took the stage to deliver her famous speech "Ain't I a Woman, Too?" Maria Stewart, a Black abolitionist, asked in 1831, "How long shall the fair daughters of Africa be compelled to bury their minds and talents beneath a load of iron pots and kettles?" This question is still painfully resonant.

The declaration claimed the right to overthrow a government that had come to evince "a design to reduce [women] under absolute despotism" and to provide new safeguards for their future security. "Such has been the patient sufferance of the women under this government, and such is now the necessity which constrains them to demand the equal station to which they are entitled," it declared. To which it added a far broader statement: "The history of mankind is a history of repeated injuries and usurpations on the part of man toward woman, having in direct object the establishment of an absolute tyranny over her."

It went on to enumerate the many ways that the US Constitution deprives women of equal rights, recognition, and standing as citizens under the law. And it names many issues that are still unresolved. It recognized women's inequality as stemming from inequalities in marriage, religion, education, and economic participation. What is more, it observed, "He has endeavored, in every way that he could[,] to destroy her confidence in her own powers, to lessen her self-respect, and to make her willing to lead a dependent and abject life."

This historic affirmation, acknowledging how living under patriarchy is destructive to women's collective self-esteem, confirms that the United States' contemporary branches of patriarchy trace to their constitutional roots. The United States is no outlier, but as the world's longest-existing democracy, it deserves unique condemnation for failing, all these centuries later, to confront the patriarchy that remains its beating heart. Pervasive inequality causes psychological injuries; this has been known for generations, and it is still true today. Nowhere is this more obvious than in abusive relationships, where a man's attempts to destroy a woman's self-esteem are visibly woven into the patterns of power and control.

Having accurately detailed the reach and intent of patriarchal constitution and law, the women convened in Seneca Falls resolved that laws that entitled men to pursue their own true and substantial happiness but that conflict with women's rights to do the same were "contrary to the great precept of nature, and of no validity." Any laws that placed women in positions of inferiority were declared of no force or authority.

The convention attendees focused on marriage laws as the source of women's greatest inequality, and after the convention at Seneca Falls, they went on to work for passage of Married

Women's Property Acts to allow a woman to keep control of her property rather than granting it legally to her husband, who maintained supremacy over his wife in all matters. The Declaration of Sentiments noted that "in the eye of the law," a married woman was "civilly dead."

Individual states passed individual laws amending to differing degrees how civilly dead a married woman was. This patchwork of redress was, and remains, the norm. Suffice it to say that, it was seventy-two years after Seneca Falls that women won the right to vote in the United States. Though it was undeniably significant, this right, like the Married Women's Property Acts, has not resulted in a rapid change in our citizenship. It is a piece of it, of course, but the prevalence of patriarchal violence guarantees our inequality. The right to vote has not led to the radical change our foremothers believed it would. Sadly, the Declaration of Sentiments is still relevant today, more than 150 years later.

The second wave of feminism in the 1960s and 1970s continued the fight and focused on sexual liberation, the fight against domestic violence, and the advancement of equal rights. In 1977, the National Women's Conference, a significant yet remarkably unknown event, was convened in Houston, Texas. A literal torch was passed from Seneca Falls to the Houston convention center, and for four days nearly two thousand delegates once more took up the causes of gender equality. The opportunity to advance these causes, though, fell apart when the conservative gadfly and "traditional family values" advocate Phyllis Schlafly gained attention across town as a powerful campaigner against abortion rights.

Divisions between women over reproductive freedom are

deeply rooted in patriarchy and follow religious, racial, economic, and political fault lines. In a Bonobo Sisterhood, reproductive autonomy will be achieved through the absence of sexual coercion. Women can achieve that; it is only because of patriarchal divisions that we have difficulty seeing this possibility. Bonobos enjoy reproductive autonomy.

NEW LAWS IN THE BONOBO SISTERHOOD

The laws emanating from the Bonobo Sisterhood will contain more positive rights—rights to do or receive—than negative rights outlawing behaviors. They will reflect the values of the sisterhood; resource sharing, protection, mutual commitment to thriving, equality, and bridge building. The laws will be the product of new alliances reflecting unprecedented possibilities for a new society.

In the meantime, changing existing laws to facilitate the development of the Bonobo Sisterhood might include addressing some of the following.

First, self-defense laws would be changed to reflect the reality of the threats that patriarchal violence poses to women. Threats themselves will be assessed and understood from the victim/target's point of view. The laws will be written from that perspective.

Second, the laws will afford women the right to participate in collective self-defense without fear of prosecution.

Third, conspiracy laws would acknowledge the ways in which male alliances enable large-scale sexual abuse. Most abusers do not operate in isolation. In particular, powerful men, such as

Harvey Weinstein and R. Kelly, who prey on women for years, are able to do so because of the drivers, assistants, PR specialists, and other people who protect them. Enablers, coconspirators, and those who fail to intervene are all a part of conspiracies to commit patriarchal violence.

Fourth, credibility must be considered. In Bonoboland, women will be believed as credible witnesses, and what they say will be considered as testimony. The current patriarchal laws gaslight women into not believing what they know to be true. Recall Heidi Schreck sitting in her car, thinking something like "stay alive" while a boy removed her panties. At that moment she knew something to be true, and in Bonoboland her truth will be acknowledged and acted upon, either in the moment if her cry is heard or afterward. Once women purge themselves of internalized misogyny, they can start to believe one another and build up one another's credibility.

DECISION MAKING FOR PEACE

The Bonobo Sisterhood will prioritize peace by putting women at the center of negotiating processes. As Swanee Hunt advocates through Inclusive Security, a Hunt Alternatives campaign that aims to involve more women in decisions about war and peace around the world, inclusive security is lasting security: when women are involved in negotiations, the agreement achieved is 35 percent more likely to hold for fifteen years or more. In reality, however, women make up only 9 percent of negotiators at official peace talks. In the style of bonobos, we will set up a Department of Peace, focused on female leadership and alliances. And what can work at an international scale can work, too, at the local level.

RESOURCE SHARING

Sarah Buel, a longtime advocate for the rights of domestic violence survivors, says, "If you haven't been abused, you have *more* of an obligation to help." She herself is a domestic violence survivor, as well as a lawyer who has devoted her life to helping women. I heard her say that at a conference in 1993, and I heard it as a bonobo call, even though at the time I did not yet know about bonobos. But it did make me think about my privilege of not having experienced abuse in my intimate relationships. I heard it as an invitation to help, as well, one I hadn't specifically heard before.

In that moment, I identified my privileged or lucky position as a resource that I could share with others. The term *battered woman* itself denotes someone who is somehow diminished by what has been done to her. What could I bring to the table? Perhaps a sense of optimism, a sense that we are entitled to live our lives free from the constant threat of sexual violence hanging over us—and the knowledge that it is possible.

Survivors' voices are at the center of the Bonobo Sisterhood movement. Patrisha McLean reminded me that you cannot know what it's like to be a survivor unless you go through it. She did so during her visit to my class with her daughter, Jackie, when they discussed decisions Patrisha had made at the time she was separating from Don. The postseparation abuse was worse than the abuse she had suffered at his hands while they were married. When one's self-esteem is shattered, it is difficult to make choices that seem rational to others. But they are choices made to survive.

Lady Gaga's epic song "Til It Happens to You" conveys the same crucial and searing message. She wrote it for the film *The Hunting Ground*, about campus sexual assault. At the Academy Awards, she performed it, and, in a wonderfully bonobolike act, she invited fifty-one survivors who had been involved in the film to join her onstage at the end. She poured her soul into that performance; you can't watch it without feeling her pain.

#MeToo has created a revolutionary Survivors' Agenda Initiative that centers on the needs and perspectives of women of color who have endured sexual violence. What the Bonobo Sisterhood will offer is a bridge among all women to create the strongest voice possible. Sharing of resources among women for the good of all women will unleash a new force of nature unlike anything we have ever seen.

Our voices are a resource. Our pain is a resource. Our joy is a resource. Our connection and our love for one another will be the resource that changes everything.

CHAPTER 9

BE BONOBO!

We hold these truths to be self-evident, that all women are created equal.

We are taught to think about women's equality in terms of our standing compared to men. This, of course, is precisely how men themselves think, which helps explain how a white man who enslaved other humans penned the original statement about the equality of men. Women will do better; we will focus on our commonality as women. In doing so, we will start to realize our strength. Therein lies our true power and a meaningful path toward equality. All women will be equal beneficiaries—as will men.

Under patriarchy, being vulnerable is what we all have in common. Not only is vulnerability to male aggression common among women, it is common among men. Men are taught to be aggressive; women are taught to divide among themselves as we chase the false hope of a few of us finding a few good men to ward off the bad ones. Worse, those of us who obtain a false sense of security by believing that we are less vulnerable than other women become participants in keeping our sisters at the mercy of the patriarchy. The fact that we are spending all our energy on this lose-lose game means we have had no plan for a collective self-defense to thwart male aggression—until now.

Start with yourself. Start with a self worth defending. Then build out with some sisters. Then change society.

Setting our default to loving other women as our equals is to give weight to the fact that we need to regard one another as resources and need to follow through on being resources for one another. Investing in your female relationships will be your liberation. Women will come to your aid where men have failed to do so, especially once you learn the Bonobo Principle.

Here's a *Washington Post* headline that caught my eye: "Three Women Discovered They Were Dating the Same Man. They Dumped Him and Went on a Months-Long Road Trip Together." The article went on:

> Three young women are touring the West together this summer, united by something they never imagined they'd have in common: They all had the same cheating boyfriend. At the same time.
>
> Instead of feeling bitter about their discovery . . . they decided the best way to cope was to move on—in a 30-year-old school bus that they bought and renovated themselves over 2 ½ months.

That is the essence of love among women.

Our society conditions us to expect that whatever their opinion of the shared boyfriend, the three young women would view one another as competition, hating one another from the start. But no; when they discovered what the man had done to them, they bonded. They did not hate him or wreak vengeance on him, either. It wasn't about him. There are fewer shorter paths to upending patriarchy than that insight. What they had in common was much bigger than the false bond they had with their shared boyfriend.

A lesson here is to adopt this idea: there is no "other woman"; there are only women.

A key difference between us and bonobos is that we human women never had the opportunity to share a reality like the bonobos' and therefore build a sisterhood based on empathy and protection. We have only ever lived under patriarchy. Our community is fractured through patriarchally imposed and widely enabled structures, especially racism and poverty. So whereas bonobos extend protection because they understand the threat that other bonobos face, our isolation from one another keeps us from seeing how we are all threatened by patriarchal violence.

We perpetuate patriarchal harms when we distance ourselves from one another's pain. The rules of patriarchal violence define all women's lives, with greater suffering visited on the most vulnerable. At each level of vulnerability there is a false safety in believing "Oh, that's not me." But there doesn't even have to be so much distance between women to otherize as a defense mechanism. Here's a composite story, drawn from many such stories, of how close it can be:

A friend is being sexually harassed by her boss. Several women in the company know what is going on. However, none of the women in the company comes to her defense. The harassed woman doesn't know where to turn. A conversation breaks out among the other women who know a little or a lot. One of those who knows a little criticizes the way the harassed woman is handling the situation. Another asks in response, "Help me, then—

what would you do in this situation?" The response comes back immediately: "I would never be in that situation."

This is a perfect example of women blaming other women for being harmed because it is so much easier to do than to challenge the system—the person and his context of power—that enabled the harm in the first place. We are socially conditioned to believe that if we are good girls who follow the rules, bad things will not happen to us. Until they do. Recall that this is exactly the state of affairs that governed before the myriad disclosures that followed the #MeToo movement. "Me too" needs to become "Not again, not her, not ever." Bonobos show us what we must do.

BE XENOPHILIC

Bonobos are prosocial toward others. They will offer food to them first before offering it to bonobos within their group or eating it themselves. In contrast to bonobos' xenophilia, chimps are xenophobic to the point of making lethal attacks on strangers. This is so well established that scientists cannot ethically conduct food-sharing experiments with chimpanzees who are strangers to one another because of the likelihood of violence.

Perhaps bonobos are not afraid of strangers because they know they have a protective sisterhood, one that effectively shields them from male violence. When you think about it, what women and girls have to fear most is male violence. Remove that threat, as we can through the Bonobo Sisterhood, and the world will open up. Abundance will become visible.

Xenophobia rests on the feeling that there is only one pie, that resources are finite. When the perception is that food and safety are scarce, we fearfully protect our own kin, whoever we define them to be. We draw circles around our kin, people like us, afraid that strangers will take what is ours. The logic of xenophobia is the logic of the lion's share, which, as Aesop's fable made clear, is the logic that the lion gets all it wants, and if anything is left over, that's everyone else's share. Xenophilia is the logic of the bonobo's share and the logic and power of the Bonobo Sisterhood.

Chances are good that you are already xenophilic. You probably give to charity. You've probably helped out strangers in the past. You've probably given money to homeless people on the streets. Being consciously xenophilic is something we can do right away, starting with recognizing our own privileges and being willing to share them with others.

When one bonobo group meets another, their members engage socially with one another in a friendly way: they share food, they groom one another, they might have sex, they laugh and share joy together. Sometimes, when one group is ready to move on, a member might decide to stay with the other one. If she does, there are no violent consequences. A choice is made; new groups form. Lethal intergroup aggression has never been observed among wild bonobos.

In this stark contrast between bonobos and chimps, between xenophilia and xenophobia, there lies hope for us.

For the Bonobo Sisterhood, for our community, it means simply this: love other women deeply, and do not be afraid of that love.

As Audre Lorde observed in "The Master's Tools Will Never

Dismantle the Master's House," "For women, the need and desire to nurture each other is not pathological but redemptive, and it is within that knowledge that our real power is rediscovered. It is this real connection which is so feared by a patriarchal world." Patriarchy fears women's strong bonds because they are a threat to our dependence on men.

Women-women alliances are based on equality. Women-women alliances are based on xenophilia. Women-women alliances are the force that ensures that the logic of the bonobo sisterhood will succeed. They reflect the power of bonobolike coalitions.

SHARE YOUR FOOD

Some theories posit that bonobos share food so much more readily than chimpanzees do because they do not have to compete with gorillas for their food on the side of the Congo River where they are located. We humans can share the abundance of food we have. The wealth disparities in a capitalist patriarchy are vast, yet women can form collectives to share the wealth much more equitably.

In the United States the food supply "is so abundant that it contains enough to feed everyone in the country nearly twice over—even after exports are considered" according to the food expert Marion Nestle. We have abundance. We need not live like chimps, and we will all live better if we live as bonobos do.

Bonobos share their food. They wait for friends to join them before they eat; studies have shown that among bonobos, sharing food is more important than the food itself. Remarkably, in an experiment, they shared food with strangers first and then with friends. This, by the way, reminds me of my grandma Sarah, who did the same thing. She always fed you, especially if you were a stranger.

My grandma Sarah helps underscore a crucial insight: many women are already choosing to be bonobo, already pointing the way toward how we can adapt the sharing of abundance to the Bonobo Sisterhood.

Examples of women feeding children, families, and other women abound.

In Albany, New York, Jammella Anderson launched Free Food Fridge Albany, a mutual aid food justice project, in August 2020. Queer and black, Jammella is an activist, doula, and trauma-informed yoga teacher who transformed her experience with food insecurity and the underserved communities in Albany into a call to act. Free Food Fridge Albany provides a network of outdoor fridges, all stocked with free food for anyone in the local underserved communities who needs or wants it.

In a video on the project's website, Anderson explains that the food in the fridges is not "the leftovers or the waste of a place. The food is made and trimmed and cut and produced for the fridge." Every day, the fridges are filled with full meals and fresh produce by local volunteers, area farmers, and restaurant owners.

In Nepal, where more than 41 percent of women lost their jobs during the covid-19 crisis, civil society organizations started a network of women-run community kitchens with the support of UN Women. These kitchens provide jobs for local women, who in turn share food with their communities.

In Los Angeles, California, Feed Black Futures, led by Ali

Anderson, "feeds Black mamas and caregivers impacted by parole, probation, and/or caring for incarcerated loved ones." It delivers fresh produce and provides families with the skills and space needed to grow their own food.

In St. Louis, Missouri, Tosha Phonix enables others to become food sharers. Phonix, a Black Muslim food justice activist and farmer, started Elevating Voices of Leaders Vying for Equity (EVOLVE) to train Black farmers and supply them with grants and business tools.

After the devastating June 2017 Grenfell Tower fire in London, England, that resulted in the deaths of seventy-two people and the injuries of over two hundred more, a group of women gathered to prepare fresh food for their neighbors. They formed what became the Hubb Community Kitchen, which now supplies several hundred meals to families in London every week in collaboration with local food redistribution organizations.

Finally, in Charlotte, North Carolina, Ebonee Bailey runs the Bulb, a mobile farmers' market that supplies local produce and related educational services to food-insecure residents. The Bulb's "take what you need, give what you can" motto epitomizes the generosity and care of the bonobo food-sharing model. When interviewed for *Time* about her food-sharing work, Bailey said, "If you want something done right, you call a woman, because we will handle it."

In her compelling book *Woman*, Natalie Angier argued that only in humans is the idea propagated that a woman needs a man to supply her food. She wrote:

Only among humans have males succeeded in stepping between a woman and a meal, in wresting control of the resources that she needs to feed herself and her children. Only among humans is the idea ever floated that a male *should* support a female, and that the female is in fact incapable of supporting herself and her offspring, and that it is a perfectly reasonable act of quid pro quo to expect a man to feed his family and a woman to be unerringly faithful, to give the man paternity assurance and to make his investment worthwhile.

Men stand between women and their food to control the terms of women's survival. But it doesn't have to be like this. This uniquely human phenomenon is a constructed and false idea that we can overcome. Indeed, we must overcome it.

As humans, we can easily share our food. Feeding children, working on food security for all, is incontrovertibly the good, right thing to do. We live during an age of abundance, a fact obscured only by the existing controls over distribution. And given technology, we can share our wealth in creative new ways. There is no reason that anyone in the United States should go hungry. There is no reason that anyone anywhere should go hungry.

PROTECT THE VULNERABLE

Older female bonobos form coalitions to protect young female bonobos against aggressive male behavior. Adult females can often win conflicts on their own, but they recognize that younger females, who do not yet know how to defend themselves, are vulnerable. Recognizing this, they step in to protect and teach them. The clues to their cooperative behavior are evident in all the ways they protect the young. Their attention and care during childbirth and child rearing suggest that they understand that young mothers and their offspring need help and nurturing. Indeed, one study concluded that this ability to form strong cooperative bonds was the evolutionary prerequisite for the emergence of human midwifery.

Alone among primates, no infanticide has been observed among bonobos. Why? It is a straight line from bonobos not killing their young to the proven power of female alliances to protect the young.

Having emulated them in midwifery, let's emulate them in alliances to protect the vulnerable. Let's emulate them by acting on the principle that if a person of any age can be abused, then every woman, of every age, is your sister.

Patriarchy fails women on so very many metrics, but none so damning as this: abuse of children is rampant among humans. According to the Centers for Disease Control and Prevention (CDC), one in seven children has experienced child abuse and/or neglect in the past year. And in 2020, "1,750 children died of abuse and neglect in the United States. . . . Rates of child abuse and neglect are 5 times higher for children in families with low socioeconomic status." Poverty equals vulnerability. Yet wealth is not protective, either. Child sex abuse is rampant in humans cross-culturally.

Consider just one metric for this: the prevalence of child pornography on the internet. According to a 2019 investigative report by the *New York Times*, "In 1998, there were over 3,000 reports of child sexual abuse imagery. Just over a decade later, yearly reports soared past 100,000. In 2014, that number surpassed 1 million for the first time. Last year [2018] there were 18.4 million." Remember, those are *reported cases* of abuse imagery, not the number of images. In 2018, the number of images of children being sexually abused was more than 45 million. The opening lines of the *Times* report read, "The images are horrific. Children, some just 3 or 4 years old, being sexually abused and in some cases tortured." Recall that Tarana Burke, the founder of the #MeToo movement, was raped at the age of seven. Her child was molested at the age of five. V wrote a book called *The Apology* in which she imagined the apology her father should have given her after his years of sexually violating her when she was a small child.

This must end. Here's how. As we are bonobo, all children are our children. And don't think about coming near our children. We will enforce this by the same mechanism we protect each other: hear the call, answer the call—not just to protect but also to nurture.

Consider another lesson courtesy of bonobos. Adult males abandon food to infants, even if the mother is not nearby, in a fascinating elaboration of food sharing among all bonobos. The hypothesis is that the adult males act as though the mother might be nearby, even if she is not. Such is the power of female alliances. It shows that the Bonobo Sisterhood can feed children and protect them from sexual abuse. As a tertiary benefit, men might even fall into line and become bonobo, too.

HAVE WANTED (BETTER) SEX

Claudine André is the founder of Lola ya Bonobo, a bonobo sanctuary in the Democratic Republic of the Congo. She says teasingly in her French accent, "I love men a lot. I'm a bonobo, you know?" Wanted sex is transparently, obviously better than unwanted sex.

Given the choice, who would opt for anything other than wanted sex? If sex were transparently, honestly wanted, wouldn't you want more of it? Wouldn't practitioners of wanted sex be better partners, in every sense of better?

A social system without compliance sex is immediately possible within the Bonobo Sisterhood because female coalitions are readily available to respond to any aggression. The result is wanted sex. Because they do not fear punishment for refusal, female bonobos determine when and how sex occurs. When they say "No," the males don't aggress. When they say "Yes," males know the sex is desired. And wanted sex is better sex.

Notable is that males successfully initiate sexual encounters about 70 percent of the time. This is not a bad rate of success! Men need not be afraid of abandoning compliance sex.

The result of female bonobos' collective self-defense is that they enjoy reproductive autonomy from choosing their sexual partners to rearing their offspring. Make no mistake about the critical importance of this for humans; male sexual coercion of females as reproductive resources is at the very foundation of a patriarchal society. Bodily integrity and sexual autonomy are at the very foundation of women's human rights. Bonobos have actualized this in their society. Now it is up to us to follow their lead.

CREATE AN ALTERNATIVE TO PATRIARCHY

You are welcomed among strangers. You are fed. You are safe. You are joyful. Bonobos have realized each of these things within their society. Humans, however, suffer from the opposite. We even know why.

When I worked in the Illinois Attorney General's Office, we established the first Women's Advocacy Division in the country. What did "women's advocacy" mean? Fighting violence against women; that was it. Fighting violence against women took up all the resources of the office. It was and remains unambiguously true that men commit the overwhelming majority of all violence. When I worked in the Office on Violence Against Women at the US Department of Justice, it was clear that male violence was to be the focus of all our efforts.

Think about that: an office of the government of the United States dedicated only to working to end violence against women. Not equality for women; not access to health care for women and the children they bear and raise; not fairness in the workplace for women. Its sole agenda is to end violence against women. And it is 100 percent clear that the concern isn't women being violent to women but men being violent to women. Violence against women is patriarchy's foot on our necks. We cannot progress until that ends, until women—and with them *everyone* who is vulnerable to the men who commit violence—can breathe. The Bonobo Sisterhood is a collective call to action. It's the only way ahead. And it's already happening, which is why we are seeing a doubling down of authoritarianism and the rhetoric and enactment of violence. Men do not want to cede power to the safety of a collective alliance.

In the meantime, it is clear how we are to move forward. We must do so together. That is how it is accomplished. You start with a self worth defending. You extend that knowledge to your immediate sisters at home, at work, in your neighborhood.

Then you build out from there. We must take inventory, asking what we ourselves can do. Then what can we do along with a group of sisters? Then how do we affect society? This is how our equality work begins.

This work would be faster if we could call on government resources to address economic inequalities and the myriad other barriers to equality among women. We must build the Bonobo Sisterhood in collaboration with those offices but without relying on them to make structural changes. There is much to do, but we must not succumb to the Good-Girl Trap of imagining it needs to be done within the available structures of patriarchy. We have to make change happen from the outside.

Women's leadership means acting without asking for permission to lead. We must unapologetically be bonobo. We must imagine an ironclad alliance and move forward together. We can begin, today and in our immediate communities, without giving any attention to what patriarchy has bequeathed us.

Imagine places where you could drop in and just be bonobo, places in which to be safe among other bonobos. Seek out and claim such places—coffee shops, gyms, churches, schools, town halls, libraries—but know that of paramount importance is creating a space for self-defense classes. Know, too, that one to several bonobos attending an existing self-defense class can infuse it with knowledge and behavior so that not only do all the students learn to protect themselves, they also learn that they have the power to protect their sisters.

Open spaces for men to join. We know that male-on-male violence has its own attributes and harms. It plays a particularly important role in establishing gender hierarchy and maintaining patriarchy. A bonobo space will welcome men who want to exit that structure, who want to be able to acknowledge the patriarchal wounds that have been inflicted upon them.

Equality, true equality for all, begins with equality among women.

An immediate step we can take is to focus on what we can do to share our resources. Women are demonstrably more generous than men. We give more and differently. Even though we control only a tiny percentage of the economy, we give way out of proportion to our share. And we can share our abundance differently. We can, for example, support microlending programs for women, which have been tried around the world to great effect. They spotlight the fact that we can and should work toward a different economy among women.

The greatest gift the bonobos give humans is the understanding that living within a Bonobo Sisterhood and by the Bonobo Principle is practical, possible, better—way, way better. Nothing prevents humans from choosing to be bonobo, from doing everything possible to exit a world of endemic violence by some men against all women and some men and entering a world of what is wanted. Wanted safety. Wanted food. Wanted opportunity. Wanted sex. Wanted family. Wanted peace and security.

Attaining this is as near as the next decision you make. What will you do when you next hear the call? What do you hope will happen when you next have to issue the call? No one pimps, harms, rapes, batters, abuses, harasses, or gaslights my sister. Everyone, starting with you, is my sister.

Start with the fun and easy: Throw a bonobo dance party. Secure a space secured by women. Call seven sisters and invite them, asking each of them to invite seven more sisters. All those who attend are equal. All are allied. Each is your sister. And no one harms any of your sisters.

We will not choose complacency. We will not choose compliance. We will choose bonobo. Close this book, choose bonobo, and make your world and the world of all your sisters better.

ACKNOWLEDGMENTS

Thank you, dear reader, for spending time with this book. A warm welcome to the Bonobo Sisterhood! I am grateful to everyone who has engaged with me over the several years of writing it, most especially my students from whom I constantly learn so much.

If not for the brilliant, unwavering, guidance of my editor, Thomas LeBien, this book would not be in your hands. I have a yellow sticky note above my desk that reads "Trust Thomas" and those words have proven worthy time after time. Thomas, you helped me find my authorial voice; your belief in this book and its power to change the world infuses these pages. Your extraordinary commitment, your steady, clear vision, and your coaching and patience have made all the difference. The vote of confidence you gave through your time has been the resource upon which I have drawn to write and finish this book.

To Gail Ross, my fiercely feminist and razor-sharp agent, thank you for your wisdom and for bringing the book to Karen Rinaldi, my publisher. Karen, you are an extraordinary bonobo sister. Thank you for believing in me and for the vigorous support and insight at every juncture. And Amanda Moon for the backup reinforcements along the way. Knowing you were there made a huge difference. To Kirby Sandmeyer, Yelena Nesbitt, Elizabeth Shreve, Amanda Pritzker, and the team at Harper-Collins for getting this book across the finish line and out into the world, thank you!

To Ashley Judd, my bonobo sister, in all the best possible ways. Our conversations throughout the writing of the book, informed by your keen observations of the bonobos in the wild, your exquisite listening, and your remarkable intellect, have been the fertile ground from which many of the most important insights have grown. You always challenge me to be my very best.

To Shepard Fairey for your breathtaking cover art that translated the energy and message of the book so perfectly. It brings tears to my eyes.

To my "squad," Brianna Banks, Holly Boux, Lilly McGuire, and Amanda Odasz: What a team! You each brought a crucial perspective to the book. Your honesty, humor, critical lenses, legal acumen, creativity, intensity, and brilliant research made the book what it is. You yourselves are a tremendous bonobo sisterhood. Thank you for working so hard amidst all the other demands you were facing in law school, studying for the bar, working, yet being such a consistent source of support.

I am deeply grateful to other current and former students including Mikelina Belaineh, Morgan Carmen, Schuyler Daum, Liran Samuni, Zoja Surroi, and Camila Tellez who provided research and other assistance.

To Callahan Miller for years of collaboration, from inventing the term "Probonobo Law"(stay tuned!) to being my teaching fellow and constant sounding board. I cherish our friendship.

To my original bonobo students in the class of 2010: Laura Jarrett, whose signature optimism is expressed in her saying "Of course!"; Brittany Rogers, who drew on a napkin what became the enduring structure of the book over coffee and croissants in Claremont; Rebecca Leventhal, Britanie Hall, and Tamara Schulman.

To Richard Wrangham for being a truly wonderful colleague and friend. Thank you for exploring this theory with me so thoroughly and for so long. Our relationship is a pure intellectual pleasure.

To other colleagues and former students: Charlotte Anrig, Sierra Bender, Victoria Budson, Samantha Burke, Anne Clougherty, Ellie Clougherty, Carvana Cloud, Lisa Cloutier, Rebecca Donaldson, Kelly Dunne, Leah Fessler, Mary Anne Franks, Anisha Gopi, Ruchira Gupta, Elizabeth Hague, Judith Herman, Lam Ho, Swanee Hunt, Hauwa Ibrahim, Valerie Jarrett, Antuan Johnson, Lisa Jones, Haley Kulakowski, Jackson Katz, Lauren Birchfield Kennedy, Elizabeth Lesser, Renee Levitt, Jenae Moxie, Sonia Marton, Rachel Sandel Morse, Sean Ouellette, Olwen Pongrace, Sarah Pongrace, Nick Sensely, Shauna Shames, Cari Simon, Esta Soler, Clara Spera, Maclen Stanley, Mary Stottele, Steven Trothen, Vanessa Tyson, and Valencia Walker.

To Harvard colleagues whose support and friendship I so appreciate: Jacqueline Bhabha, Kristi Dobson, Rakesh Khurana, Elizabeth Knoll, Duncan Kennedy, Catharine MacKinnon, John Manning, Jenny Mansbridge, Martha Minow, Ruth Okediji, John Palfrey, Katy Park, Martin Surbeck, David Wilkins, and Michelle Williams.

To Michael Bischof, Alvin Notice, and Kathy Lewis: I hope this book honors the memories of Cindy Bischof and Tiana Notice. Thank you for your courageous collaboration on protecting others from harm. And to Patrisha McLean and others who shared so generously their stories for this book.

To my bonobo circle: Michele Fishel, Ann Hill, Catherine Lemagueresse, Laura Levy, Shoushan Kouyoumijan, Maria

Manning, Cynthia Mufarreh, Betsy Myers, Dena Sacco, Alexa Smith, and Christina Wilgren.

To my family, especially my brother, Jack, for being the best sibling one could have. And Sheryl, Maris, Joe, Ruth, and Sarah for sustaining me. And my bonus nieces Claudia and Ruby. To the Fisher family for your patience and support while I absented myself from many activities while writing this book. Hopefully, Louise, Tate, Faren, and Althea will benefit from a better world. To Jadwiga Milokowska for holding my feet to the fire, and for, along with Noemi Carlos, caring so exceptionally well for my mother. You gave me the peace of mind that enabled me to write this book.

To Sarah Andrysiak for the morning walks with our dogs, for being such a solid, clear-minded, and generous friend.

To my mentor Jane DiRenzo Pigott, I channel you in order to be my very best self. Your guidance, honesty, support, love, and intellect animate these pages, and my life, for that matter. Our long walks on Lake Michigan feed my soul.

To Harvey Berkman, "There is no better friend."

To Roberta Oster for your enduring friendship, unwavering support, and intellectual partnership that helped me to develop so many of the thoughts in the book.

To Cindy Kahn, my best friend and soulmate, since the first day we met in law school. I am so excited to work with you on the next chapter!

And finally, and most important, to Terry, for everything. You are the source of my hope; you are an exceptional human being, and you are my greatest gift in this life. You are living proof that a truly equal life partnership is possible. Your kindness, wisdom, equanimity, and love are my wellspring.

NOTES

Introduction

xvi He explained that primates use: Richard Wrangham and Dale Peterson, *Demonic Males: Apes and the Origins of Human Violence* (London: Bloomsbury, 1997).

xvi less studied and less well known: Kay Prüfer et al., "The Bonobo Genome Compared with the Chimpanzee and Human Genomes," *Nature* 486, no. 7404 (2012): 527–31, https://doi.org/10.1038/nature11128.

xvii *Patriarchal violence* is the term: Diane L. Rosenfeld, "Sexual Coercion, Patriarchal Violence, and Law," in *Sexual Coercion in Primates and Humans: An Evolutionary Perspective on Male Aggression Against Females*, edited by Martin N. Muller and Richard W. Wrangham (Cambridge, MA: Harvard University Press, 2009), 424–47.

xviii LGBTQ people experience: "National Statistics," National Coalition Against Domestic Violence, https://ncadv.org/STATISTICS.

xviii Here's the snapshot: 14th Annual Domestic Violence Counts Report National Executive Summary National Network to End Domestic Violence https://nnedv.org/wp-content/uploads/2020/03/Library_Census_2019_national_summary.pdf

xviii That same day: Ibid.

xix "Bonobo females live": Amy R. Parish, "Two Sides of the Same Coin: Females Compete and Cooperate," Archives of Sexual Behavior 2021 https://doi.org/10.1007/s10508-021-02230-2

xix butterfly politics sense: butterfly politics here refers to how Catharine MacKinnon uses it in her book *Butterfly Politics*. She says, "What it means is that the right small simple intervention into an unstable political system can ultimately produce large complex systematic changes." https://www.hup.harvard.edu/catalog.php?isbn=9780674237667

xix Women from all over: "Variations on the campaign's theme gained steam with an international audience in other countries across Europe, Africa, the Middle East and South America, adding their own linguistic spin and cultural insight into a global problem.

"To date, there have been more than 2.3 million #MeToo tweets from 85 countries; on Facebook, more than 24 million people participated in the conversation by posting, reacting, and commenting over 77 million times since October 15." http://peacewomen.org/resource/metoos-global-moment-anatomy-viral-campaign (last accessed June 3, 2022).

xix The Women's Marches: The first Women's March was the largest single-day protest in US history at that point. Held the day after President Donald Trump's inauguration, the protests extended around the world. The Women's March has continued to organize a yearly March on Washington, and over the past several years, it has also arranged protests to end family detention, object to Brett Kavanaugh's confirmation as Supreme Court justice, and rally for abortion justice. See https://www.womensmarch.com.

Chapter 1: Answer the Call

1   In the Wamba forest: Natalie Angier, "In the Bonobo World, Female Camaraderie Prevails," *New York Times*, September 10, 2016, https://www.nytimes.com/2016/09/13/science/bonobos-apes-matriarchy.html.

2   an emergency order of protection: An order of protection (sometimes called a restraining order or protection from abuse) is a court-sanctioned order that is meant to protect victims of domestic violence from their abusers. The remedies given to the victim may vary, but typically an order of protection prohibits the abuser from contacting or going near the victim. See, e.g., IL R 20 CIR Rule 8.05.

2   domestic violence courts: A compendium compiled by the Center for Court Innovation confirmed the existence of 208 such courts within the US as of December 2009. https://www.courtinnovation.org/sites/default/files/national_compendium.pdf

4   On a typical day: "15th Annual Domestic Violence Counts Report," National Network to End Domestic Violence, May 2021, https://nnedv.org/wp-content/uploads/2021/05/15th-Annual-DV-Counts-Report-Full-Report.pdf, 3.

6   Cindy L. Bischof Memorial Foundation: Established in 2008, the Cindy L. Bischof Memorial Foundation works to pass laws that would allow judges to order GPS monitoring bracelets to domestic violence and stalking offenders. See "About Cynthia L. Bischof," Cynthia L. Bischof Memorial Foundation, http://www.cindysmemorial.org/?page_id=2.

7   danger assessment: The danger assessment is a tool used by domestic violence advocates, health care providers, and law enforcement officials to estimate how likely an abused woman is to be killed by her intimate partner. See https://www.dangerassessment.org.

8   one of the legal policy proposals: I also proposed the creation of batterer detention facilities to house offenders with appropriate supervision, intervention, rehabilitation, and work release so that victims and survivors would not have to be displaced from their homes, forced to seek shelter elsewhere. See Diane L. Rosenfeld, "Why Doesn't He Leave?: Restoring Liberty and Equality to Battered Women," *Directions in Sexual Harassment Law*, Catharine MacKinnon and Reva Siegel eds. Yale Univ Press, 2004. 535.

13   so predictable: I used the phrase "so predictable," meaning "as to be preventable," in an op-ed; Diane L. Rosenfeld, "Law Enforcement Sends Mixed Signals," *Chicago Tribune*, July 29, 1994. It became something of a catch-phrase in the movement against domestic violence homicide.

14   We know that just after: Patricia Tjaden and Nancy Thoennes, "Extent, Nature, and Consequences of Intimate Partner Violence," US Department of Justice, July 2000, https://www.ojp.gov/pdffiles1/nij/181867.pdf, 37.

14   In the nineteenth century: John Stuart Mill, "The Subjection of Women," 1869. Though John Stuart Mill might have been the sole author of the article, many of the arguments in it were adopted from his wife, Harriet Taylor Mill.

15   "Murder Has Abuse Victims Terrified": Meadow Rue Merrill, "Murder Has Abuse Victims Terrified," *Boston Globe*, September 12, 1999.

18   In the United States: "2014: Crime in the United States: Persons Arrested," FBI, May 20, 2015, https://ucr.fbi.gov/crime-in-the-u.s/2014/crime-in-the-u.s.-2014/persons-arrested/main.

18   Eighty-five percent of intimate partner: Callie Marie Rennison, "Bureau of Justice Statistics Crime Data Brief: Intimate Partner Violence, 1993–2001," US Department of Justice, February 2003, https://bjs.ojp.gov/content/pub/pdf/ipv01.pdf.

18   "John beat Mary": Jackson Katz, "Violence Against Women—It's a Men's Issue," TEDxFiDiWomen, November 2012, https://www.ted.com/talks/jackson_katz_violence_against_women_it_s_a_men_s_issue?language=en.

19   Green Dot: In an effort to reduce rates of violence, Green Dot programs provide bystander intervention training courses to increase the likelihood that community members will interfere when they witness violence and to change community norms that allow such violence to take place. See "Green Dot," Alteristic, https://alteristic.org/services/green-dot/.

19   made the point: Dorothy Edwards, Futures Without Violence National Summit (Boston, 2011).

21   In 2003: John Consiglio, "Wife Killing Epidemic," *Glamour Magazine*, August 2003, pp 206-209.

21   One was Scott Peterson: Carolyn Marshall, "Jury Finds Scott Peterson Guilty of Wife's Murder," *New York Times*, November 13, 2004, https://www.nytimes.com/2004/11/13/us/jury-finds-scott-peterson-guilty-of-wifes-murder.html.

21   Another case was: Andrew Blankstein and Jean Guccione, "Actor Robert Blake Acquitted in Shooting Death of His Wife," *Los Angeles Times*, March 17, 2005, https://www.latimes.com/archives/la-xpm-2005-mar-17-me-blake17-story.html.

22   He was accused: Jennifer Tanaka, "Behind Her Smile," *Chicago*, June 22, 2007, https://www.chicagomag.com/Chicago-Magazine/September-2003/Behind-Her-Smile/

24   Women in abusive relationships: Susan Weitzman, *Not to People Like Us: Hidden Abuse in Upscale Marriages* (New York: Basic Books, 2001).

24   I remember a case: Ret. Sgt. Anne O'Dell, Stop Domestic Violence Training Materials, on file with author.

25   Anecdotal data: Claire Cain Miller, "Men Do More at Home, but Not as Much as They Think," *New York Times*, November 12, 2015, https://www.nytimes.com/2015/11/12/upshot/men-do-more-at-home-but-not-as-much-as-they-think-they-do.html.

Chapter 2: Men's Castles, Women's Shelters

27   The last male bonobo: Natalie Angier, "In the Bonobo World, Female Camaraderie Prevails," *New York Times*, September 10, 2016, https://www.nytimes.com/2016/09/13/science/bonobos-apes-matriarchy.html.

27   The woman in the kitchen: Róisín Ingle, "Patrisha McLean: My 'Deeply Controlling' Ex-Husband Don McLean," *Irish Times*, November 14, 2020, https://www.irishtimes.com/life-and-style/people/patrisha-mclean-my-deeply-controlling-ex-husband-don-mclean-1.4407458.

29   "He was just screaming": Althea Legaspi, "Don McLean's Daughter
      Alleges Mental, Emotional Abuse by 'American Pie' Singer," *Rolling Stone*,
      June 23, 2021, https://www.rollingstone.com/music/music-features/don-
      mclean-jackie-roan-yellowthorn-1187117/.

29   Yet the type: The World Health Organization (WHO) estimates the
      prevalence of intimate partner violence committed by males against
      females at one in three relationships worldwide. Male sexual coercion over
      females as reproductive resources is prevalent in all societies. The Power
      and Control Wheel developed by the Duluth Project is a widely used and
      accepted description of the types of abuse used by offenders. Interestingly,
      Patrisha McLean uses the Power and Control Wheel as the basis for a
      brilliant, bonobo-like initiative she created called "Finding Our Voices" in
      which women provide testimonials along with portraits Patrisha takes and
      then displays throughout Maine. Victims and survivors mark up copies of
      the Power and Control Wheel, amplifying the similarities of patriarchal
      violence in heartbreaking detail. So far, the project has included people
      from the governor of Maine to an ex-convict. https://findingourvoices.net

30   Black women, Brown women: Alvarez, Fred, "Victims of Domestic
      Violence to Be Armed With Cellular Phones" (Oct. 7, 1998) https://
      www.latimes.com/archives/la-xpm-1998-oct-07-me-30034-story.html.
      Belknap, Joanne, Ann T. Chu, and Anne P. DePrince. "The Roles of
      Phones and Computers in Threatening and Abusing Women Victims of
      Male Intimate Partner Abuse." *Duke Journal Of Gender Law & Policy* vol.
      19, 2012, pp. 373-76. https://scholarship.law.duke.edu/cgi/viewcontent.
      cgi?article=1232&context=djglp.

30   a feature, not a bug: Critically, isolation is part of a campaign of emotional
      abuse by an offender to erode the self-esteem of the other partner.
      The technique of isolation makes the victim more dependent on the
      abuser for her sense of reality. In isolation, gaslighting is more effectively
      accomplished.

31   "Human patriarchy has": Richard W. Wrangham and Dale Peterson,
      Demonic Males: Apes and the Origins of Human Violence (New York:
      Houghton Mifflin Harcourt, 1996), 242.

33   The first-known law of marriage: Angela Browne, *When Battered Women
      Kill* (New York: Free Press, 1987), 164.

34   "When you see your wife": Ibid., 164–65.

34   Girls and women are socialized: Jackie McLean's experience captures
      this perfectly in her fear of her father's temper. She writes how he warned
      her "to stay small, not to speak about my stories. . . . I felt like I was not
      allowed to exist. Like he wanted me to disappear." https://findingourvoices.
      net/powercontrol?itemId=natz06p99hp9parogbpybqdxw3i1ld

34   In the 1950s: See Nancy Walker, *Women's Magazines 1940-1960: Gender
      Roles and the Popular Press* (Boston: Bedford/St. Martins, 1998), 15.

35   When controlling their harem: Hans Kummer, *In Quest of the Sacred
      Baboon: A Scientist's Journey* (Princeton, NJ: Princeton University Press,
      1997).

35   The idea, enshrined: Elizabeth Plumptre, "What to Do If You Feel
      Like You're Walking on Eggshells in Your Relationship," Verywell Mind,
      November 15, 2021, https://www.verywellmind.com/how-to-handle-
      walking-on-eggshells-in-your-relationship-5207935.

36   According to Sir William Blackstone: William Blackstone, *Commentaries on the Laws of England* (Oxford, UK: Oxford University Press, 1765–69).
37   Alongside the doctrine: Ibid., vol. 0, 432.
38   "the civil law": Ibid., 433.
39   "as an indicator": Reva B. Siegel, "'The Rule of Love': Wife Beating as Prerogative and Privacy," *Yale Law Journal* 106 (June 1996): 2117–209, https://documents.alexanderstreet.com/d/1000679743.
39   "during the Reconstruction Era": Ibid.
40   "struck . . . his wife": *State v. Rhodes*, 61 N.C. 453, 457 N.C., 1868, https://la.utexas.edu/users/jmciver/357L/61NC453.html.
40   And third, *State v. Rhodes*: Ibid.
41   "Our conclusion is": Ibid.
41   "Trifling" refers to: *De minimis* is "Latin for 'of minimum importance' or 'trifling.' Essentially, it refers to something or a difference that is so little, small, minuscule, or tiny that the law does not refer to it and will not consider it." "De Minimis," in Gerald N. Hill and Kathleen Hill, *The People's Law Dictionary: Taking the Mystery Out of Legal Language* (New York: MJF Books, 2002), 135.
42   Moreover, for centuries: Jacquelyn C. Campbell and Peggy Alford, "The Dark Consequences of Marital Rape," *American Journal of Nursing* 89, no. 7 (July 1989): 946–49, https://doi.org/10.2307/3426372.
42   "not because those relations": *State v. Rhodes*. 7 (July 1989): 946–49, https://doi.org/10.2307/3426372.
42   "For, however great": Ibid.
43   "Husband and wife": 1. W. Blackstone, *Commentaries on the Laws of England*, 418 n. 103 (R. Welsh & Co. ed 1897).
44   "Who made you king": Sara Bareilles, "King of Anything," *Kaleidoscope Heart*, 2010.
46   Women face disproportionately: "The average prison sentence for men who kill their female partners is two to six years. . . . By contrast women, who kill their partners are sentenced on average to 15 years." Mona Chalabi, "Are Women Punished More Harshly for Killing an Intimate Partner?," *Guardian*, January 12, 2019.
47   When women kill: Margaret Lazarus, Renner Wunderlich, and Stacey Kabat, "Defending Our Lives," Cambridge Documentary Films, 1993.
49   "I think we just": Emma Specter, "Please Stop Asking FKA Twigs—and All Domestic-Abuse Survivors—'Why Did You Stay?,'" *Vogue*, February 18, 2021, https://www.vogue.com/article/fka-twigs-domestic-abuse-survivors-why-did-you-stay.
49   Compared to the number: Alexia Cooper and Erica L. Smith, "Homicide Trends in the United States, 1980–2008," US Department of Justice, November 2011, https://bjs.ojp.gov/content/pub/pdf/htus8008.pdf, 18; "When Men Murder Women: An Analysis of 2013 Homicide Data," Violence Policy Center, September 2015, 3.
49   Lest you think: Brandi Booth et al., "Captive-Taking Incidents in the Context of Domestic Violence: A Descriptive Analysis," *Victims & Offenders* 2 (April 2010): 183–98.
50   As just one example: Rachel Louise Snyder, "A Raised Hand," *New Yorker*, July 15, 2013, https://www.newyorker.com/magazine/2013/07/22/a-raised-hand.

50 "broke into the family home": "Not Without Warning," *Boston Globe*, October 16, 2008.

50 On a previous occasion: Snyder, "A Raised Hand."

55 She dutifully checked: Diane L. Rosenfeld, "Correlative Rights and the Boundaries of Freedom: Protecting the Civil Rights of Endangered Women," Harvard Civil Rights—*Civil Liberty Law Review*, Vol 43, p. 257 (2008).

Chapter 3: The Phallacy of the Male Protection Racket

60 In 2018, the journalist: E. Jean Carroll, *What Do We Need Men For?: A Modest Proposal* (New York: St. Martin's Press, 2019).

60 "What Do We Need Men For": Ibid., 170

62 "In the system of chivalry": Susan Griffin, *Rape: The Politics of Consciousness* (New York: HarperCollins, 1986), 11.

69 "prevents women from enjoying": Holly Kearl, *Stop Street Harassment: Making Public Places Safe and Welcoming for Women* (New York: Praeger, 2010), 72.

73 "I am a spy": P. Carl, *Becoming a Man: The Story of a Transition* (New York: Simon & Schuster, 2020), 13–14.

73 "knows what it is": P. Carl recognized that it "is taboo in the trans community to use someone's 'dead name' (pretransition name)." He consciously broke that taboo in his book to offer us critical insights into gender construction and performance. "You must know Polly, as much as I will begrudge telling you, because Polly knows so much about Carl and vice-versa." Ibid., 15.

75 In the Sambia tribe: Gilbert H. Herdt, *Rituals of Manhood: Male Initiation in Papua New Guinea* (Berkeley: University of California Press, 1982).

78 "Weighing heaviest on": Susan Faludi, "The Naked Citadel," *New Yorker*, September 5, 1994, 62–81.

80 "According to the Citadel": Susan Faludi, *Stiffed: The Betrayal of the American Man* (New York: HarperCollins, 2011), 117.

80 Studies consistently show: See, e.g., Peter H. Neidig, Harold E. Russell, and Albert F. Seng, "Interspousal Aggression in Law Enforcement Families: A Preliminary Investigation," *Police Studies* 15, no. 1 (1992): 30–38, https://policing.umhistorylabs.lsa.umich.edu/files/original/5528df2d5b5c33cfeaa930146cfe20ccb5cad0cd.pdf.

80 "the extra amount": Sarah M. Kaufman, Christopher Polack, and Gloria Campbell, "The Pink Tax on Transportation," NYU Rudin Center for Transportation, November 2018, https://wagner.nyu.edu/files/faculty/publications/Pink%20Tax%20Survey%20Results_draft6.pdf, 2.

80 75 percent of women had experienced: Ibid., 5.

81 "The results of the survey": Ibid., 6.

82 In the movie: Stanley Kubrick, *Full Metal Jacket*, Warner Bros., 1987.

82 "Short of homicide": "We do not discount the seriousness of rape as a crime. It is highly reprehensible, both in a moral sense and in its almost total contempt for the personal integrity and autonomy of the female victim and for the latter's privilege of choosing those with whom intimate relationships are to be established. Short of homicide, it is the 'ultimate violation of self.'" *Coker v. Georgia*, 433 U.S. 584, 1977, https://courtroomcast.lexisnexis.com/acf_cases/9123-coker-v-georgia.

Chapter 4: Patriarchal Violence

84   in the Kanyawara community: Kimberly G. Duffy, Richard W. Wrangham, and Joan B. Silk, "Male Chimpanzees Exchange Political Support for Mating Opportunities," **Current Biology** 17, no. 15 (2007): R586–87, https://doi.org/10.1016/j.cub.2007.06.001.

84   Violence Against Women Act: "All persons within the United States shall have the right to be free from crimes of violence motivated by gender." Violence Against Women Act, Civil Rights for Women, 42 USC, Section 13981, 2000, https://uscode.house.gov/view.xhtml?req=granuleid:USC-2000-title42-section13981&num=0&edition=2000.

85   But in 2000: *United States v. Morrison*, U.S. 598, 146 L. Ed. 2d 658, 120 S. Ct. 1740, 2000, https://cite.case.law/us/529/598/.

85   And just five years after that: *Town of Castle Rock, Colorado, v. Jessica Gonzales et al.*, 545 U.S. 748, 125 S. Ct. 2796, 2005, https://1x937u16qcra1vnejt2hj4jl-wpengine.netdna-ssl.com/wp-content/uploads/socialjustice/Town%20of%20Castle%20Rock,%20Colo_%20v_%20Gonzales.pdf.

86   "Sexual abuse works": Catharine MacKinnon, *Feminism Unmodified: Discourses on Life and Law* (Cambridge, MA: Harvard University Press, 1987), 7.

87   Barbara Smuts's work: Barbara Smuts, "The Evolutionary Origins of Patriarchy," *Human Nature* 6 (1995): 1–32, https://doi.org/10.1007/BF02734133.

88   "The basic unit": Gerda Lerner, *The Creation of Patriarchy* (New York: Oxford University Press, 1985), 212.

88   The anthropology of law: Richard W. Wrangham, "The Evolution of Patriarchy," Tanner Lectures, Stanford University, 2022.

89   Thus, I recount them here: *United States v. Morrison*.

90   Jessica Gonzales, now Lenahan: *Town of Castle Rock, Colorado, v. Jessica Gonzales et al.*

94   "too big problem": Pamela Coukos, "Deconstructing the Debate over Gender and Hate Crimes Legislation," *Georgetown Journal of Gender and the Law*, Inaugural Issue (Summer 1999): 11.

99   "The rule is simple": Deborah Tuerkheimer, *Credible: Why We Doubt Accusers and Protect Abusers* (New York: HarperCollins, 2021), 9.

101   "Male hegemony over the symbol system": Gerda Lerner, *The Creation of Patriarchy*, Woman and History, vol. 1 (New York: Oxford University Press, 1986), 219–20.

105   "Battering in animals": Richard W. Wrangham and Dale Peterson, *Demonic Males: Apes and the Origins of Human Violence* (New York: Houghton Mifflin Harcourt, 1996), 146.

Chapter 5: Compliance Sex

109   Deep in the forests: Takeshi Furuichi and Chie Hashimoto, "Sex Differences in Copulation Attempts in Wild Bonobos at Wamba," *Primates* 45 (2004): 59–62, https://doi.org/10.1007/s10329-003-0055-7.

110   "[raise] the specter": Kate Manne, *Entitled: How Male Privilege Hurts Women* (New York: Crown, 2020), 58.

111   Katie Way wrote: Katie Way, "I Went on a Date with Aziz Ansari. It Turned

into the Worst Night of My Life," Babe, January 13, 2018, https://babe. net/2018/01/13/aziz-ansari-28355.

114 "he said, 'Don't worry'": Kristen Roupenian, "Cat Person," *New Yorker*, December 4, 2017, https://www.newyorker.com/magazine/2017/12/11/cat-person.

116 "Why was I": Nancy Jo Sales, *Nothing Personal: My Secret Life in the Dating App Inferno* (New York: Hachette, 2021), 143.

122 "This idea—that the rules": Amia Srinivasan, *The Right to Sex: Feminism in the Twenty-First Century* (New York: Farrar, Straus and Giroux, 2021), 20-21.

124 "To a nontrivial degree": Jennifer S. Hirsch and Shamus Khan, *Sexual Citizens: A Landmark Study of Sex, Power, and Assault on Campus* (New York: Norton, 2020), 96.

124 In Ariel Levy's 2005 book: Ariel Levy, *Female Chauvinist Pigs: Women and the Rise of Raunch Culture* (New York: Free Press, 2005).

125 The 2008 documentary: *The Price of Pleasure: Pornography, Sexuality, and Relationships*, Media Education Foundation, 2008.

125 "all of the feminists thought": Levy, *Female Chauvinist Pigs*, 47.

126 "The new sexual revolution": Ibid., 70.

126 "The room was packed": Ibid., 72.

127 "My students belonged": Srinivasan, *The Right to Sex*, 41.

127 "For porn does not inform": Ibid., 64.

128 "During sex, he moved her": Roupenian, "Cat Person."

130 "At these gatherings": Diane L. Rosenfeld, "Who Are You Calling a 'Ho'?: Challenging the Porn Culture on Campus," in *Big Porn Inc.: Exposing the Harms of the Global Pornography Industry*, edited by Melinda Tankard Reist and Abigail Bray (North Melbourne, Victoria, Australia: Spinifex Press, 2011), 41-42.

130 Time, and perhaps: "College Party Themes," DormHigh, https:// dormhigh.com/college-party-themes/.

130 "When it comes to frat parties": College OTR (2009) 'The Top 5 Frat Party Themes', http://www.collegeotr.com/college_otr/top_5_frat_party_themes_18285 (accessed 10 April, 2011).

130 "just make sure": Lace Nguyen, "7 Theme Parties You Have to Do at Least Once," Her Campus, October 13, 2013, https://www.hercampus.com/ school/wash-u/7-theme-parties-you-have-do-least-once/.

131 "The party may change": Hannah Tager, "Saint Paul's to Saint Ann's, Our Harmful Hook-Up Culture," *Saint Ann's Ram*, October 2015, https://issuu. com/saintannsram/docs/19-1_online_version, 7.

132 "Within minutes of him": Sales, *Nothing Personal*, 227–28.

134 "choking is really risky": Debby Herbenick et al., "Diverse Sexual Behavior and Pornography Use: Findings from a Nationally Representative Probability Survey of Americans Aged 18 to 60 Years," *Journal of Sexual Medicine* 17, no. 4 (April 2020): 623–33, https://linkinghub.elsevier.com/ retrieve/pii/S1743-6095(20)30047-3.

134 normalized in women's magazines: "Some women's magazines have celebrated choking as an exciting form of 'sex play'—even recasting it as a 'daring' sex act which allegedly gives women power. In 2016, *Women's Health* said that choking can 'be an exhilarating experience.' In order to

enjoy it, the article said, women just needed to learn to 'relax.'" Sales, *Nothing Personal*, 228.

134   Just a few weeks: Brian Rogers, "As Domestic Violence Claims Another Victim in Houston, Prosecutors Target Strangulation Assaults," *Houston Chronicle*, March 7, 2018, https://www.chron.com/news/article/houston-domestic-violence-strangulation-prosecutor-12732988.php.

139   "Since seeking out": Leah Fessler, "A Lot of Women Don't Enjoy Hookup Culture—So Why Do We Force Ourselves to Participate?," Quartz, May 17, 2016, https://qz.com/685852/hookup-culture/.

Chapter 6: A Self Worth Defending

145   While observing members: Martin Surbeck and Gottfried Hohmann, "Intersexual Dominance Relationships and the Influence of Leverage on the Outcome of Conflicts in Wild Bonobos (*Pan paniscus*)," *Behavioral Ecology and Sociobiology* 67, no. 11 (2013): 1767–80, https://doi.org/10.1007/s00265-013-1584-8.

145   Kelly Herron was four miles: Kayna Whitworth, Kelly McCarthy, and Nia Phillips, "Female Jogger in Seattle Uses Self-Defense Tactics to Fend Off Brutal Assault," ABC News, March 10, 2017, https://abcnews.go.com/US/female-jogger-seattle-defense-tactics-fend-off-brutal/story?id=46034147.

146   "The most important thing": Gloria Steinem, *The Truth Will Set You Free, but First It Will Piss You Off! Thoughts on Life, Love, and Rebellion* (New York: Random House, 2019), 20.

156   "I think more awareness": "Miss USA Defends Her Controversial 'Self Defense' Answer," HuffPost, https://www.huffpost.com/entry/miss-usa-defends-her-controversial-self-defense-answer_n_5b576e36e4b0860924774319.

157   "In a society where": Amanda Marcotte, "Taekwondo Is Great but Not the Solution to Campus Rape," Slate, June 9, 2014, https://slate.com/human-interest/2014/06/miss-usa-on-campus-sexual-assault-nia-sanchez-a-black-belt-in-taekwondo-wants-women-to-defend-themselves.html.

159   The Trans Defense Fund: Trans Defense Fund LA, https://transdefensefundla.org/.

159   Researchers at the Williams Institute: "Transgender People over Four Times More Likely Than Cisgender People to Be Victims of Violent Crime," Williams Institute, UCLA School of Law, March 23, 2021, https://williamsinstitute.law.ucla.edu/press/ncvs-trans-press-release/.

162   "throwing a detective": Matthew Wills, "How American Women First Learned Self-Defense," JSTOR Daily, March 29, 2021, https://daily.jstor.org/how-american-women-first-learned-self-defense/.

162   "used their bodies": Ibid.

162   "Indeed, self-defense training": Martha E. Thompson, "Empowering Self-Defense Training," *Violence Against Women* 20, no. 3 (2014): 351–59, https://doi.org/10.1177/1077801214526051.

163   "While of course preparation": Martha McCaughey and Jill Cermele, "Changing the Hidden Curriculum of Campus Rape Prevention and Education: Women's Self-Defense as a Key Protective Factor for a Public Health Model of Prevention," *Trauma, Violence & Abuse* 18, no. 3 (July 2017): 287–302, https://doi.org/10.1177/1524838015611674.

164   "Self-defense training empowers": Ibid.

164   "I think it's because": Lisa Wade, "Why Don't More Men Hit Each Other Below the Belt?," Pacific Standard, June 14, 2017, https://psmag.com/social-justice/why-dont-more-men-hit-each-other-below-the-belt.

165   "Well, I don't know": https://www.huffpost.com/entry/miss-usa-defends-her-controversial-self-defense-answer_n_5b576e36e4b0860924774319

168   our collective rage: Three excellent books on feminist rage explore the topic from many different dimensions, yet none advocates for self-defense or a collective self-defense strategy. See Soraya Chemaly, *Rage Becomes Her: The Power of Women's Anger* (New York: Atria, 2018); Brittney Cooper, *Eloquent Rage: A Black Feminist Discovers Her Superpower* (New York: St. Martin's, 2018); and Rebecca Traister, Good and Mad: The Revolutionary Power of Women's Anger (New York: Simon & Schuster, 2018).

168   feminist utopian novel: Charlotte Perkins Gilman, *Herland*, 1915.

169   dynamics of target rape: For a discussion on the term "target rape" as distinguished from date or acquaintance rape, see Diane L. Rosenfeld, "Uncomfortable Conversations: Confronting the Reality of Target Rape on Campus," 128 Harv. L. Rev. F. 359 (2015). https://harvardlawreview.org/2015/06/uncomfortable-conversations-confronting-the-reality-of-target-rape-on-campus/

Chapter 7: Building the Bonobo Sisterhood

175   rescued bonobos in the Democratic Republic: Brian Hare and Suzy Kwetuenda, "Bonobos Voluntarily Share Their Own Food with Others," *Current Biology* 20, no. 5 (March 9, 2010): R230–31, https://doi.org/10.1016/j.cub.2009.12.038.

176   I first heard: Jessica Contrera, "He Was Sexually Abusing Underage Girls. Then, Police Said, One of Them Killed Him," *Washington Post,* December 17, 2019, https://www.washingtonpost.com/graphics/2019/local/child-sex-trafficking-murder/.

177   "'hundreds' of child pornography": Ibid.

178   "prostituting herself out": Ibid.

180   The #MeToo, founded: The #MeToo movement was founded by survivor and activist Tarana Burke in 2006. "In 2017, the #MeToo hashtag went viral and woke up the world to the magnitude of the problem of sexual violence. What had begun as local grassroots work had now become a global movement — seemingly overnight. Within a six-month span, our message reached a global community of survivors. Suddenly there were millions of people from all walks of life saying 'me too.' " https://metoomvmt.org/get-to-know-us/history-inception/. The movement focuses on "assisting a growing spectrum of survivors—young people, queer, trans, the disabled, Black women and girls, and all communities of color." Ibid. For a deep and poignant explanation of the work, see Tarana Burke, *Unbound,* (New York: Flatiron Books, 2021).

187   In the documentary: *Rape Is...* is a documentary that "explores the meaning and consequences of rape. . . . from a global and historical perspective, but it focuses mainly on the domestic cultural conditions that make this human rights violation the most underreported crime in America. Many types of sexual assault are not considered a serious crime

by the legal system and our society refuses to see the true cost of this brutal denial of basic rights." https://www.cambridgedocumentaryfilms. org/filmsPages/rapeIs.html. It is available on YouTube. It was made by Cambridge Documentary Films and coproduced by Diane Rosenfeld.

187 Salamishah Tillet says: Salamishah Tillet is a Pulitzer Prize-winning contributing critic at large for the *New York Times*, an author and professor. Her poem and work is featured in *Rape Is . . .*

188 self in *Unbound*: Tarana Burke, *Unbound* (New York: Flatiron Books, 2021).

188 This is the most critical point: "Sexual abuse during adolescence and being an ethnic minority tended to increase the risk of sexual revictimization. Having been sexually abused in childhood not only increased Black women's risk of sexual violence as adults, it also increase their risk of prostitution." Melissa Farley, "Prostitution: An Extreme Form of Girls' Sexualization" in *The Sexualization of Girls and Girlhood: Causes, Consequences, and Resistance*, eds. Eileen L. Zurbriggen and Tomi-Ann Roberts (New York: Oxford Univ. Press, 2013) https://prostitutionresearch. com/wp-content/uploads/2016/08/Sexualization-of-GirlsProstitution2013. pdf

188 Experts across the board: According to World Without Exploitation, the number is as high as 84 percent, according to multiple studies. https:// www.worldwithoutexploitation.org/stats

189 what I am talking about: Tarana Burke, *Unbound* (New York: Flatiron Books, 2021).

191 A lot of consciousness raising: Historian Gerda Lerner wrote, "It was under patriarchal hegemony in thought, values, institutions, and resources that women had to struggle to form their own feminist consciousness. I define feminist consciousness as the awareness of women that they belong to a subordinate group; that they have suffered wrongs as a group; that their condition of subordination is not natural, but is societally determined; that they must join with other women to remedy these wrongs; and finally, that they must and can provide an alternate vision of societal organization in which women as well as men will enjoy autonomy and self-determination." Gerda Lerner, *The Creation of Feminist Consciousness* (New York: Oxford Univ. Press, 1993), 14.

191 *Upscale Marriages*: Susan Weitzman, Ph.D., *Not to People Like Us: Hidden Abuse in Upscale Marriages*, (New York: Basic Books, 2000).

192 "While Black women": Angela Y. Davis, *Women, Race & Class* (London: Penguin Classics, 2019), 97.

193 Our sisters of color: Ruby Hamad states, "There is no sisterhood. How can there be, when white supremacy has done such a thorough job of setting White Womanhood apart from the rest of us? . . . women of color have to not only battle white patriarchy and that of their own culture, but must also contend with colonialism, neocolonialism, imperialism, and other forms of racism. Given white women have never had to deal with racial and colonial oppression, it is not surprising—though it is certainly regrettable—that so many of them still regard feminism as a movement purely concerned with gender, leaving racialized women to keep trying to draw their attention to the ways in which various oppressions affect our lives. Until white women reckon with this, mainstream Western feminism cannot be anything more than another iteration of white supremacy." Ruby

Hamad, *White Tears/Brown Scars: How White Feminism Betrays Women of Color* (New York: Catapult, 2020), 162.

194   commercially sexually exploited: A report on racial and gender disparities in the US sex trade shows that survivors are disproportionately women of color. https://prostitutionresearch.com/racial-gender-disparities-in-the-us-sex-trade/.

197   In bonobos, the females emigrate: Takeshi Furuichi, *Bonobo and Chimpanzee: The Lessons of Social Coexistence* (Springer, 2019), 46.

198   One of my favorite examples: For more about Valerie Jarrett's life, see her memoir, *Finding My Voice*, https://www.penguinrandomhouse.com/books/566230/finding-my-voice-by-valerie-jarrett/.

198   Valerie served as the chair: President Obama created the Council through an executive order signed on March 9, 2009, early in his first term: https://obamawhitehouse.archives.gov/administration/eop/cwg.

199   through their mothers: Martin Surbeck, Roger Mundry and Gottfried Hohmann, "Mothers matter! Maternal support, dominance status and mating success in male bonobos" (Pan Panicus) Proc. R. Soc. B.278: 590-598 http://doi.org.ezp-prod1.hul.harvard.edu/10.1098/rspb.2010.1572

200   exclusion of women: Gerda Lerner, *The Creation of Patriarchy* (New York: Oxford Univ. Press, 1986).

202   sought his care: Dr. Denis Mukwege, *The Power of Women: A Doctor's Journey of Hope and Healing* (New York: Flatiron Books, 2021).

204   defenseless mothers first: Mukwege, 272-273.

206   Alexandra authored a book: Alexandra Brodsky, *Sexual Justice: Supporting Victims, Ensuring Due Process, and Resisting the Conservative Backlash* (New York: Metropolitan Books, 2021).

206   Amanda Nguyen is the founder: Rise, https://www.risenow.us/.

Chapter 8: Law in Bonoboland

212   Back in the Wamba forest: Nahoko Tokuyama and Takeshi Furuichi, "Do Friends Help Each Other? Patterns of Female Coalition Formation in Wild Bonobos at Wamba," *Animal Behaviour* 119 (July 2016): 27–35, https://doi.org/10.1016/j.anbehav.2016.06.021.

212   men kill three to four women: "In 2019, there were 1,795 females murdered by males in single victim/single offender incidents that were submitted to the FBI for its Supplementary Homicide Report." Violence Policy Center, *When Men Murder Women: An Analysis of 2019 Homicide Data* (Washington, DC, 2021). 3 https://www.vpc.org/studies/wmmw2021.pdf.

213   time in school: "Among undergraduate students, 26.4% of females and 6.8% of males experience rape or sexual assault through physical force, violence, or incapacitation." RAINN https://www.rainn.org/statistics/campus-sexual-violence.

216   Just as the development: Barbara Smuts, "The Evolutionary Origins of Patriarchy," *Human Nature* 6 (March 1995): 1–32, https://doi.org/10.1007/BF02734133.

216   "centuries of laws": Heidi Schreck, *What the Constitution Means to Me* (New York: Theatre Communications Group, 2020), 57.

221   The convention's Declaration of Sentiments: The Declaration of Sentiments, E. C. Stanton (New York, 1848).

221 "iron pots and kettles": Brittney Cooper, *Eloquent Rage* (New York: St. Martin's Press, 2018), 34.

223 National Women's Conference: "Fifty-seven years after winning the vote, over two thousand delegates gathered in Houston, Texas, in November 1977. The federally funded conference was the most purposely diverse and demographically representative group ever assembled in the United States." https://americanhistory.si.edu/creating-icons/national-women's-conference-1977.

225 negotiating processes: For an extended consideration of the importance of gender equality, see Valerie M. Hudson, Bonne Ballif-Spanvill, Mary Caprioli, and Chad F. Emmett, *Sex & World Peace* (New York: Columbia Univ. Press, 2012).

Chapter 9: Be Bonobo!

228 the original statement: Declaration of Independence, July 4, 1776.

229 Here's a *Washington Post* headline: Cathy Free, "Three Women Discovered They Were Dating the Same Man. They Dumped Him and Went on a Months-Long Road Trip Together," *Washington Post*, July 15, 2021, https://www.washingtonpost.com/lifestyle/2021/07/15/boyfriend-cheat-girlfriend-roadtrip/.

231 A friend is being sexually harassed: Personal correspondence on file with author.

231 scientists cannot ethically conduct: "Chimpanzees cannot be paired with strangers in experiments due to ethical concerns over their xenophobia." Jingzhi Tan and Brian Hare, "Prosociality among non-kin in bonobos and chimpanzees compared," Hare & Yamamoto, *Bonobos: Unique in Mind, Brain and Behavior* (New York: Oxford Univ. Press, 2017), 141.

232 When one bonobo group: Takeshi Furuichi, "Female Contributions to the Peaceful Nature of Bonobo Society," *Evolutionary Anthropology* 20, no. 4 (2011): 131–42, https://doi.org/10.1002/evan.20308.

233 "For women, the need": Audre Lorde, "The Master's Tools Will Never Dismantle the Master's House," in *Sister Outsider: Essays and Speeches* (Berkeley, CA: Crossing Press, 2007), 112.

233 "is so abundant": Marion Nestle, *Food Politics: How the Food Industry Influences Nutrition and Health*, revised and expanded tenth anniversary edition (Berkeley: University of California Press, 2013), 1.

234 In Albany, New York: "Who We Are," Free Food Fridge Albany, https://freefoodfridgealbany.com/who-we-are.

234 In Nepal, where more than: "Women-Managed Community Kitchens Support Vulnerable Women in Nepal," UN Women, August 19, 2021, https://www.unwomen.org/en/news/stories/2021/8/feature-women-managed-community-kitchens-support-vulnerable-women-in-nepal.

235 "feeds Black mamas": "About Feed Black Futures," Feed Black Futures, https://feedblackfutures.org/general-1-1.

235 In St. Louis, Missouri: Hannah Wallace and Tosha Phonix, "In St. Louis, Tosha Phonix Is Growing Food Justice," Civil Eats, July 1, 2021, https://civileats.com/2021/07/01/in-st-louis-tosha-phonix-is-growing-food-justice/.

235 a group of women gathered: Victoria Murphy, "Meghan Markle Checks In with the Women of the Hubb Community Kitchen from Her

New Home in L.A.," *Town & Country*, April 17, 2020, https://www.townandcountrymag.com/society/tradition/a32185253/meghan-markle-hubb-community-kitchen-video-call-la-home/.

235   They formed what became: Rasha Ali, "Duchess Meghan Reunites with Hubb Community Kitchen Women on Zoom Call amid Coronavirus," *USA Today*, April 17, 2020, https://www.usatoday.com/story/entertainment/celebrities/2020/04/17/duchess-meghan-zoom-chats-hubb-community-kitchen-during-coronavirus/5152019002/.

235   Finally, in Charlotte: "FAQs," The Bulb, https://www.thebulbgallery.org/faqs.

235   "If you want something": Abby Vesoulis and Mariah Espada, "'We Will Handle It': An Army of Women Is Taking On the Hunger Crisis in Local Communities," *Time*, March 3, 2021, https://time.com/5942123/women-solve-hunger-us/.

235   "Only among humans": Natalie Angier, *Woman: An Intimate Geography* (London: Virago, 2014), 302.

237   one study concluded: Elisa Demuru, Pier Francesco Ferrari, and Elisabetta Palagi, "Is Birth Attendance a Uniquely Human Feature? New Evidence Suggests That Bonobo Females Protect and Support the Parturient," *Evolution and Human Behavior* 39, no. 5 (May 2018): 502–10, https://doi.org/10.1016/j.evolhumbehav.2018.05.003.

237   no infanticide has been observed: Furuichi, "Female Contributions to the Peaceful Nature of Bonobo Society."

237   "1,750 children died": "What Are Child Abuse and Neglect?," Centers for Disease Control and Prevention, https://www.cdc.gov/violenceprevention/childabuseandneglect/fastfact.html.

237   "In 1998, there were": Michael H. Keller and Gabriel J. X. Dance, "The Internet Is Overrun with Images of Child Sexual Abuse. What Went Wrong?," *New York Times*, September 29, 2019, https://www.nytimes.com/interactive/2019/09/28/us/child-sex-abuse.html.

238   Recall that Tarana Burke: Tonya Mosley, "'Me Too' Founder Tarana Burke Says Black Girls' Trauma Shouldn't Be Ignored," NPR, September 29, 2021, https://www.npr.org/2021/09/29/1041362145/me-too-founder-tarana-burke-says-black-girls-trauma-shouldnt-be-ignored.

238   Her child was molested: Tarana Burke, Unbound (New York: Flatiron Books, 2021) 238-239.

238   V wrote a book: Eve Ensler, *The Apology* (New York: Bloomsbury, 2019).

238   The hypothesis is: Kara Walker and Brian Hare, "Bonobo Baby Dominance: Did Female Defense of Offspring Lead to Reduced Male Aggression?," in *Bonobos: Unique in Mind, Brain, and Behavior*, edited by Brian Hare and Shinya Yamamoto (Oxford, UK: Oxford University Press, 2017), 49–64.

238   "I love men": "How Bonobos Help Explain the Evolution of Nice," NPR, January 28, 2021, https://www.npr.org/transcripts/959599401.

239   Notable is that males: Takeshi Furuichi and Chie Hashimoto, "Sex Differences in Copulation Attempts in Wild Bonobos at Wamba," *Primates* 45 (2004): 59–62, https://doi.org/10.1007/s10329-003-0055-7.

INDEX

abortion rights, (*see also* reproductive autonomy) 217, 223
abundance, xxi, 175, 182, 190, 202, 208, 214, 231, 233–234, 236, 242
Abused Women's Advocacy Project, 16–17
acquaintances, strangers vs., 62, 146–47, 169–71
adultery, 32
Aesop's fables, 232
African American (see also Black), 47, 130, 160, 177, 197
ageism, 129
AIDS, 209
"Ain't I a Woman, Too?" (Truth), 221
Alexander, Marissa, 47–48
Alliance for HOPE International, 135
all-male spaces, 73–83
"American Pie" (McLean), 28
Anderson, Ali, 234–35
Anderson, Jammella, 234
André, Claudine, 238
Angier, Natalie, 235–36
Ansari, Aziz, 110–14, 119, 127
anti-racism, 190–95
Apne Aap Women Worldwide, 196–97, 203, 208–9
Apology, The (V), 238
Australia, 68–69

baboons, 64
Backpage.com, 176–77
Bailey, Ebonee, 235
"Bananarama," 78
Banks, Brianna, 182–86
battered women. *See also* domestic violence; endangered women
avoiding term, 20–21, 226
battered women's shelters, xvii–xviii, 4, 5, 30–31–51, 52, 55–56, 193

Becoming a Man (Carl), 73–74
Belaineh, Mikelina, 66, 68
Berger, Wilma, 161–62
Bhabha, Jacqueline, 207
Bischof, Cindy L., 6–8
Bischof, Cindy L., Memorial Foundation, 6–7
Bischof, Michael, 6–8
Black abolitionists, 221
Black farmers, 235
Blackstone, William, 36–38, 43
Black trans women, 160
Black women and girls, xviii, 30–31, 47–48, 160, 176, 181–83, 190–95, 197, 218, 221
Blake, Robert, 21
Boies Schiller Flexner, 182
Bolger, Dana, 206
Bompusa bonobo community, 145
Bonobo call, 10–11, 16, 154, 158–58, 203
Bonobo dance party, 140–141
Bonobo Principle, 83–87, 176–83, 190–95, 242–43
bonobos,
being like, 228–43
chimpanzees vs., xvi, 231, 233
DNA and, ix
egalitarianism and, x
exit from Good-Girl Trap and, 99, 105–6
fear and, xv
female alliances and, x–xiii, xv, 1, 27, 57, 145, 212
female sexuality and, xii, xxii, 109, 110, 137–38
food sharing and, xv, 175, 233–36
goals of human feminist movement and, xix
Judd and, 209
male status and, xii, 199

The central idea in The Bonobo Sisterhood is that there is a need for a strong support system between human women, and that there is a successful model of this in the social world of bonobos. In designing the cover, I wanted to showcase the kindred relationship between bonobo females and human women while simultaneously conveying the radiant dynamics of sisterhood. Both the bonobo and the woman on the cover look directly at the viewer, implying that the time is NOW to engage the world with these important ideas about sisterhood. To symbolize the strength of sisterhood I designed an unbreakable chain made out of linked female symbols. The female symbol chain also incorporates a fist to represent the revolutionary power of female alliance.

—SHEPARD FAIREY, ARTIST AND ACTIVIST

ABOUT THE AUTHOR

Diane L. Rosenfeld, JD, LLM, is a lecturer on law and the founding director of the Gender Violence Program at Harvard Law School, where she has taught since 2004. A bold and dynamic advocate for ending gender violence, Rosenfeld has appeared in major media outlets including ABC's *Nightline; Deadline: Crime* with Tamron Hall; *Katie* (with Katie Couric), *CNN Headline News*; *Fox and Friends*; the *New York Times*, the *Washington Post*, the *Boston Globe*, the *Chicago Tribune*, and NPR's *All Things Considered* and *Morning Edition*. She is featured in the award-winning documentaries, *The Hunting Ground* (2015), *It Happened Here* (2014), and *Rape Is . . .*(2003), which she coproduced with Academy Award–winning Cambridge Documentary Films.

Rosenfeld served as the first senior counsel to the Office on Violence Against Women at the US Department of Justice and as an executive assistant attorney general in Illinois. She is the recipient of multiple awards for her teaching, mentoring, and change-making legal policy work.

She lives outside of Boston with her husband and their dog.